THE CONDEMNATIONS OF THE REFORMATION ERA

THE CONDEMNATIONS
OF THE
REFORMATION ERA

Do They Still Divide?

Edited by
KARL LEHMANN and **WOLFHART PANNENBERG**

Translated by
Margaret Kohl

FORTRESS PRESS   MINNEAPOLIS

THE CONDEMNATIONS OF THE REFORMATION ERA
Do They Still Divide?

First English-language edition published 1990 by Fortress Press. Translated by Margaret Kohl from the German edition with the approval of Herder and Vandenhoeck & Ruprecht.

Original German edition published 1988 by Herder, Freiburg im Breisgau, and Vandenhoeck & Ruprecht, Göttingen, under the title *Lehrverurteilungen—kirchentrennend?* copyright © 1986 Verlag Herder, Freiburg im Breisgau. English translation copyright © 1989 Augsburg Fortress.

Cover and interior design by Publishers' WorkGroup

Library of Congress Cataloging-in-Publication Data

Rechtfertigung, Sakramente, und Amt im Zeitalter der Reformation und heute. English
   The condemnations of the Reformation era : do they still divide? / edited by Karl Lehmann and Wolfhart Pannenberg : translated by Margaret Kohl.
      p. cm.
   Translation of: Lehrverurteilungen, kirchentrennend?. 1, Rechtfertigung, Sakramente, und Amt im Zeitalter der Reformation und heute.
   Written by the Ecumenical Study Group of Protestant and Catholic Theologians.
   Includes bibliographical references.
   ISBN 0-8006-2398-3
   1. Excommunication. 2. Reformation. 3. Counter-Reformation. 4. Christian union. 5. Justification. 6. Sacraments and Christian union. 7. Clergy—Office. 8. Catholic Church—Relations—Protestant churches. 9. Protestant churches—Relations—Catholic Church. I. Lehmann, Karl, 1936– . II. Pannenberg, Wolfhart, 1928– . III. Ökumenischer Arbeitskreis Evangelischer und Katholischer Theologen (Germany). IV. Title.
BX9.5.E97R4213 1990
280'.042—dc20   89-37506
                                                                              CIP

Manufactured in the U.S.A.   AF 1-2398
94   93   92   91   90   1   2   3   4   5   6   7   8   9   10

CONTENTS

v

ABBREVIATIONS

References marked with an asterisk (*) represent translations in which the German text which is the basis of the present translation deviates from NR or the episcopally sponsored translation of the texts of the Council of Trent or of the Second Vatican Council.

AA	Vatican II: Decree *Apostolicam Actuositatem*
AÄDO	*Amt, Ämter, Dienste, Ordination. Ergebnisse eines Gesprächs*, ed. J. Rogge and H. Zeddies (Berlin [GDR], 1982)
AAS	*Acta Apostolicae Sedis*
AG	Vatican II: Decree *Ad Gentes*
Apol.	Apology of the Augsburg Confession (1530)
AS	Smalcald Articles (1537)
BC	*The Book of Concord: The Confessions of the Evangelical Lutheran Church*, trans. and ed. T. G. Tappert (Philadelphia, 1959)
BSLK	*Die Bekenntnisschriften der evangelisch-lutherischen Kirche* (Göttingen, 1930; 10th ed. 1986)
CA	Augsburg Confession (1530)
can.	canon
CD	Vatican II: Decree *Christus Dominus*
CIC	*Codex Iuris Canonici*
CR	*Corpus Reformatorum*, ed. C. G. Bretschneider and H. E. Bindseil (Halle, 1834–60)
CT	*Concilium Tridentinum* (Freiburg, 1901ff.)
Deferrari	*The Sources of Catholic Dogma*, trans. by R. J. Deferrari from the 13th ed. of H. Denzinger, *Enchiridion Symbolorum* (St. Louis and London, 1955)
DS	H. Denzinger and A. Schönmetzer, eds., *Enchiridion symbolorum definitionum et declarationum de rebus fidei et morum* (Freiburg, 1965 and frequently)
DV	Vatican II: Dogmatic Constitution *Dei Verbum*
Ed. pr.	Editio princeps
EKD	Evangelische Kirche in Deutschland
Epit.	Epitome (Formula of Concord)
Eucharist	*The Eucharist: Final Report of the Joint Roman Catholic–Lutheran Commission* (1978)

FC	Formula of Concord (1577)
GS	Vatican II: Pastoral Constitution *Gaudium et Spes*
HC	Heidelberg Catechism
Inst. Institutio	J. Calvin, *Institutio Religionis Christianae* (1559)
Jedin	H. Jedin, *Geschichte des Konzils von Trient* I-IV (Freiburg, 1950–75). Partial English translation by E. Graf, *History of the Council of Trent* (Edinburgh, 1961)
Kaczynski	*Enchiridion Documentorum Instaurationis Liturgicae* I (1963–73), ed. R. Kaczynski (Turin, 1976)
LC	M. Luther, Large Catechism (1529)
Leun. C.	Leuenberg Concord (or Agreement)
LG	Vatican II: Dogmatic Constitution *Lumen Gentium*
Lima	*Baptism, Eucharist and Ministry,* Faith and Order Paper No. 111, World Council of Churches (Geneva, 1982). (Lima Document)
LThK	*Lexikon für Theologie und Kirche*, ed. J. Höfer and K. Rahner, 2nd ed. (Freiburg, 1957–)
LW	*Luther's Works*, American Edition, ed. J. Pelikan and H. T. Lehmann, 54 vols. (Philadelphia and St. Louis, 1955–86)
LWF	Lutheran World Federation
Malta	*The Gospel and the Church*, Report of the Joint Lutheran/Roman Catholic Study Commission, 1972. (Malta Report)
Meyer/Vischer	H. Meyer and L. Vischer, eds., *Growth in Agreement: Reports and Agreed Statements of Ecumenical Conversations on a World Level* (New York and Geneva, 1984). (Includes Lima, Malta, Ministry, etc.)
Ministry	*Ministry in the Church*, Lutheran–Roman Catholic conversation, 1981.
MSA	P. Melanchthon, *Werke in Auswahl*, ed. R. Stupperich (Gütersloh, 1951ff.)
NR	J. Neuner and H. Roos, eds., *Der Glaube der Kirche in den Urkunden der Lehrverkündigung* (Regensburg, 1938; 11th ed. 1983)
OE	Vatican II: Decree *Orientalium Ecclesiarum*
PO	Vatican II: Decree *Presbyterorum Ordinis*
Rennings	*Dokumente zur Erneuerung der Liturgie*, I: *Dokumente des Apostolischen Stuhls 1963–73*, ed. H. Rennings (Kevelaer, 1983)

Res.	M. Luther, "Resolutiones disputationum de indulgentiarum virtute" (1518)
Rit. Rom	Rituale Romanum (1614)
SC	Vatican II: Constitution *Sacrosanctum Concilium*
SD	Formula of Concord: Solid Declaration
SmC	M. Luther, Small Catechism (1529)
STh	Thomas Aquinas, *Summa Theologiae*, Latin/Eng., Blackfriars (London and New York, 1963–)
Suppl.	Supplementum
ThQ	*Theologische Quartalschrift* (Tübingen, 1819ff.)
TRE	*Theologische Realenzyklopädie* (Berlin and New York, 1977ff.)
Treatise	P. Melanchthon, "Treatise on the Power and Primacy of the Pope" (1537)
UR	Vatican II: Decree *Unitatis Redintegratio*
VELKD	Vereinigte evangelisch-lutherische Kirche Deutschlands (United Evangelical Lutheran Church of Germany)
WA	M. Luther, *Werke* (Weimar, 1883ff.). (Weimarer Ausgabe)

The Reformed Confessions for which no official edition exists may be found in E. F. G. Müller, ed., *Bekenntnisschriften der reformierten Kirche* (Leipzig, 1903); W. Niesel, ed., *Bekenntnisschriften und Kirchenordnungen der nach Gottes Wort reformierten Kirche* (Zollikon, Zurich, 1938, 1985); P. Jacobs, ed., *Reformierte Bekenntnisschriften und Kirchenordnungen in deutscher Übersetzung* (Neukirchen, 1949); and O. Weber, ed., *Der Heidelberger Katechismus* (Gütersloh, 1978).

TRANSLATOR'S PREFACE

One or two points may perhaps be of use to English-speaking readers of these documents.

The German word *evangelisch* has, as is normal practice, been translated as "Protestant." However, readers should bear in mind the confessional situation which was the background of the study. Protestant churches in Germany belong for the most part to the Lutheran tradition and—although some Reformed theologians were coopted to the working parties (see the minutes of 14/15 September 1982 and the membership lists)—the main weight on the Protestant side lay on the Lutheran tradition. The word "Protestant" is therefore sometimes used to describe positions with which members of non-Lutheran Protestant churches may not always be able to identify themselves. The Independent/Baptist tradition particularly is not taken into account here. Readers will also occasionally find the phrase "the two churches" used to cover the Roman Catholic and the Protestant traditions en bloc. Here the historical situation should be borne in mind.

In the individual documents the Revised Standard Version of the Bible has been used for biblical quotations except where a modification was required to bring out the nuance of the German text. Quotations from the documents of the Second Vatican council have been taken from *Vatican Council II: the Conciliar and Post Conciliar Documents*, ed. A. Flannery, revised ed. (Dublin, Leominster, New Town NSW, 1988).

I should like to thank Professor Alasdair Heron for valuable advice most patiently and generously given. Any remaining faults of judgment are mine, not his.

MARGARET KOHL

EDITORS' PREFACE

*The Origin and Growth
of the Study*

It has been generally accepted that doctrinal differences were the essential reason for the disintegration of the Western church into different denominations. At the same time, it must be pointed out that other elements contributed to the division of the churches in the sixteenth century, not differences of doctrine alone. Political, cultural, social, and economic factors were involved, as well as the laws that go to maintain any already existing institution. Nor must we forget the part played by individual human characteristics.

All these things were woven into a web that is often hard to penetrate. The historians have tried to unravel the tangle, each in his own way, while the systematic theologians have attempted to weigh the significance of all the individual threads. Notwithstanding the importance of all these "nontheological" factors, pure conflict about the truth has often pushed into the background the other aspects of the church's fellowship. It would therefore seem all the more necessary to follow up a phase of ecumenical dialogue in which endeavors centered on the discovery of buried common ground, adding to it a comprehensive and thorough investigation of the problem of the mutual doctrinal condemnations: What were the sixteenth-century fathers about, when they condemned the doctrines of the other side? In what form did they do what they did, and with what consequences? Do our discussion partners today still fall under the condemnations of that earlier time because they are in the succession of its decisions simply by virtue of their membership of their respective churches?

1. The Origin and Course of the Investigations

The present document owes its existence to these questions and themes. On 17 November, 1980, during his visit to Germany, Pope John Paul II met Protestant Christians in Mainz. On that occasion, Regional Bishop* Eduard Lohse, as chairman of the Council of the Evangelical Church in Germany,** pleaded the urgent need for improved ecumenical cooperation with regard to Sunday services, eucharistic fellowship, and mixed marriages.[1] In the Joint Ecumenical Commission set up after this meeting (1981 to 1985) it was soon pointed out on the Catholic side that these burning practical problems could not be dealt with unless fundamental and hitherto insufficiently clarified theological

---

*Landesbischof. Protestant bishops in Germany have "territories," not dioceses. In spite of the title, these territories are not identical with the federal states (Bundesländer). In this work, the title Landesbischof will be translated simply as Bishop.—TRANS.

**Rat der Evangelischen Kirche in Deutschland.—TRANS.

questions were also solved. Indeed, these fundamental questions had actually to take precedence, since the pastoral tasks in question could not be solved on a merely pragmatic basis.

At the very beginning, at the constituting session of the Joint Ecumenical Commission held in Munich on 6/7 May, 1981, it was already agreed that working through the questions mentioned above should actually serve to strengthen the common witness of the churches involved. Yet the "condemnations" of the sixteenth century stand in the way of this common witness and call it into question. The commission resolved that the Ecumenical Study Group of Protestant and Catholic Theologians should be entrusted with the task of "ironing out the past" through a clarification of the mutual doctrinal condemnations.[2]

In a letter of June 1981 addressed to the chairmen and scholarly directors of the study group, Bishop Lohse and Cardinal Ratzinger described the heart of the task before them in the following words: "During the discussions in Munich, it once again became clear that our common witness is counteracted by judgments passed by one church on the other during the sixteenth century, judgments which found their way into the Confessions of the Lutheran and Reformed churches and into the doctrinal decisions of the Council of Trent. According to the general conviction, these so-called condemnations no longer apply to our partner today. But this must not remain a merely private persuasion. It must be established by the churches in binding form." From the very beginning it was stressed that this did not imply a "frivolous relationship to our own history. On the contrary, it means that, accepting our own history, we also accept new insights that have meanwhile emerged, new challenges and new experiences" (Minutes of the meeting held on 6/7 May, 1981, no. 2, p. 3; cf. the full text on pp. 168f. below).

In the autumn of 1981 this task was supplemented by another. The Joint Ecumenical Commission also asked itself which statements in the convergence texts could be accepted by the churches. The examination of this question was also passed on to the Ecumenical Study Group. This was a necessary step, for the task of discovering whether the rejections of long ago still apply to our partner today must not be restricted to a historical investigation in the narrow sense. The state of the question today must be drawn into the whole context, at least as a ferment and catalyst. To "work through" the condemnations and to examine the reception given to the convergence texts are therefore two sides of the same coin. At the same time, common sense made it obvious that here not all ecumenical convergence documents could be called upon and made the subject of separate investigation.

Under the chairmanship of Hermann Cardinal Volk and Bishop Hermann Kunst, and under the scholarly guidance of the editors, the Ecumenical Study Group of Protestant and Catholic Theologians worked from the summer of 1981 until the autumn of 1985 on the investigation for which the commission had asked. In order that it might fulfill its function, the study group was expanded by Reformed theologians and by a number of experts who had not originally belonged to it. All in all, over thirty theologians worked continually on the texts in three different working parties (justification, sacraments, ministry; see pp. 164ff. below). A number of other theologians were asked for expert opinions on particular subjects. The whole Ecumenical Study Group (see pp. 163f. below)—not all its members participated in the working parties—discussed the results in five plenary sessions, each lasting several days. Thus fifty theologians in all took part in the total process of the work and its evaluation. From the early summer to the early autumn of 1985, these theologians also participated in a differentiated, written vote.

Three working parties were formed to consider the following subjects:

1. *Justification* (faith, baptism, penance): chairman, Karl Lehmann.
2. *Sacraments* (in general, and especially the Lord's Supper): chairman, Theodor Schneider.
3. *Ministry* (including the ecclesiological presuppositions and the question of Scripture and tradition): chairman, Wolfhart Pannenberg.

Other open questions (e.g., the veneration of saints, the celibacy of the clergy, monastic vows, and the veneration of the Virgin Mary) were not supposed to be explicitly included. But the method of treating the fundamental questions was intended to throw general theological light on these remaining points of dispute or divergence.

From the very beginning there was close contact between the leaders of the Ecumenical Study Group and the Joint Ecumenical Commission. The scholarly directors took part in the meetings of the Joint Ecumenical Commission from the second conference until the tenth (and last). Quite early on, and regularly thereafter, individual preliminary results were put forward and discussed. In the final phase of the deliberations, the two chairmen, Bishop Kunst and Cardinal Volk, also participated in an advisory capacity in the meetings of the Joint Ecumenical Commission. On 24/25 October, 1985, the chairmen of the Ecumenical Study Group were then able to submit the whole undertaking to the chairmen of the Joint Ecumenical Commission, now Bishop

Eduard Lohse and Bishop Paul-Werner Scheele (see pp. 174f. below). At the same time, the Final Report of the Joint Ecumenical Commission on the Examination of the Sixteenth-Century Condemnations was passed (fourteen pages). This was submitted to the public in January 1986 (see pp. 178f. below). It is of course no substitute for the differentiated results of the investigations, but it does attempt an initial summing up, a preliminary formulation, and an evaluation of the outcome of the work, which it is hoped may be of service for the future course of the reception.

In February 1986, the Council of the Evangelical Church in Germany (EKD) and the German Episcopal Conference gave intensive consideration to the results. The Council of the EKD has passed on the final report and the separate investigations to its member churches, and in the course of the next two to three years their synods are to study the results and pass the appropriate resolutions. The German Episcopal Conference has also accepted the documents for examination, and has set up a working party which will put forward recommendations for a more precise evaluation. The already existing contact with the Secretariat for Promoting Christian Unity in Rome is to be intensified. The churches will also remain in close touch with regard to the reception process.

2. The Need for the Investigation
and Its Methods

The questions laid before the Ecumenical Study Group have to be approached with a large measure of understanding. The result of working through the doctrinal condemnations will not ipso facto be a further convergence between the churches. Many people will therefore take a skeptical view of the laborious working procedure involved, with its differentiated thought processes. Even from a scholarly point of view, the procedure of working through these earlier condemnations is open to question and to doubts.

It has already been pointed out, however, that many of the sixteenth-century doctrinal condemnations run counter to the "fundamental agreement" between the churches which is continually asserted. In addition, ecumenical sincerity requires us to face up to this difficult task, for statements of this kind are also part of the binding doctrine of the church in question, even if the weight given to them varies. As long as these statements have not been officially considered—at least in theological instruction—they will inevitably continue to be passed on. It would not be honest simply to allow quiet dust to gather around them, as it were. It is impossible in the long run tacitly to pass them by, even though this is no doubt common practice today. No Catholic theologian, for example, can simply invalidate the binding force of such doctrinal statements simply of his own accord. Nor can the solemn obligation to accept the Confessions which apply in any given case be overlooked in Protestantism either, particularly in the Lutheran churches. The service of ordination includes an "injunction" based on particular Confessions, which are often listed by name. Even more modern orders for ordination have not abandoned this custom. What point would there be in binding oneself, not only to the whole body of confessional documents, but to the condemnatory judgments they include, and to do so in solemn form, while at the same time more or less ignoring these judgments? Common honesty toward the inheritance we have received and toward our own present conduct therefore enjoins us, in the context of our specific and binding commitment, to turn our attention to the condemnations also.

If, now, we look back to the agreement about the foundations of our faith arrived at in the ecumenical conversations of recent years, the tension between this agreement and the mutual condemnations becomes even greater, indeed unendurable. Fundamental agreement and a "fundamental consensus" are certainly not as yet a *full* consensus leading to complete community and eucharistic fellowship between the churches. But how can we understand and judge the mutual condemnations in a new way, in the light of these recognitions, if we understand a condemnation in its original sense of a total rejection or casting off? For a condemnation is not pronounced because of a rupture on the human level. Condemnatory judgments are theologically legitimate only if they are based on an interpretation of the ultimately binding doctrine of faith and its ultimately valid practice. Consequently, condemnations usually involve the end of communion between the churches. The *damnamus* ("we condemn") stands and falls with an opposition in doctrine that touches the very foundation of faith and the gospel. But not every doctrinal difference has to be censured by an anathema. It is also possible for some doctrinal differences to remain—differences which must not be glossed over or ignored for what they are but which are not sufficient to divide the churches, or no longer do so (see pp. 27f. below). This may even be the case in questions where a greater measure of understanding still has to be acheived before full communion between the churches can be restored.

The task the Ecumenical Study Group was given and which it has fulfilled brings us face-to-face with a fundamental contradiction. On the one hand the creeds and dogmas of the church retain their validity. Yet on the other hand they are supposed to lose their force, inasmuch as they no longer apply to the present state of doctrine in the other church. This problem brings to mind the procedure and discussion leading up to the Leuenberg Agreement (or Concord). The connection was in fact already touched on in the letter written by Bishop Lohse and Cardinal Ratzinger in June 1981—that is to say, when the task was officially outlined for the first time. The passage runs: "The path entered upon in the Leuenberg Agreement between the Lutheran and the Reformed churches ought to find a corresponding continuation between the Protestant churches and the Roman Catholic Church." This agreement between the Protestant churches in Europe takes the form of a text which was finally adopted in 1973. It seeks on a European level to bring into being a communion between the Lutheran, Reformed, and United (Lutheran and Reformed) churches, the Church of the Czech Brethren, and the Waldensian Church.[3] However, similar though the problems are, in working out the individual documents the Ecumenical Study Group was from the outset unable to ignore the considerable differences also existing between the methodology involved in the task assigned to it and the Leuenberg Agreement (or Concord):

1. With regard to the texts under discussion, there was from the very beginning no intention of arriving at a "concord," which is a binding agreement and a direct attempt to restore the communion of the churches. If any such concord were to be successfully arrived at, it would have to be worked out in a series of later steps. The investigations of the Ecumenical Study Group are, at most, preliminary work for this later stage.

2. It is true that the Protestant churches had ceased to be in communion with one another. They had also in some cases reproached one another with having completely failed to understand the Reformation properly, or with not having grasped its implications and its scope. But these different churches have also, often enough, been interpreted merely as different theological schools within the Reformation. The churches belong to the same "type." The relationship between the churches of the Protestant tradition and the Roman Catholic Church has a different structure altogether, and therefore raises problems of its own.

3. The attitude of the Protestant churches toward the Confessions differs from the Catholic Church's commitment to its dogma; and this is particularly true of the churches belonging to the Reformed tradition. The Confessions can from the outset be more directly and firmly

relativized among the Protestant partners because of the relation to Scripture, and because the Confessions themselves were so strongly molded by historical circumstances. Modern dogmatic hermeneutics provides the Catholic theologian with an instrument which links together continuity and change in a differentiated way.

Because of these and other differences, the Leuenberg Agreement did not as a whole fundamentally influence the findings of the Ecumenical Study Group as it sought to fulfill the task assigned to it, although methodologically the Agreement had a "trigger" function and led to individual convergences. Many points of contact emerge rather from an inner closeness to the problems of the critical-historical method and of ecumenical dialogue.

The following questions proved useful as a *methodological* approach in the practical work on the many condemnatory pronouncements:

1. Against whom is a given doctrinal condemnation directed?
2. Was this condemnatory pronouncement a correct rendering of the target position?
3. Does it still apply to the position adopted by today's partner?
4. If it does, what importance and what significance does the remaining difference have?

A comparison of the two perspectives (that is to say, the retrospective, historical view, and the analysis of the present state of doctrine) raises the question: Can the formulations of that earlier time still be maintained today at all points? And this question leads to the further inquiry: Can the partner churches *still, today,* be viewed as the addressees of the condemnations? Perhaps it would be preferable to say rather that today's doctrine is no longer determined by the error that the earlier rejection wished to guard against.[4] It is in this sense that the "shorthand," codelike formulations in the documents should be interpreted, when they say that the doctrinal condemnations are "no longer applicable," "do not apply," or can be "revoked."

An understanding of the method used is extremely important for the reception process, since there is also considerable skepticism about the procedure itself. The Introduction (cf. pp. 14ff.), other individual documents, and also the Final Report of the Joint Ecumenical Commission on the Examination of the Sixteenth-Century Condemnations (cf. esp. pp. 182ff.) attempt a synthesis, so there is no need to repeat that here. It must not be forgotten that the individual documents are themselves, in their turn, highly concentrated syntheses of more extensive trains of thought and analyses. Even less can these individual documents present all the reasons and evidence underlying the whole argumentation. Moreover, in inquiring how far the sixteenth-century condemnations have ceased to apply to today's partner, we are faced with an unusually wide spectrum. Here we stand before a multiplicity of highly differentiated judgments that cannot easily be reduced to a single definition, even after a repeated reading of the texts. Above all, however, for this we lack a comprehensive hermeneutic. The instrument we have at our disposal is, for this specific field, relatively simple and restricted. Here there is always a lurking danger that we may reduce the matter to simplistic formulas—for example, that all the sixteenth-century condemnations were merely "misunderstandings," that the parties to the dispute were merely at cross-purposes, and so forth.

Avoiding this oversimplification, we may mention at least a few different types drawn from the whole spectrum of different kinds of judgment. There are rejections on the Protestant side which have as their target—as we can see today—not the binding doctrine of the Catholic Church but theological opinions of the time. We can discover condemnations which apply to extreme positions and marginal assertions on the other side. These are often not the doctrine of the church; they are personal opinions. Some condemnations were directed at extreme theses which, in this one-sided, exaggerated form, did not represent the full, comprehensive doctrine of the partner even then, let alone today. Views that were originally stated in oppositional, exclusive terms may today not infrequently prove to be complementary. Doctrinal elements that seemed to be lacking turn up in other contexts and in other terminology. Both partners occasionally stick fast in antitheses because they are each imprisoned within the confines of a particular terminology, particular ways of thinking, and so forth, which are conditioned by the circumstances of intellectual and theological history. Problems of definition and different kinds of approach can ultimately distort what is in fact common ground.

These brief indications must suffice, for the results still have to be individually worked out, and this is a process which certainly cannot take place in this opening explanation and introduction.

3. The Publication of the Results

This volume gathers together the eight individual texts that comprise the total project. The texts have undergone a final formal harmonization, and continual consultations between the working parties took place. But it cannot be denied that the individual documents vary in form, not merely because they deal with different subjects but also because they were produced by three different working parties. Moreover, the same time for study and consultation was not available in all cases. Some texts were modified and revised nine times. In other cases no such intensive work went to the building up of a consensus—for example, in the papers on "the minor sacraments," the anointing of the sick, confirmation, and marriage. The Joint Ecumenical Commission did not want to prolong its life for more than approximately four years and wished to complete the limited task assigned to it within that period. More extensive studies—particularly on the subjects that are less frequently the subject of ecumenical discussion—would, however, have claimed considerably more time. And this time was not available, for a number of different reasons (e.g., the period of office of the EKD, other claims on the time of members of the Ecumenical Study Group, and the extensive nature of the documents). Here above all, tasks for the future also become plain.

It seemed necessary to offer the reader at least some information about the background of the undertaking—the people involved and the context of the project in the churches contributing to the investigations. Lists of members of the various bodies have therefore been included (cf. pp. 163f.) as well as the letters, minutes, and reports that document the origin of the study and its completion (cf. pp. 168ff.). The subject index is especially designed to gather together headings that are thematically not much stressed in the studies and are rather scattered but that are nonetheless important for an understanding of the whole.

With the publication of these texts, the Ecumenical Study Group has fulfilled its chief task. It will probably publish two further volumes of material. These will include the important preliminary studies, working papers, studies and excursuses relating to the total document published here. The first volume will present contributions on the doctrinal condemnations in general and on the doctrine of justification. The second will contain material on the doctrine of the sacraments and the ministry.

The completion of this publication is an occasion for the editors to express their very sincere thanks. In the name of the Ecumenical Study Group, they have to thank the churches for the confidence placed in them and for support in many different ways. Very particular gratitude, however, is due to the colleagues who for almost five years set aside many of their own scholarly plans and devoted themselves to the work with immense pains, exceptional discipline, and a discretion that has nowadays become a rarity. The editors thank Dr. Lothar Kugelmann, Munich, for his work in editing and preparing the manuscripts for press. He also undertook the task of verifying all quotations and references.

Karl Lehmann
Wolfhart Pannenberg

1

INTRODUCTION

---

*The Condemnatory Pronouncements of
the Sixteenth Century Which Stand
between the Roman Catholic Church
and the Churches of the Reformation*

The changed situation of Christianity in the world, and the ecumenical movement which grew up in that context, have softened the confrontation of earlier centuries and have brought a new awareness of the ties that bind us through our faith in Jesus Christ. This is particularly true of the ecumenical conversations that have taken place between the Roman Catholic Church and the Protestant churches since the Second Vatican Council; but it may also be said of converging developments in the life of the churches on both sides. Today our awareness of the ties of faith between the churches is stronger than our remembrance of the reasons for the division that came about in the sixteenth century. Yet the mutual condemnations, rejections, and differing doctrines that were expressed at that time still stand between the churches, hindering further progress on the way to full mutual recognition and communion. The reexamination of these condemnations and doctrinal differences is therefore an urgent task for the churches on their way to ecumenical understanding.

This reexamination can only be a matter of taking the truth seriously, together. The antitheses that developed in the age of the Reformation must not be trivialized. Mutual misunderstandings undoubtedly existed, and were also reflected in some of the mutual condemnations. But there were also profound differences in the interpretation of the gospel itself. Under the conditions of the time, these were hard to overcome and were, to all intents and purposes, never removed. But today the churches share a largely common, supradenominational interpretation of Scripture, and a common awareness of the historical contingency of theological formulations. And on this basis new convergences have grown up in our understanding of the content of faith. In this process, one-sided emphases have been corrected, emphases which were partly the cause of the division but which partly grew up as its consequence, and in the wake of the controversial theology that developed out of the separation.

We may pick out two examples of particular relevance for the life of the church. On the Roman Catholic side, the theology of the Word was taken up, and the importance of preaching in congregational worship was stressed; while on the Protestant side, the Eucharist came to be recognized as central element in the worship or liturgical life of the church, a new order being accordingly introduced. Both sides were concerned to find ways of emphasizing the link between the presence of Christ in the Lord's Supper and the liturgical anamnesis of his sacrificial death; and these endeavors led to a large measure of agreement. Both sides are at one in their belief that Jesus Christ and his gospel are the source, center, and norm of Christian life. The recollection of this fact must lead divided Christendom to repentance and to endeavors to overcome the divisions of the church, which violate the unity of Christ's body and are in contradiction to the Lord's own prayer for the unity of believers.

I. THE PRESUPPOSITIONS FOR A REEVALUATION OF THE DISPUTED QUESTIONS OF THE REFORMATION PERIOD

a. The progress already achieved toward surmounting the old disputed questions is in the first instance due to a renewed and deepened study of the Holy Scriptures of the Old and New Testaments. This study has brought Catholic and Protestant theologians closer together. The more differentiated appraisal of the wording of scriptural statements, in the framework of their historical contexts, has eliminated one-sided stresses on both sides. This development has been forwarded in recent years by the fact that the most authoritative documents of the Roman Catholic Church have encouraged Catholic scholars to explore the meaning of the biblical writings, giving greater weight to their historical genesis and to the literary character of the individual texts. This encouragement was given above all in Pope Pius XII's encyclical *Divino afflante Spiritu* and in the Second Vatican Council's Constitution on Divine Revelation *(Dei Verbum)*. This initiated a renewal which bound the whole of theology more closely to the biblical origins of faith. Here Catholic exegesis was able to draw on the methodological findings of Protestant biblical studies.

This development had great importance for the ecumenical theological dialogue, especially since Protestant exegesis also arrived at a more differentiated view of the biblical testimonies of faith and devoted more attention to the link between theological and historical problems. In their common conviction that the biblical testimony has normative significance for the Christian faith, Catholic and Protestant theologians learned particularly how to distinguish more precisely the different stages in the formation of the tradition deposited in the writings of the New Testament. The recognitions that were acquired in this process were especially important for Christology, but also for an understanding of the Lord's Supper and justification particularly.

b. Historical research in the fields of liturgy, church history, and the history of dogma provided further impulses toward new thinking.

Today, research sees the historical interactions more clearly and knows better how to distinguish between New Testament origins and their developments in the patristic church. This is especially important with regard to the growth of the episcopal office in the early and patristic church, and for the view of the Eucharist as sacrifice. But it also has an important bearing on the interpretation of the papal office in its relationship to the Petrine tradition of the New Testament. No less important for an understanding and evaluation of the Reformation was the more precise distinction between the mental approach of patristic and medieval Latin writings, as well as between the theology of high scholasticism and the late scholasticism which Luther studied and which was his main target of attack. Important also, finally, has been research into Luther's own theology, study of the other Reformers, and the investigation of sixteenth-century Catholic controversial theology.

In spite of all differences of opinion in particular cases, more differentiated judgments about the old controversial themes are emerging on both sides. Today, for example, the Catholic side recognizes more freely the contribution made by the Reformation to a renewed understanding of the gospel in the light of Scripture, and more readily admits the justification of the criticism leveled by Luther and Calvin at the theology and ecclesiastical life of their time. On the other hand, the Protestant side increasingly recognizes that scholastic theology interpreted the biblical message for the questioning men and women of its own time, and with the intellectual possibilities open to it; for the human mind is never more than incompletely and imperfectly able "to comprehend . . . what is the breadth and length and height and depth, and to know the love of Christ which surpasses knowledge" (Eph. 3:18f.). Better historical understanding makes it possible to grasp the different ways of thinking and terminology on both sides—differences which make mutual understanding difficult, especially in the doctrine of justification but also in the understanding of the Lord's Supper as eucharistic sacrifice. Here the limitations imposed by the terminology of the time become evident on both sides—limitations of terminology which also affected the understanding of the substance itself. Some of these limitations were common to Catholics and Protestants alike, having their roots in the intellectual tradition of Western Christianity, Augustinianism, and the Latin Middle Ages. The statements of the Protestant doctrine of justification, and the other Protestant doctrinal formulations, were not as directly identical with scriptural doctrine as the Reformers believed. But the decisions of the Council of Trent, which aimed to clarify Catholic doctrine in the face of the insufficiency of late medieval theology and the Reformers' criticism, also show themselves to be a new formulation of the ancient message for the people and church of an age that was no longer the age of the apostles.

Moreover, the many-faceted character of the conflict process which started with Luther has become clearer, as well as the far-reaching influence of the "nontheological factors," which at that time made theological agreement difficult. Among these factors were the interweaving of theological argumentation with ecclesiastical, political, and economic interests, as well as—to an increasing degree—painful experiences on both sides, which roused a mistrust hard to overcome. So the other side often came to be interpreted in the light of fringe groups and extremist positions.

c. Progress in biblical studies and historical research has led directly to the insight that it is apparently not uncommon for people to mean the same thing by different words—and also that the same words can mean different things. It is certainly true that conversation between the churches must never shun the labor of expressing in a common language what all affirm and that to which all testify. Where a difference of language remains, we may suspect that there is still disunity in substance as well. And, above all, fellowship in the one church, whatever form this may take, requires a common language for a common creed. At the same time, however, when we talk in different, indeed opposing, languages—as happens in our churches—we must remember that if we want to discover whether there is a real difference of doctrine, it is not sufficient merely to compare different words. This is particularly true when we hurl exaggerated theses and extremist positions at one another (as often in the sixteenth century), whether out of undue zeal, or whether—according to academic convention—in the interests of a clear-cut discussion.

It must also be said, however, that this insight occasionally flashed through the minds of some people even in the Reformation period; for example, when in the Augsburg Confession of 1530 Melanchthon continually attempted to explain to his Catholic opponents that, even if the Reformers seemed to be expressing themselves in a new way, they still desired only to bring out the ancient traditional doctrine of the Bible and the church, to which they too knew themselves to be bound. Or when, even at that time, a few Catholic controversial theologians maintained the view that some points of controversy were merely what they called "a duel about words." But in a way that can only be called tragic, this insight never gained a wide enough influence at that time. Today it counts as so axiomatic that without it ecumenical discussion would be inconceivable.

d. This insight is linked with a second one. Why, then, do we choose one or the other mode of expression, clinging to it with an insistence that is even prepared to pay the price of bitter strife? The reason is that the different "words" we "fight for" spring from and reflect particular different "concerns" and emphases in the interpretation of a message: whether it be faithfulness to tradition; or whether it be the desire to face up responsibly to the questions and possible interpretations of the present time; or whether it be anxiety about the consequences for proclamation and pastoral care. It is seldom, probably, that these "concerns" and interpretative emphases are open to criticism in themselves—although they may certainly become so if they lead to one-sidedness because of the fears and anxieties that prompt them in any given case. On the other hand, no one way of expressing the truth of faith can ever take account of all its aspects at once, giving equal weight to them all. This means that it is the function of theological interpretation to present what seems to be of the first importance for the men and women to whom the gospel has to be proclaimed, according to the charge given us, and in the light of the church's situation; and theology has to distinguish this from what is less urgent, even though it is also important and true. But as a result theological presentations of the truths of faith are always partly conditioned by some kind of judgment about what is most important. And in this sense they are certainly "relative," in the double sense of the word: related to the most urgent concern, and for that very reason also limited in comparison with the whole truth.

e. In considering differences about concepts and their terminology, and disagreements about the interpretative stress in any given case, we must also remember the following: even a binding doctrinal decision requires further interpretation. A confessional document, or conciliar texts, certainly never merely represent the thinking of an individual; in however comprehensive or however limited a way, they express "the memory of the church," as the fellowship of believers, and have a significance pointing to the future. Yet in the form in which they are expressed, if not in the truth they embody, they are historically conditioned. They are "enunciated . . . in terms that bear the traces of [the changeable conceptions of a given epoch]" (Declaration of the Congregation for the Doctrine of the Faith, "Mysterium Ecclesiae," of 24 June, 1973, sec. 5).

This is, on the one hand, an advantage: the doctrine of the church speaks to the men and women of a particular time in order to utter the truth of faith in their own historical hour and in relation to their own particular needs and problems. But it also involves a limitation. It means that dogmatic formulations of the past, true though they may be, cannot always be easily communicated to a later time "to the same extent" (ibid.). Of course this must not lead to the forgetting of some truth of faith, let alone to its denial. Yet it applies even to statements of faith of which Luther would say, "Nothing in this article can be given up or compromised" (AS II.1, 5: BC 292). Consequently, traditional doctrine has continually to be reinterpreted. And since this process of further and continuing interpretation has long since taken place in the Catholic and the Protestant churches alike, and is once again taking place at the present time, the positions maintained in the sixteenth century no longer confront one another in unaltered form.

f. To a degree that can hardly be exaggerated, the insights described here have led to fruitful progress in conversations between the Roman Catholic Church and the churches of the Reformation. They have also been—and are still—fostered in a positively dramatic way by the challenges and the threats to the Christian faith experienced in recent years and at the present time. In this way, these insights have encouraged a new, hitherto undreamed of openness in the attempts of Catholic theologians to arrive at a better understanding of the theology of the Reformation and, conversely, in the endeavors of Protestant theologians to understand Roman Catholic theology. On the Catholic side this has come about with particular intensity, and in what may be called exemplary fashion, where Luther and Lutheran theology are concerned. But it is also true of the approach to Calvin and other Reformers, and to the theological tradition that derives from them. What may be called Luther's "new beginning" (although according to his reforming intention it was really a renewal of origins and the removal of abuses) came increasingly to be accepted as a theological question and challenge; and Catholic theologians have freed themselves more and more from the assumption—never before called into question—that whatever was new in Luther's theology—especially in the understanding of justifying faith—which as such found no support in pre-Lutheran ecclesiastical and theological tradition (above all, in the tradition of late medieval times) was through its very novelty ipso facto heretical. Whether what is new in Luther's theology is heretical is something that has to be asked and proved. It must not be assumed. And this applies to the theology of the other Reformers as well.

On the other hand, Catholic theologians have also asked in recent times whether, in its anti-Reformation decrees, the Council of Trent really met the target of the Reformers' intentions and of true Reformation doctrine, and whether its answer was appropriate—indeed, whether the Council was not often substantially in agreement with the Reformers. So—to the joy of all who have at heart the unity in faith of the one church—Catholic theologians have come to participate in research into the theology of Luther, Zwingli, and Calvin, while Protestant theologians contribute to research into Catholic doctrine and its history. Indeed, Catholic theologians help their Protestant fellow Christians to comprehend Luther more fully, while Protestant theologians assist Catholic fellow Christians in arriving at a profounder understanding of the church's doctrine and its roots.

This situation would have been inconceivable fifty years ago. It is a truly spiritual happening, for faith is permitted to see in it the workings of the Holy Spirit, who guides the church "into all the truth" (John 16:13). The other side of the coin must of course be the admission of heavy guilt: Why did we for so long fail to see—or why were we not prepared to admit—the extent to which we stand on the one, *common* foundation, laid down by the one Lord? So we are faced all the more inexorably today with a question: When, in the sixteenth-century condemnations, Catholic Christians and followers of the Reformation mutually accused one another of apostasy—of a departure from the true faith—did they not, even then, go too far? Or at least: Do these condemnations still apply to our discussion partner in church and theology today—and apply in such a way that even now we have to reiterate the statement: "Accordingly we are and remain eternally divided and opposed the one to the other" (AS II.2, 10:*BC* 294)?

II. THE FORM OF THE CONDEMNATORY PRONOUNCEMENTS, THE NEED FOR THEIR REEXAMINATION, AND THE PROCEDURE TO BE ADOPTED

In their reexamination of the mutual rejections of the sixteenth-century period, the churches concerned start from the conviction that the decisions of the church which crystallized in the condemnatory pronouncements of the time contain intellectual and spiritual judgments which state what is permanently valid and binding, even for Christians today. Indeed we must gratefully recognize that the separated churches have drawn life and strength from the spiritual heritage of that era down to the present day. Just because we are convinced of the truth of these statements, they remain for us worthy of reflection. We must therefore think about them afresh, making them our own in a new way in order to understand more profoundly and fully, in a situation that has in many respects changed, statements that were expressed in a historically conditioned and limited way.

The first point to remember here is that the rejections took various forms. There are assertions, especially in the Protestant Confessions, which certainly utter no formal anathema but which imply one in substance, the opponent often being expressly named. On the other hand, explicit condemnations, especially on the Catholic side, are often quite reserved in form. They are conditional, no opponent being expressly named: "If anyone shall have said . . . (*Si quis dixerit . . .*)." Yet in these cases too (e.g., in the condemnatory pronouncements of the Council of Trent) it is generally possible to identify the view against which the statements are directed—at least in the opinion of the writers or the conciliar fathers themselves. And on the opposing side these statements were in fact so viewed—that is, as a rejection of their doctrines, even if those concerned felt that they had been misunderstood.

Today a careful investigation of all the relevant points of view is required before we can even decide whether the condemnations correctly defined the opinion held by the opponent of the time or whether they were directed against a view he never maintained. Even more must we ask whether the rejections of that earlier time still apply to our partner today or whether the truth contained in these assertions cannot be appreciated and recognized by both sides, even while we perceive the limitations of their formulation. Here it must be noted that neither the Protestant Confessions, nor even the decrees and canons of the Council of Trent, may be read primarily as texts directed against the genuine doctrine of the other side, for which that other church was prepared to answer. In the condemnations relating to the doctrines of justification and the sacraments especially, it is evident that the Protestant Confessions were mainly directed against late scholastic positions; and conversely, the Council of Trent had as its target Protestant positions as they had been presented to the conciliar fathers from the lists of errors laid before the Council—lists that had often been drawn up at second or third hand.

It must further be remembered that even at the time when they were formulated, not all the condemnations accused the opponent of denying fundamental articles of faith. Some of the condemnatory pronouncements of the Council of Trent were aimed, not at a denial of revealed truths, but at assertions made against doctrines that were accounted theologically sound, or against a general law of the church. The terms "faith" and "heresy" can also have a correspondingly wide range of meaning.[1] On the Lutheran side, on the other hand, the Formula of Concord, "in a period of persecution" of the gospel, rejected any concession, even in the "indifferent things" (adiaphora) affecting "ecclesiastical rites," subjecting them to its condemnatory judgment.[2] Here too that judgment is particularly related to the situation of the time.

In addition, past doctrinal condemnations must be newly examined today even when they affect central questions of faith; and the doctrinal content itself which people then believed divided them must be jointly considered and adopted afresh.[3] The need for this reexamination is affirmed on the Protestant side as well, in view of the historical contingency of the confessional statements and the corresponding rejections. Both require "interpretation, application, or reformulation" in a changed situation.[4] But this is true in a particular way of the condemnations, because they originated in historical situations of controversy. They are therefore influenced by their particular context in a different way from the fundamental assertions of faith, which claim a general applicability bridging the times. Consequently, common strivings on behalf of these fundamental assertions of faith can make it evident that the rejections of a former day "do not affect [our partner today] because the doctrine of that partner is not determined by the error which the earlier condemnation wished to refute."[5] In the light of this recognition, judgments about those against whom the earlier condemnations were directed will change as well. This is important for ecumenical understanding, because none of today's churches should be expected to break with the tradition that lends them their particular character. On the other hand, inadequacies can certainly be discovered in the opposing formulations of the period, inadequacies of which the adversaries of that former time were not aware.

The chapters that follow will concentrate on three complexes. These were the focuses of the sixteenth-century controversies, and they are still of central importance today for the churches' understanding of faith and for their life. These three complexes are faith and justification, the sacraments, and the ministry. Of course there is a whole series of other topics about which controversy developed between the churches. But subjects such as monasticism, the veneration of saints, and Mariology did not provide the real reason for the schism, nor, taken by themselves, can they justify its continuation. Can we, on the basis of our common recognition of the authority of Scripture, the trinitarian and Christological creeds of the early church, and the fundamental forms of liturgical life and worship, reach an understanding about faith in justification, about the sacraments, and about the ministry of the church? If we can, then confidence in the possibility of a substantial understanding about the remaining differences would seem to be well founded, an understanding that respects differing developments in theology, institutional structure, and spirituality in the churches.

The special situation in the relationship between the churches of the Reformation and the Roman Catholic Church does not permit us to view the formulation of a common basic understanding of the gospel and of the gift of the sacraments as in itself a sufficient basis for withdrawing the mutual condemnations where our partner today is concerned. This proved possible in the Leuenberg Agreement, where the relationship between Protestant churches was at issue, because for these the fellowship of the churches springs directly from their common understanding of the gospel. Hence there were no differences about the interpretation and order of the church's ministry that were capable of dividing them. It is true that in the dialogue between the Reformation churches and the Roman Catholic Church also, understanding about the proclamation of the gospel and the administration of the sacraments is considered to be fundamental. But it must at the same time be remembered that here profound differences exist about the understanding of the church, both in regard to the interpretation of the ministry and its order and with respect to the way in which the church arrives at authoritative doctrinal decisions. Consequently, in the discussion of individual questions, the authority of the church and its magisterium or teaching office in its specific historical utterances must continually be borne in mind. So in the case of each individual topic, we have to ask whether the full reality of Christ's church can be recognized in the other church today, in spite of the condemnations uttered in the past.

In this procedure, we may presuppose a large measure of enduring agreement about the foundations of the Christian faith and its tradition. This was already brought out even in the first part of the Augsburg Confession of 1530.[6] Also presupposed and included in our thinking are the results of the commissions jointly set up by the Protestant churches and the Roman Catholic Church to consider questions relating to the gospel and the church, the Lord's Supper, and the ministry. These for their part are to be evaluated in the wider framework of the ecumenical dialogue between theologians belonging to the churches concerned and the convergence declarations of the World Council of Churches on baptism, Eucharist, and ministry (Lima 1982). In our discussions of the condemnations standing between the Protestant and Roman Catholic churches, our aim has been to determine how far the common ground and convergence in the understanding of faith that was formulated in the results of these dialogues take us *where the condemnations still dividing the churches are concerned.* The common understanding in substance hitherto achieved in the documents of the ecumenical dialogue[7] finds explicit expression here only where it is relevant for this particular purpose.

III. THE AUTHORITY OF HOLY SCRIPTURE AND ITS INTERPRETATION AS FOUNDATION FOR AN UNDERSTANDING OF THE BELIEFS DISPUTED IN THE MUTUAL CONDEMNATIONS

All the churches find the (fundamental) criterion for their understanding of faith in the Holy Scriptures of the Old and New Testaments, as the testimony of the apostolic proclamation, which is the source and norm of the church and its teaching. Yet in the disputes of the Reformation period, the interpretation of scriptural authority and the principles of scriptural interpretation themselves became the object of dispute. The controversial theological discussions about the relation between Scripture and tradition may today count as having lost their acrimony. For on the one hand the Protestant churches also recognize that the biblical writings grew up in the transmission process of the gospel's proclamation (the *viva vox evangelii*—the gospel's living voice) and are permanently related to this process as well as to the testimony of the Holy Spirit which effects faith.[8] And on the other hand, in the Second Vatican Council the Roman Catholic Church stated that the one Word of God is the content of Scripture and tradition (*DV* 10: *unum Verbi Dei sacrum depositum*—"a single sacred deposit of the Word of God"), stressing that to this Word of God the church's teaching office is bound: "This Magisterium is not superior to the Word of God but is its servant. It teaches only what has been handed on to it" (ibid.).

The Second Vatican Council did not explicitly teach that Scripture and its interpretation have a critical function, over against the process in which the church's tradition came into being, after reception of the scriptural canon.[9] But it did say that the church's whole proclamation has to be "nourished and ruled by Scripture" (*DV* 21) and that the study of Holy Scripture is the very soul of all theology (*DV* 24). If these statements are read together with the guidelines for the interpretation of Scripture formulated in *DV* 12, which binds interpretation to the literal and historical sense of the writings,[10] agreement about the function of Scripture as the criterion for the church's doctrine seems at least possible, and in many respects already implicitly to exist. This is all the more true since, according to the Catholic view also (a view already found in high scholasticism), it is possible to talk about a substantial sufficiency of the content of Holy Scripture in questions of faith, even if according to Catholic doctrine the church does not draw its certainty about all revealed truths from Scripture alone (*DV* 9). In this sense, tradition is given the function of interpreting Scripture.

The inner link between Scripture and the church's tradition also finds expression in the establishment of the scriptural canon. The Council of Trent therefore declared the canon of Old and New Testament writings passed down by the church to be binding, including the writings judged apocryphal on the Protestant side (*DS* 1504; cf. 3006). Protestants too do not overlook the fact that the canon is the result of a transmission process, since the biblical writings were handed on in the church. But this fact is interpreted to mean that, under the guidance of the divine Spirit, the canonical writings imposed themselves on the judgment of the church as authoritative because of the inspired character of their content. According to this view, therefore, the church's judgment is to be understood as a recognition that the biblical writings prevailed of themselves, under the efficacious guidance of the Spirit. It is not to be taken as meaning that the canon might have taken a form different from the one it now has. The differences that emerged here ought to be surmountable today, through a deeper reflection about the relation between Scripture and tradition, especially since in both Catholic and Protestant theology exegetical practice has to all intents and purposes been brought into line. What is important for the churches on both sides is that the canon as a whole—that is to say, Scripture as a unity within the diversity of its tradition—is binding for the church's faith and doctrine.

The real point of controversy was, and is, not so much the position of Holy Scripture itself as the question about its correct interpretation, or—to be more precise—the binding nature of the interpretation given by the teaching office of the church (*DS* 1507; cf. 3007). This doctrine was further developed by Vatican I (*DS* 3011, 3006ff.) and by Vatican II. According to what is said there, it is the living teaching office of the church alone which has the task of arriving at an authoritative interpretation of Scripture and tradition (*DV* 10; *LG* 25). Under certain conditions this may even be infallible. According to Catholic interpretation, the teaching office is therefore subordinate to the Word of God, but above the interpretation of that Word by any individual.

The fact that the interpretation of Scripture is in a particular way the task of the church and its teaching office[11] was not denied on the Protestant side either (the interpretation meant here being the interpretation of a total complex, not an individual passage).[12] But according to the Protestant view, this is a matter quite generally for those who preach the gospel, which is also one of the functions of a bishop, according to the Augsburg Confession (28.5ff., 21: *BC* 82ff.). However, the proclamation always remains dependent on the testimony of the divine Spirit (CA 5.2: "Where and when it pleases God" [*ubi et quando visum est Deo*], *BC* 31; cf. Calvin, *Inst.* 1, 7). The scriptural interpretation of theological doctrine, the office of visitation, and the task to "judge doctrine and condemn doctrine that is contrary to the Gospel" (CA 28.21: *BC* 84)—all belong to the preaching office. Preaching is also dependent on its hearing and reception by the congregation. This means that the congregation is co-responsible for pure doctrine and the right administration of the sacraments. It also excludes any monopoly by the ordained ministry with regard to the interpretation of Scripture. According to the Protestant view, when the church listens to the gospel, the results are to be found in its proclamation, and substantially in its Confessions,[13] and these results continually require interpretation and examination in the light of Scripture and its ongoing exegesis. However, even the Protestant churches do not expect that a total revision of their doctrine will be required in the light of Scripture,[14] since the church's doctrine has always been drawn from the testimony of Scripture and from the gospel to which Scripture witnesses. But they do expect that ongoing scriptural exegesis will provide new instruction about the content of the gospel, and that this will give rise to new and, if necessary, modified interpretations of the confessional texts that have been passed down.

To this extent there is fundamental agreement in this question between the Protestant and the Catholic viewpoints, even if no full consensus has as yet been achieved—above all in the question of infallibility and, closely linked with that, the question about the critical function of Scripture. But in the light of the situation in which the gospel is preached at present, both Catholic and Protestant churches have to ask themselves afresh, in the light of their own respective presuppositions, how the church can today teach with authority.[15]

Today the antithetical positions of controversial theology with regard to the relation between scriptural authority and church doctrine have been mitigated to a considerable degree in theological discussion, especially where the discussion of factual theological questions is concerned. On the other hand there is as yet no explicit consensus about the critical function of Scripture over against the formation of the church's tradition. Consequently even greater weight must be given to the question about the practical application of Scripture in judging factual theological questions in which there used to be acrimoniously maintained counterpositions and mutual condemnations.

Today it is possible to say the following: Far-reaching agreement in the interpretation of Holy Scripture, clearer insight about the historical contingency of traditional doctrinal formulations, and the new spirit of ecumenical dialogue, in awareness of the ties linking Christians of different denominational traditions through their faith in the one Lord, have all contributed essentially to the achievement of a large measure of mutual understanding. This understanding is not confined to the fundamental acknowledgment of the one Lord Jesus Christ. It applies also to central themes of Christian doctrine. Today we have to say that a whole series of sixteenth-century condemnatory pronouncements rested on misunderstandings about the opposite position. Others were directed at extreme positions that were not binding on the church. Again others do not apply to today's partner. In the case of a further group, new factual recognitions have led to a considerable degree of agreement. Where some of the condemnations are concerned, however, it must be said that even today we were unable to establish a sufficient consensus. At the same time, it must be asked whether this group of condemnations alone can justify continued division between the churches, in view of the changed relationship between them and between their members.

This is not to say that today we could simply sweep aside the condemnations uttered at that earlier time. They are still important as salutary warnings, both for the members of the churches in which they were originally formulated, and for members of the other Christian confession in question. In each individual tradition, they warn us not to fall short of the clarifications already achieved in the sixteenth century in that particular church. In each given case, they warn members of the other church against interpreting and expressing their own tradition in such a way that antitheses that more recent theological development have made surmountable, break out anew, lending the rejections fresh topical force.

Just because today these warnings are directed equally to the Christians of our own church and to those of other churches, the governing bodies of the churches may perhaps ask themselves the following question: In view of the changed relationship to one another of the churches and their members, must the divisive effect of the condemnations still be maintained—true though it is that further agreement about the positive content of doctrine is certainly still required, on our way to complete unity? This question must be asked, even about those condemnations where no sufficient consensus can yet be established. For the one-sided emphases against which the condemnations are directed can certainly find supporters in each of the Christian churches today; but these views are censured by the churches themselves as curtailed forms of their own understanding of faith. To avert this danger is a common task for all the Christian churches today.

2

JUSTIFICATION

The Justification of the Sinner

I. THE ANTITHESES,
AS THEY WERE HITHERTO UNDERSTOOD

It is not easy to sum up both precisely and clearly the contrasting ways of understanding the justification of the sinner that have been put forward by Roman Catholic and Protestant theologians in the name and at the commission of their churches from the time of the Reformation down to the most recent past. The difficulty is due mainly to the fact that the confessional documents of the different churches are not expressly and deliberately related to one another, but choose different sequences of ideas, and therefore different structures as well. The reasons for this are connected with the situation in which the various documents were drawn up. But it means that we can seldom set text over against text, statement over against statement, comparing the two in each given case.

For a considerable time, however, it has been possible to find a list of essential doctrinal differences—in the sphere of justification as well as in other disputed theological questions—by turning to the relevant theological investigations, to statements made on behalf of the churches, and to the dogmatic textbooks which describe and explain church doctrine. These differences are frequently termed "distinguishing doctrines"; and they have again and again provided the clue or point of reference for comprehending the difference between the divided churches, and for judging the depth of that division. This is still the case today. But ever since the rise of the ecumenical movement, these doctrines have also provided the point of departure for all attempts at overcoming ancient conflict and all efforts to find a deeper agreement in faith which will make a continuing division between the churches seem theologically unjustifiable. In this study too, these distinctions, in spite of their gross over-simplification of the points at variance (or just because of that), can initially perform an important service, providing a starting point for a differentiated theological judgment. They must now be reexamined and reevaluated on the basis of new insights which have been given to the churches and theology today.

As far as the doctrine of justification is concerned, the "distinguishing doctrines" are generally considered to include the following opposing positions.

1. The Reformers teach the complete *depravity of human nature.* Through this, human beings have lost their liberty and power to do what is morally good, and to fulfill God's commandments out of love of him, and not merely outwardly, for their own credit or out of fear of punishment. The Roman Catholic doctrine, on the other hand, insists that human nature is *not entirely* depraved. The liberty to do good is certainly profoundly impaired, but it has not been entirely lost; and it is good, even if not perfect, to perform what God commands out of fear of his punitive judgment. This is not something to be condemned.

The Formula of Concord says:

> We believe, teach, and confess that original sin is not a slight corruption of human nature, but that it is so deep a corruption that nothing sound or uncorrupted has survived in man's body or soul, in his inward or outward powers.

And:

> We believe that in spiritual and divine things the intellect, heart, and will of unregenerated man cannot by any native or natural powers in any way understand, believe, accept, imagine, will, begin, accomplish, do, effect, or cooperate. . . . Hence according to its perverse disposition and nature the natural free will is mighty and active only in the direction of that which is displeasing and contrary to God.[1]

And Luther maintained, contrary to the papal rejection (DS 1486):

> After sin, free will is no more than a name, yea, a name without a substance—and when the will doeth what is in it, it sins mortally.[2]

But Roman Catholic doctrine says:

> If anyone shall say that after the sin of Adam man's free will was lost and destroyed, or that it is a thing in name only, indeed a title without a reality, a fiction, moreover, brought into the Church by Satan: let him be anathema.
>
> If anyone shall say that all works that are done before justification, in whatever manner they have been done, are truly sins or deserving of the hatred of God, or that the more earnestly anyone strives to dispose himself for grace, so much the more grievously does he sin: let him be anathema.
>
> If anyone shall say that the fear of hell, whereby by grieving for sins we flee to the mercy of God or refrain from sinning, is a sin or makes sinners worse: let him be anathema.[3]

2. The Reformers consider *concupiscence* (desire) to be the essential element in the depravity of human nature. It is hence understood as sin, not in the ethical sense, as actual sin, but as the sin rooted in the person which lies at the root of all ethical sins; and it can also be used as a term for original sin. The Roman Catholic Church, however, explicitly de-

scribes concupiscence as *not* being sin, as long as the human being does not assent to it, thereby falling into actual sin.

> For they [the testimonies of Augustine and Paul] clearly call lust sin, by nature worthy of death if it is not forgiven, though it is not imputed to those who are in Christ.[4]

> Accordingly we reject and condemn the teaching . . . that evil desires are not sin but concreated and essential properties of human nature, or the teaching that the cited defect and damage is not truly sin on account of which man outside of Christ is a child of wrath.[5]

Roman Catholic doctrine says in objection to this doctrine of the Lutheran Confessions:

> But this holy Synod confesses and perceives that there remains in the baptized concupiscence of an inclination, but although this is left to be wrestled with, it cannot harm those who do not consent, but manfully resist by the grace of Jesus Christ. Nay, indeed, "he who shall have striven lawfully, shall be crowned" (II Tim. 2:5). This concupiscence, which at times the Apostle calls *sin* (Rom. 6:12ff.; 7:7, 14–20), the holy Synod declares that the Catholic church has never understood to be called sin, as truly and properly sin in those born again, but because it is from sin and inclines to sin. But if anyone is of the contrary opinion, let him be anathema.[6]

3. The Reformers teach *the complete passivity of human beings toward God*—because of the complete depravity of human nature and because salvation has its sole foundation in Christ: where the justification of the sinner is concerned, any cooperation on the part of the human being is impossible. The teaching of the Roman Catholic Church, on the other hand, insists that if human beings are touched by God's justifying grace and are literally "converted," they themselves cooperate with God, inasmuch as they freely assent to God's justifying activity and accept it.

Luther can put the matter as follows:

> Thus the human will is placed between the two like a beast of burden. If God rides it, it wills and goes where God wills. . . . If Satan rides it, it wills and goes where Satan wills; nor can it choose to run to either of the two riders or to seek him out.[7]

And the Formula of Concord says:

> Yet he [the human being] can do nothing whatsoever toward his conversion . . . and in this respect is much worse than a stone or block, for he resists the Word and will of God until God raises him from the death of sin, illuminates him, and renews him.[8]

Roman Catholic doctrine says, however:

> If anyone shall say that man's free will moved and aroused by God does not
> co-operate by assenting to God who rouses and calls, whereby it disposes
> and prepares itself to obtain the grace of justification, and that it cannot
> dissent, if it wishes, but that like something inanimate it does nothing at all
> and is merely in a passive state: let him be anathema.[9]

4. The Reformers teach that *justifying grace* is completely identical
with God's forgiving love and his ever-new commitment. It is therefore
a reality on God's side alone. Roman Catholic doctrine, on the other
hand, insists that justifying grace is by its very nature *(formaliter)* a
reality in the soul of the human being. It has its source in the love of
God and *inwardly renews and remolds* the human being. Melanchthon
asks in the Apology of the Augsburg Confession:

> Why do they [i.e., the opponents] not expound here "grace" as "God's
> mercy with us"?[10]

And Luther explains:

> Here, as ought to be done, I take grace in the proper sense of the favour of
> God—not a quality of soul, as is taught by our more recent writers.[11]

But Roman Catholic doctrine says:

> If anyone shall say that men are justified either by the sole imputation of
> the justice of Christ, or by the sole remission of sins, to the exclusion of
> grace and charity, which is poured forth in their hearts by the Holy Spirit
> and remains in them, or even that the grace by which we are justified is
> only the favor of God: let him be anathema.[12]

5. Pointing to solemn statements of Holy Scripture, the Reformers
emphatically stress that human beings receive the gift of justification
through faith alone—that is to say, solely through trust in the mercy of
God, who for Christ's sake does not impute our sins to us. But the
teaching of the Roman Catholic Church insists that faith and trust
justify only if they are united with the hope and love conferred by God,
and are joined by a corresponding active cooperation with God's grace.

The Augsburg Confession says:

> Men cannot be justified before God by their own strength, merits, or
> works but are freely justified for Christ's sake through faith when they
> believe that they are received into favor and that their sins are forgiven on
> account of Christ, who by his death made satisfaction for our sins. This
> faith God imputes for righteousness in his sight (Rom. 3, 4).[13]

And in the Smalcald Articles we can read in Luther's own words:

Inasmuch as this must be believed [namely, justification by grace as a gift, through the redemption which is in Christ Jesus, by his blood (Rom. 3:23–25)] and cannot be obtained or apprehended by any work, law, or merit, it is clear and certain that such faith alone justifies us. . . . Nothing in this article can be given up or compromised, even if heaven and earth and things temporal should be destroyed.[14]

On the other hand, Roman Catholic docrine says:

If anyone shall say that by faith alone the sinner is justified, so as to understand that nothing else is required to cooperate in the attainment of the grace of justification, and that it is in no way necessary that he be prepared and disposed by the action of his own will: let him be anathema.

If anyone shall say that justifying faith is nothing else than confidence in the divine mercy which remits sins for Christ's sake, or that it is this confidence alone by which we are justified: let him be anathema.[15]

And, as has already been mentioned, the Council of Trent rejects every interpretation of justification that is formulated "to the exclusion of grace and charity" (can. 11, see above).

6. The Reformers contended with equal emphasis that—because of God's promise—this faith creates *the assurance of salvation*, grace, and the forgiveness of sins. Otherwise it would not be true faith. The doctrine of the Roman Catholic Church, on the other hand, insists that, since their love is imperfect, Christians can never be certain whether they are really in a state of grace. They must therefore "work out [their] own salvation with fear and trembling" (Phil. 2:12). Talking about the view to be taken of the church's teaching office, Luther asserted:

Why did Christ say, "Whose soever sins ye remit, they are remitted unto them" if not because they are not remitted unless a man believe they are remitted when the priest remitteth them? . . . Nor doth the remission of sin and the bestowal of grace suffice, but a man must also believe that it is remitted.[16]

I have said: No man can be justified unless through grace, and then in such a fashion that it is necessary for him to believe with a firm trust that he is justified, and in no way to doubt that he attaineth grace. For if he doubteth and is uncertain, then he will indeed not thereby be justified, but rejects grace.[17]

This finds a full echo in the Confessions:

Faith alone, looking to the promise and believing with full assurance that

God forgives because Christ did not die in vain, conquers the terrors of sin and death. If somebody doubts that his sins are forgiven, he insults Christ because he thinks that his sin is greater and stronger than the death and promise of Christ.[18]

But Roman Catholic doctrine says:

If anyone shall say that it is necessary for everyman in order to obtain the remission of sins to believe for certain and without any hesitation due to his own weakness and indisposition that his sins are forgiven him: let him be anathema.

If anyone shall say that man is absolved from his sins and justified, because he believes for certain that he is absolved and justified, or that no one is truly justified but he who believes himself justified, and that by this faith alone absolution and justification are perfected: let him be anathema.[19]

7. Finally, the Reformers teach in the strongest terms that, although good works performed out of faith in God's grace are certainly the consequence and fruit of grace, they are in no way a "merit" in the sight of God. The doctrine of the Roman Catholic Church, on the other hand, insists that the good works of those who are justified, performed in the power of grace, are in the true sense meritorious before God, not because of the human achievement as such, but by virtue of grace and the merits of Christ.

Some of the Reformers' texts quoted above already made it clear that according to Protestant interpretation it is of the essence of God's justifying act to exclude all merit. Their opponents "say they earn grace and eternal life by merit. Such a trust is simply wicked and vain."[20] The Confessions are full of statements of this kind. Luther can sum up his whole criticism of the doctrine of the medieval church in the sentence:

[The righteousness fanatics] are not willing to receive grace and eternal life for nothing from him [God]; they desire to earn both through their works.[21]

And:

[Those men] philosophize godlessly against theology . . . who say that by doing what lies within his power a man may earn God's grace and life.[22]

Roman Catholic doctrine, however, says:

If anyone shall say that the one justified sins, when he performs good works with a view to an eternal reward: let him be anathema.

If anyone shall say that the good works of the man justified are in such a way the gifts of God that they are not also the good merits of him who is justified, or that the one justified, by the good works which are done by him through the grace of God and the merit of Jesus Christ (whose living member he is), does not truly merit increase of grace, eternal life, and the attainment of that eternal life (if he should die in grace), and also an increase of glory: let him be anathema.[23]

If we sum up all the above antitheses in this oversimplified way, questions arise as if of themselves; and to these we have to find an answer: Are the antitheses in fact correctly defined? Have any new points of view emerged that can help us to evaluate them? Can we discover new possibilities for a tenable theological agreement?

II. NEW INSIGHTS, AND THE PATHS LEADING TO THEM

Where the doctrine of the justification of the sinner is concerned, the path to any such agreement seems to be particularly firmly blocked, not only because here the doctrinal differences are formulated in an especially oversimplified way, but also because they are maintained with particular intransigence. But this makes it all the more essential to see that the barricades can be torn down only if we remain unswervingly on the Christological foundation expressed—with particular reference to the doctrine of justification—in the Lutheran-Catholic dialogue that took place in the United States.

Christ and his gospel are the source, center, and norm of Christian life, individual and corporate, in church and world. Christians have no other basis for eternal life and hope of final salvation than God's free gift in Jesus Christ, extended to them in the Holy Spirit.[24]

In faith we recognize that the nearer we draw to Jesus Christ, the closer we come to one another. This recognition is important, because the whole subject and content of the doctrine of justification is nothing other than the gospel of Jesus Christ. An agreement in the doctrinal differences about justification will therefore bring us closer to Christ and to one another. But the doctrine of justification was the fundamental difference on which the ways parted in the sixteenth century. A treatment of this doctrine therefore remains the essential task in all attempts to arrive at an understanding between the Roman Catholic Church and the churches of the Reformation. Every other consensus will be built on sand unless it is supported by a genuine consensus about the doctrine of justification.

In our dialogue about the justification of the sinner, essential progress has in fact been made, in the light of our fundamental reference to Christ and his gospel. The motive forces are the same that we described in the introduction to this study as driving forward the ecumenical dialogue in general. In the question about justification, these forces make themselves felt in a quite specific way.

In the field of biblical studies, Catholic and Protestant theologians—supported by their common conviction about the normative importance of the biblical witness for the Christian faith—have learned to distinguish more clearly between the fundamental biblical assertion about the justification of the sinner and the later theological form given to biblical testimony in a "doctrine of justification." It is undoubtedly the biblical testimony which this doctrine takes up and interprets; yet the testimony itself still remains distinct from the form given to it in its interpretation. Consequently the scriptural witness, because it is primal and normative, remains a critical, and a dynamic, criterion for the doctrine.

But investigations by both Protestant and Catholic scholars into the substance of the apostle Paul's message of justification (especially in the Epistles to the Galatians and the Romans) have also shed new light on the doctrinal differences of the sixteenth century. The interpretation of these texts in the light of their conceptual and historical premises has increased our insight into the event of justification as a totally unmeritable, divine act on behalf of sinful men and women. These receive the gift of justification solely through faith in Jesus Christ, who was crucified for us and is risen; and through this very faith they are also totally claimed by God. This fundamental Pauline recognition pushes into the background all the extremes and over-statements of the "distinguishing doctrines" of the different churches.

Research into church history and the history of theology has made it plain that the late scholastic doctrine of grace and justification differs fundamentally from the doctrine of the high scholastic period, even though the same concepts and words are often employed. In addition, it has shown, above all, that the Council of Trent—contrary to what would at first sight appear to be the case—did not wish to lay down either the late scholastic or the high scholastic doctrine of grace as the authoritative form of expressing Catholic belief. And, contrary to the fears of the Reformers, the Council explicitly affirmed the basis which it shared with them: faith in Christ as the sole source of justification—even if it at the same time rejected the postulate that the righteousness of Christ was *formaliter* ("formally," in the sense of its essential nature) the believer's righteousness also (*DS* 1560).

Hermeneutics and a study of the language of theology have brought us to the point where hardly anyone fails to recognize that scholasticism employs the intellectual and linguistic categories of Aristotelian metaphysics as a way of thinking about the relation between faith and reality. On the other hand, it is now accepted that Luther and the other Reformers rejected this way of speaking because they wanted to help the language of the Bible to come into its own in a new way. There does not have to be any exclusive antithesis here, as is shown by the fact that Melanchthon could once again adopt the scholastic, Aristotelian mode of expression without thereby betraying the cause of the Reformers; and this is even more true of later Lutheran and Reformed theology— although the Protestant writers used scholastic-Aristotelian language in modified form.

Today the Catholic Church and its theology unreservedly recognize the wholly personal and "non-proxy" character of faith, on which everything that takes place between God and human beings depends; and this recognition goes hand in hand with a full acceptance of all the confidence and joy of being a Christian. On the other hand, the Protestant churches and their theologians today can more easily understand the pastoral concerns of the Reformers' opponents, who were afraid that the wording of the Protestant doctrine of justification might endanger the earnestness of ethical endeavor—although according to Protestant doctrine also, this endeavor has to be one of the consequences of faith.

Since each partner thus recognizes the "concerns" and emphases of the other, this must provide the starting point for an understanding of the doctrinal and credal formulations about justification on both sides, so that the concerns which both affirm may be a mutual support instead of a hindrance.

It is in actual fact the case that the conversations carried on for decades at all levels about the controversial questions of the doctrine of justification have led to hopeful results. This came about first of all in specialist theology, but the advance has meanwhile showed itself also in the dialogues of official interchurch commissions. More indeed: the hopes for a consensus that have emerged in the doctrine of justification (in spite of all the continuing differences about individual points) really first gave Protestants and Catholics the courage to approach "from this liberated center" (Karl Barth's phrase) the other points of controversy with which the following sections of our present study are concerned.

The theological reasons for these hopes must now be put before the reader. In so doing, we must never forget that the Catholic, Lutheran, and Reformed doctrines of justification are in each given case a whole. From a given point within a theological "doctrinal structure" (insofar as any such structure is aimed at) down to the final single assertion, everything is, fundamentally speaking, interlocked. This means that we must not make any attempt to break up this unity into individual, isolated elements, which we then go on to compare in equal isolation, discovering harmony or continued dissension, as the case may be. On the other hand, we can never say everything all at once. The tradition of controversial theology, with its "distinguishing doctrines," compels us to go into the details, in a detailed comparison. The totality of the particular tradition in each given case must be taken into account by a recollection of the reference which every individual question bears to the whole. In order to make this easier, we may start by laying down four principles, which may act as a key in the interpretation and evaluation of individual questions and the disputed condemnations related to them.

1. *The formulas of the doctrine of justification (and the dispute about them!) may sound abstract, but they have a specific background and a practical reference to Christian life in the church.* For Protestant criticism was aimed at the praxis of the time, and at the contemporary theological understanding of *penitence and confession.* Consequently, the fundamental assertions about justification through faith in Jesus Christ alone concentrate on what takes place in the sacrament of penance, in the confession of sin and the promise of forgiveness in Christ's name. The Council of Trent's Decree on Justification, on the other hand, seeks to understand justification *by way of baptism,* as it were, and in the context of *life lived out of baptism until the final judgment.* In this way the doctrine of justification is, so to speak, applied Christology and a summary doctrine of the sacraments, although the emphases differ. And because of this, the dispute about formulations may in any given case be more than a "duel about words." But if we take into account the structural differences in the understanding of justification which are due to the different practical emphases, then some misunderstandings, at least, can be eliminated. This is especially so, since the positive pastoral concerns of the Tridentine Decree on Justification, in respect of Christian life and conduct, certainly have their place in Protestant teaching as well—in the doctrine about the Word of God, in the distinction and relation between law and gospel, justification and sanctification, and, not least, in the doctrine of baptism.

2. This first principle, as well as the insights offered in the introduction to this study, lead on to a second principle: *It must not be our aim to prove that we are at one in the structure of our thinking and our trains of thought, let alone in our mode of expression.* What we have to ask is the following question: Are the "concerns" and interpretative stresses which are of primary importance in the doctrine of the one partner nevertheless so clearly maintained in the doctrine of the other that they can neither be overlooked nor misunderstood? If they are, then a condemnation no longer has to be maintained today. The different doctrinal forms in the various churches can then be viewed as complementary—in the doctrine of justification, above all. Remaining problems may be left to scholarly discussion between theologians (although this discussion must be put to the test in the church's praxis!). This has always been church procedure, in the churches of the Reformation too, and the unity of the community of faith has never foundered as a result. This being so, it is all the more important to lay bare hidden common foundations underlying these "concerns" and emphases.

3. In coming, then, to these varying concerns and emphases, we can start unreservedly today from the following, third principle: *No one can condemn and accuse of departing from the Christian faith those who— experiencing the misery of their sins, their resistance against God, and their lack of love for God and their neighbor—in faith put their whole trust in the saving God, are sure of his mercy, and try in their lives to match up to this faith*—even though Christians and theologians who (following the Reformers) think in this way must always be asked whether, because of their profound sense of sin, they do not think too little of God's regenerative power. *Nor, on the other hand, can anyone condemn and accuse of departing from the Christian faith those who, deeply penetrated by the limitless power of God, stress above all, in the event of justification also, God's glory and the victory of his gracious acts on behalf of men and women, holding human failure and halfheartedness toward these gracious acts to be, in the strict sense, of secondary importance*—even if Christians and theologians who (following the Council of Trent) think in this way must always be asked whether they take the misery of sin sufficiently seriously.

In the sixteenth century, Catholic theology was afraid that the result of the Reformers' doctrine of justification could be summed up as: no freedom, no new being, no ethical endeavor, no reward, no church (depreciation of baptism). Protestant theology was afraid that the result of the Catholic doctrine of justification could be summed up as: the triviality of sin, self-praise, a righteousness of works, purchasable salvation, a church intervening between God and human beings. Our third principle urges us to lay bare the innermost center of the interpretation of justification maintained on both sides and to recognize it unreservedly in its Christian truth, *together with* the mutual tension of the two understandings. This must be the starting point for judging all further individual developments.

Even in the sixteenth century, attention was occasionally drawn to this tension-laden *community* in faith—for example, when—especially at the beginning of the confessional formulations—the great fundamental truths were called to mind, over which no dispute exists, in spite of the diverging paths of interpretation.[25]

4. The Tridentine Decree on Justification is one of the textual complexes which we have to examine, with a view to determining whether condemnations have to be maintained. In our historical interpretation of this decree, a fourth principle applies: *In case of doubt, the view closest to Augustine must be preferred.* For it is obvious to anyone familiar with the history of theology how much the first three canons of the decree, as well as the corresponding first four chapters, are expressed in the language, and in the "climate of thought," so to speak, of the dispute between Augustine and Pelagius. We know also, however, that a recollection of the Pelagian controversy was one of the main impulses for the development of the theology of the Reformers: they believed—and not without authoritative witnesses from the late medieval period itself—that the theology and devotional practice of the church of the late Middle Ages were "Pelagian," by which we mean that human nature, and human abilities in general, were ascribed a "capacity for achievement" before God. Seen in this light, the canons mentioned may be seen as a hint on the part of the Council: they are to be read in such a way that the doctrine of Augustine, the theologian who in the West has always been known as *the* "teacher of grace" (*Doctor gratiae*), provides— if not the touchstone (for only the Holy Scripture is that), at least the compass for an evaluation of the Protestant doctrine of justification.

It is true that the ground thus shared in the sixteenth century was not preserved in the eras that followed. Today no problem can be settled by an appeal to Augustine, either in Protestant or in Catholic theology. Yet our principle helps to clarify what was meant *at that time*, and it therefore also helps us in the attempt to avoid pinning down the antitheses between Catholic and Protestant doctrine to interpretations which draw a sharper line of demarcation against the Protestant viewpoint than the Council itself intended.

III. ANCIENT CONDEMNATIONS, AND WHY THEY NO LONGER APPLY TO OUR PARTNER TODAY

If we start from these principles, in a new examination of the respective positions and rejections, it emerges that a number of differences were caused by insufficient mutual understanding—in part also by misinterpretation and excessive mistrust. Others were due to different modes of thought and expression. But undoubtedly difficulties remain, and they still have to be worked through.

1. In its judgment about *the radical depravity of the unredeemed human being* in the eyes of God, and about his subjection to the divine judgment, Catholic doctrine does not fall short of the insights of the Reformers (cf. I.1 above): grace is not something *added* to human endeavors, as it were. It *enables* the human being to take the first step toward salvation, and hence all succeeding steps as well. More: grace *is* salvation, and all human endeavors, every step from the first to the last, are the gift of grace, because Christ's saving work is the beginning of everything (cf. *DS* 222ff., 238ff., 371ff.). So it is no contradiction when the Protestant view stresses that "before" justification human beings, irrespective of their liberty and obligation to fulfill God's commandments "externally"—for example, in the sense of "civil righteousness" (cf. CA 18 and FC II)—are so completely imprisoned by the power of evil that they can allow themselves to receive the grace of justification only as a gift. And when Catholic doctrine still recognizes some good in the sinner, it does so to the glory of God, who cannot allow his work to be *entirely* spoiled by human beings, but in the event of justification makes it prevail anew through the power of his grace. According to the Catholic view, this also shows at the same time the inner theological connection between "creation" and "redemption": the justifying act of God is directed toward the man or woman in need of redemption, who is not totally "replaced" by God's grace, but who is *awakened* to a new life (thus also, incidentally, FC SD I.34–49: *BC* 514–30).

When Catholic doctrine recognizes human liberty, it is either a liberty, not over against God and toward God, but with regard to the things of this world (which the Lutheran Confession did not deny either; cf. CA 18.1: *BC* 39); or it is already a liberty issuing from the call and power of grace. And it is to *this* liberty, evoked by God and made efficacious for the very first time, that the Council of Trent ascribes the works (including the works of repentance) which are done on the basis of justification. Outside the saving activity of God, liberty is merely what Peter Brunner calls "liberty inside a prison."

The churches found it the more difficult to understand one another partly because the mutual condemnations are aimed at extreme positions on the opposing side which, in the course of the polemic, were often viewed as typical of the other position. Thus the Augsburg Confession condemns "the Pelagians and others who teach that without the Holy Spirit, by the power of nature alone, we are able to love God above all things, and can also keep the commandments of God in so far as the substance of the acts is concerned" (CA 18, Ed. pr: *BC* 40). This is really aimed at the theology of Gabriel Biel. Conversely, when the Council of Trent condemns the position that God is the origin of sin in the real sense (Decree on Justification, can. 6: *DS* 1556), it has in mind two exaggerated utterances made by Luther and Melanchthon in 1520/21—statements that were later modified or corrected and did not find their way into the Lutheran Confession.

The Protestant view can even today still give rise to the misunderstanding that God justifies a person quite arbitrarily, without that person's being affected or involved. According to Protestant conviction, justification is necessarily bound up with the preaching of God's law, which indicts the sinner and awakens his desire for the free pardon of the gospel.

The Catholic viewpoint can even today still give rise to the misunderstanding (which can also be met with on the Protestant side) that the divine grace which is the presupposition for justification is really no more than a matter of course. The view can also be so distorted that the cooperation of the human being is made the determining condition and presupposition of baptismal grace. But against this is the conviction that all human "preparation" for baptismal grace must be seen as no more than the effect of divine grace (Decree on Justification, cap. 6: *DS* 1526).

If misunderstandings of this kind are avoided, then there is today no longer any reason for us to condemn one another in this question. So the condemnations in cans. 5, 7, and 8 of the Tridentine Decree on Justification[26] and in the Formula of Concord no longer apply to today's partner.[27]

The scope of the rejections in SD, Epit. II, 4–5, must be clarified below under sec. 3.

2. Insofar as the concept of "concupiscence" is a summing up of our understanding of the depravity of sin, the dispute about this term cannot create any new problem, once the mutual condemnations about the interpretation of the depravity of sin have themselves in fact become null and void (cf. sec. 1 above). What remains is a question of definition. This is by no means unimportant, either historically or factually; but it is a question that can be solved, and it was understood as such even by Melanchthon in the Apology 2, and by the Council of Trent in can. 5 of the Decree on Original Sin (cf. I.2 above).

The present state of research into the history of dogma and theology allows us to offer the following clarifications about this point.

a. As regards the interpretation of original sin (and accordingly concupiscence), there are three different schools of thought in medieval scholasticism (which is the real target of Protestant polemic here):

• Original sin is the *cor incurvatum in seipsum* (the heart turned in upon itself). As such, it is identical with concupiscence. Here a strong undertone stresses sensual desire—also, and especially, in the sexual sense (Augustinian, Peter Lombard).

• Original sin is *formally* (i.e.—in the scholastic sense—essentially) lack of the original righteousness effected by grace *(iustitia originalis);* while *materially* it is concupiscence, understood as the inclination toward sin of the powers of the soul, which no longer act in a harmonious order that is related toward God (Thomist);

• Original sin is the mere deprivation and lack of the original state of righteousness which the human being ought to have *(carentia et privatio originalis iustitiae debitae inesse);* concupiscence is not included in the concept of original sin (Scotist, nominalist).

The Reformers attacked this *third* school, which was supported by Duns Scotus, William of Ockham, and Gabriel Biel, interpreting it to mean that original sin is merely an external imprisonment which leaves no traces in human beings themselves, so that after the Fall "the natural powers of man have remained whole and uncorrupted, and that man by nature possesses a right understanding and a good will. . . . Again, that man is able by his natural powers to observe and keep all the command-ments of God. Again, that man is able by his natural powers to love God above all things and his neighbor as himself."[28] According to the Protes-tant view, on the other hand, concupiscence is the third element in original sin, the others being lack of the fear of God and lack of true faith in God. Concupiscence is therefore not merely a possible inclina-tion to evil in the ethical sense. It signifies the striving of human beings to be as God.[29] Nor, as Luther already stressed, can it be done away with in a single moment (cf. Lecture on the Epistle to the Romans, WA 56, 273, 4ff.). It remains as sin, even after baptism. It was to this view, conversely, that the Catholic side took exception (cf. *DS* 1452f.), seeing it as undermining the efficacy of baptism.

b. The background of the dogmatic use of the word "concupiscence" in Protestant and Catholic theology is the biblical understanding of *epithymia* as the *selfish desire* of the old man, which under the law is continually inclined to "gratify the desires of the flesh" (Gal. 5:16f.; cf. Rom. 7:7, 10). Even in the lives of the justified, concupiscence is still efficacious as an inclination toward sin, and can thus always be the "address" for sin's seductive power. The apostle Paul therefore urges believers to be vigilant toward their desires, and to fight against the power of sin which still assails us (cf. Rom. 6:12–14). If we become aware of this direct *link* between desire and sin, but also its conceptual *difference*, then we can understand the theological importance of the term "concupiscence" in the context of the different conceptions of sin and justification held in Protestant and Catholic theology—conceptions which are not necessarily mutually exclusive.

c. In the conversations of the Reformation period which aimed at a settlement, people were able to arrive at an understanding through recourse to the high scholastic view "that original sin has been removed 'formally' but remains 'materially.'"[30] In 1541, in Worms, Melanchthon and Eck reached agreement in the following words:

> With regard to this sickness in the regenerate, we are agreed that the "matter" of original sin remains, whereas the "form" has been removed through baptism. But we call the "matter" of sin that which derives from sin, that which inclines to sin, and indeed the depravity of human nature itself which, as regards the fact itself, is something that strives against the law of God, so that Paul then accordingly calls it "sin." In this sense they are accustomed in the schools to teach briefly that in the baptized the matter of original sin remains, while what is formal—the guilt—is taken away.[31]

d. The Council of Trent indirectly rejects the late scholastic concept of concupiscence, reverting to the second (Thomist) version and thereby substantially confirming the agreements already arrived at. Of course it must be noted that the Council expressed an opinion about concupiscence only where it was a question of whether it remained in *those who had been baptized,* that is to say, in the *justified.* The Council has nothing to say about the question of concupiscence in those who are still in original sin—a question which is discussed in the Apology and the Formula of Concord (c.f. I.2 above).

e. The doctrines laid down at Trent and by the Reformers are at one in maintaining that original sin, and also the concupiscence that remains, are in contradiction to God, a disqualification in his eyes which precedes all ethical or unethical action. They also agree that the remaining concupiscence (whatever its closer definition may be) is the object of the lifelong struggle against sin, the struggle which is possible for the person who has been justified, and which can be expected of him by virtue of the faith in Christ which has been graciously bestowed. Finally, Trent and the Reformers agree that after baptism, concupiscence in the person justified no longer cuts that person off from God; in Tridentine language, it is "no longer sin in the real sense"; in Lutheran phraseology, it is *peccatum regnatum,* "controlled sin," which is only damnable hypothetically, as it were—that is, only if God were not to forgive (c.f. Apol. 2.38: *BC* 105; cf. I.2 above).

f. In view of the complicated history of the term "concupiscence" to which we have now drawn attention, it does not seem fruitful to discuss the question of remaining sin, in the Protestant sense, merely in the context of this concept. The discussion must center on *the fact.* Here it must be said that, by deepening its own traditional foundations, modern Catholic theology has come much closer to the Protestant view in considering the concept of concupiscence, taking sharper cognizance of human nature as a totality. It no longer pursues the tendency, still detectable in the Middle Ages, to detach a physical nature, "still" marked by concupiscence, from a spiritual nature "already" freed from concupiscence through justification.

3. The *passivity of the human being toward God's justifying act* has been frequently misunderstood. According to Protestant doctrine, it means that human beings can do no more than simply allow God's grace to be bestowed on them, fully and entirely. It does not mean that in this bestowal the man or woman does not respond to God, person to person. Exaggerated formulations by the Reformers—understandable enough in the situation of conflict—were rejected both by the Council of Trent ("like something inanimate," can. 4: *DS* 1554; Deferrari 258) and the Formula of Concord ("a stone or a block," SD II.59: *BC* 532). Here the two were in substantial agreement.

Both are concerned to make it clear that before the face of God, human beings cannot in any way cast a sideways glance at their own endeavors—not even "partly," and not even after their regeneration through the Holy Spirit, and on the basis of that regeneration. Neither the Council nor the Formula of Concord is concerned to deny that human beings are in a very real sense involved. Why should Luther especially pour forth a torrent of words, *exhorting* people to an "audacious" faith, if this faith were not the human being's response to the word of promise which moves his whole heart? But a response is not a "work." The response of faith is itself brought about through the uncoercible word of promise which comes to human beings from outside themselves. There can be *"co*operation*" only* in the sense that in faith the heart is involved, when the Word touches it and creates faith. Catholic theology begs its Protestant discussion partner to concede that this is the meaning of Catholic doctrine also. On the other hand, it itself admits that the word "cooperation" is open to misunderstanding.

With this, as far as their application today is concerned, the condemnatory pronouncements in can. 4 of the Decree on Justification (*DS* 1554) and the rejections 4 to 5 in the Formula of Concord, Solid Declaration II,[32] are null and void.

4. When *the essence of grace or righteousness* before God is defined on the one hand as an objective *reality* on God's side *"outside ourselves,"* and on the other hand as *a reality in the human soul*, a "quality" intrinsically "adhering" to the soul (cf. I.3 above), this does not seem to be merely a misunderstanding, or even a different mode of expression or another use of words. It is evidently a clear difference, indeed an antithesis in the interpretation of the actual matter under discussion (and this becomes especially clear when we look at the history of the two views, and their impact). It is therefore no more than consistent when Protestant theology links the righteousness of the believer with the righteousness of Christ *extra se* ("outside himself"), in which the believer participates, and yet at the same time sees the justified person, as far as he himself is concerned, as still a sinner (*simul iustus et peccator*, at once righteous and as sinner); and when it also sees the heart of the event of justification as being a single, total (though continually new) divine act: in the forgiving pardon, in the non-imputation of sin, in the imputation of the righteousness of Christ—all of which are different words for the same thing, namely, that the human person is again standing in a proper relationship to God. It is equally consistent when the Catholic viewpoint sees the event of justification as a process composed of different stages, because grace never prevails at a single stroke in the human soul, because of the person's continued resistance (cf. 2 above). Indeed, the renewing power of grace never prevails completely and entirely to the end of a person's life. But does this really bring us up against an antithesis which cuts through everything we have in common, and makes mutual condemnation compellingly necessary?

New Testament exegesis teaches us today that the Protestant way of talking about the righteousness which exists and is efficacious "outside us" (extra nos) has a proper biblical foundation. God has made Christ himself righteousness for us (1 Cor. 1:30). Consequently, a person is righteous in God's sight only if he is joined with Christ through faith and baptism, and has died with him to sin and to his own sinful self (cf. Rom. 6.6f.; 7:4). Yet the idea of grace "poured into" the soul and "adhering" to it (adhaerens) clearly also has a sound biblical basis. For the love of God which remains "outside us" is nonetheless "poured into our hearts" (Rom. 5:5), being identical with the gift of the Holy Spirit (Gal. 3:2–5; 5:6; Rom. 8:23; 2 Cor. 5:5); and as such it unites us with Christ, fills us with confidence and joy, and makes us capable of a new life, which we nonetheless never owe to ourselves in any way, since it is fellowship with Christ and the gift of the Spirit.

In this way New Testament exegesis has initiated a step forward to which we cannot ascribe too great an importance, because it has taken the rigidity out of the old disputes. It has shown us the indissoluble connection between what Catholic tradition calls "uncreated" and "created" grace (gratia increata and gratia creata) and what Protestant theology knows as "forensic" and "effective" justification. Systematic theology, both Catholic and Protestant, has taken advantage of this opportunity offered to it by exegesis. In addition, research into the history of theology no longer permits Catholic theology to reproach Protestantism with failing sufficiently to take into account the fact that justification issues, and must issue, in a new life. When can. 11 of the Decree on Justification (DS 1561) condemns the doctrine that grace is merely the favor of God, this does not really hit the target of the Lutheran view; it only seems to do so. The fact that the righteousness of the believer lies "outside ourselves, in Christ" (extra nos in Christo), as the Heidelberg Catechism says, also means that as such it becomes ours. The pregnant distinction that Luther makes (especially in Antilatomus) between "grace" and "gift" is intended to preserve the insight that "external" grace touches and claims the person of the believer himself. Through the Holy Spirit it makes sin "controlled sin" (peccatum regnatum), impels its expulsion, and thus determines the believer's whole practical conduct. It is significant that Rom. 5:5, the very biblical passage that can. 11 cites almost word for word, is Luther's central authority for the distinction and relationship between grace and gift.

On the other hand, the same recognitions drawn from the history of theology no longer permit Protestant theology the reproach that the notion of grace as a habitus—an enduring disposition of human existence which inclines it to new activity—is the equivalent of trust in one's own strength, and is hence the equivalent also of loving God by means of one's own natural powers, a notion which, as we know, Melanchthon untiringly contested in the Apology.[33] In addition, recent Roman Catholic research has shown that the Council of Trent *expressed itself* in terms of the *habitus* doctrine, but it deliberately did *not* say by definition that justifying grace was to be understood as *habitus*.

None of this is subject to any doubt, provided that Protestant doctrine and Catholic doctrine are properly understood. Consequently the following facts emerge:

• Catholic doctrine does not overlook what Protestant theology stresses: the personal character of grace, and its link with the Word; nor does it maintain what Protestant theology is afraid of: grace as an objective "possession" (even if a conferred possession) on the part of the human being—something over which he can dispose.

• Protestant theology does not overlook what Catholic doctrine stresses: the creative and renewing character of God's love; nor does it maintain what Catholic theology is afraid of: God's impotence toward a sin which is "merely" forgiven in justification but which is not truly abolished in its power to divide the sinner from God.

This means that the mutual rejections applied even in the sixteenth century only to indistinct and misleading *formulations*. They certainly no longer apply to the partner's actual *view*. This is true especially of cans. 10 and 11 of the Decree on Justification (*DS* 1560f.) and to the rejections of the Formula of Concord which are related particularly, directly or indirectly, to the statements in can. 11 (SD III, first group of rejections, 3–7,[34] and second group of rejections, 5–6[35]).

5. If the preceding reflections are tenable, then today the difference about our *interpretation of faith* is no longer a reason for mutual condemnation either, even though in the Reformation period it was seen as a profound antithesis of ultimate and decisive force. By this we mean the confrontation between the formulas "by faith alone," on the one hand, and "faith, hope, and love," on the other (cf. I.5 above).

In the first place, there is a misunderstandng here that pervades all the antitheses, whether genuine or supposed. When the fathers of the Council of Trent talk about *the word* "faith" (in all the semantic tension between *fides* and *credere*—the faith of the heart and notional belief), they follow medieval tradition in thinking first about the assent of the understanding to the revealed Word of God, and about the "objective" belief expressed in the church's creed and its proclaimed doctrine. This being so, and on the basis of the "catalogue of errors" in Protestant statements which was before the Council, the conciliar fathers interpreted Protestant talk about justification "by faith alone" *(sola fide)* as if this excluded the efficacy of the sacraments, the importance of good works, and the need for a binding creed requiring "assent."

The Reformers, on the other hand, going back to Paul, understood faith as the forgiveness and fellowship with Christ effected by the word of promise itself (cf. HC 21). This is the ground for the new being, through which the flesh is dead to sin and the new man or woman in Christ has life *(sola fide per Christum)*. But even if this faith necessarily makes the human being new, the Christian builds his confidence, not on his own new life, but solely on God's gracious promise. Acceptance in Christ is sufficient, if "faith" is understood as "trust in the promise" *(fides promissionis)*.

It must be noted in this context, however, that although in Luther and Melanchthon the distinction *and* the connection between faith and works are always clear *in substance*, the way in which *the terms* "sanctification," "regeneration," and "renewal" *are used* varies. It is only in the Reformed Confessions (from 1559 onward) and in the Formula of Concord that the terms are so firmly defined that they are distinguished from justification itself and applied to the moral renewal that follows it. In scholastic usage, on the other hand, these words mean preeminently the regeneration, renewal, and sanctification (through sanctifying grace) which are founded on the sacrament of baptism (and repentance). The terms are still used in a similar sense in the Augsburg Confession (CA 2: *BC* 29: "born again through Baptism and the Holy Spirit") and in the Large Catechism ("Hence to sanctify is naught else than to bring to the Lord Christ, that we may receive that good to which we of ourselves could not come" (WA 30 I, 91; cf. *BC* 415f.).

At the same time, it is important to remember the following:

• It is pointless to dispute the question about the burden of proof and with which partner it lies. For both sides—admittedly under the presuppositions of the exegesis of that day—claim the support of Paul, the one side stressing the central importance of the concept of faith in Rom. 3:21—4:25 and Gal. 2:14—3:29, the other appealing to 1 Cor. 13:13 and stressing the unity of faith, hope, and love, with the preeminent importance of love.

• The New Testament witness does not merely bear out the unique character of justifying faith. It also supports the theological unity of faith and love, since the proclamation of the apostle Paul defines inclusively, not exclusively, the relationship between "faith," "the confession of faith" (Rom. 10:9), love of God (1 Cor. 8:3), and faith issuing in love of our neighbor (Gal. 5:6). In this sense the exhortation to works of love in James 2:14–26 should not be understood as essentially a contradiction of the Pauline interpretation of faith, but as its parenetic complement.

• The decisive point about the Protestant understanding of faith—unconditional trust in the merciful God, here and in the final judgment—is no longer a problem for contemporary Catholic theology, being supported by the above-mentioned progress made in New Testament exegesis (see II.1 above, and 4 in the present section), by advances in systematic theology, and above all by the texts of the Second Vatican Council.[36]

• Absolute trust in the mercy of God, which was decisive for the Protestant concept of faith, had never been overlooked even in the pre-Reformation tradition. It was always included in the concept of hope, which according to the doctrine of the great high scholastic theologians depends, not on God's mercy *and* the merits of the human being, but *exclusively* on the almighty mercy of God. Without hope there can never be a living faith *(fides viva)*.

• Conversely, when the Reformers talk about justification "through faith," they are bringing out the meaning of the scholastic phrase about justification through *gratia gratum faciens* ("sanctifying grace"); inasmuch as in faith a person lays hold of, and receives, God's mercy:

> Similarly, at every mention of faith we are also thinking of its object, the promised mercy.[37]

> And since this faith alone receives the forgiveness of sins, renders us acceptable to God, and brings the Holy Spirit, it should be called *gratia gratum faciens* (grace that makes us acceptable to God) rather than love, which is the effect resulting from it.[38]

In Augsburg too, in 1530, agreement was arrived at about the doctrine of justification by assigning the scholastic idea of grace to the Protestant concept:

> The forgiveness of sins comes about formally through sanctifying grace and through faith.[39]

• Because faith means that a person is possessed by the Holy Spirit, the Reformers also ascribed to faith all the marvelous regenerating consequences for the life of human beings which Catholic tradition understands as the specific effects of the love of God, issuing from God's grace.

• Even though, according to the Protestant view, justification comes about through faith alone, yet even justifying faith is not mere naked faith. Luther rejected talk about justification on the basis of "faith formed by love" (*fides caritate formata*); but he did so, not out of disparagement of God's love, but because he was afraid of the view that something humanly ethical could play a decisive part in the salvific process; for it was nominalist doctrine that human beings can love God above everything "simply of their own natural powers" (*ex puris naturalibus*). In the 1531 Lectures on Galatians, Luther is still saying:

> If they were to call "formed faith" the true and theological or, as Paul calls it the unfeigned faith (I Tim. 1:5), which God calls faith, then this gloss of theirs would not offend me. For then faith would not be distinguished from love; it would be distinguished from a vain idea of faith, as we also distinguish between a counterfeit faith and a true faith.[40]

We may follow Cardinal Willebrand and say: "In Luther's sense the word 'faith' by no means intends to exclude either works or love or even hope. We may quite justly say that Luther's concept of faith, if we take it in its fullest sense, surely means nothing other than what we in the Catholic Church term love" (1970, at the General Assembly of the World Lutheran Federation in Evian).

If we take all this to heart, we may say the following: if we translate from one language to another, then Protestant talk about justification through faith corresponds to Catholic talk about justification through grace; and on the other hand, Protestant doctrine understands substantially under the one word "faith" what Catholic doctrine (following 1 Cor. 13:13) sums up in the triad of "faith, hope, and love." But in this case the mutual rejections in this question can be viewed as no longer applicable today—that is, cans. 9 and 12 of the Decree on Justification (*DS* 1559 and 1562) and the corresponding condemnations in the Formula of Concord SD III, first group of rejections 1–2 (*BC* 547f.); cf. HC, esp. 20.

In saying this we have no intention of denying the still existing difference in the two formulas. Nor do we wish to restrict this difference to a *mere* (and hence fortuitous) choice of words. On the contrary, the difference reflects different concerns and emphases on which practical Christian life and the self-understanding of Protestant and Catholic Christians can depend. According to Protestant interpretation, the faith that clings unconditionally to God's promise in Word and Sacrament is sufficient for righteousness before God, so that the renewal of the human being, without which there can be no faith, does not in itself make any contribution to justification. Catholic doctrine knows itself to be at one with the Protestant concern in emphasizing that the renewal of the human being does not "contribute" to justification, and is certainly not a contribution to which he could make any appeal before God (cf. also 7 below). Nevertheless it feels compelled to stress the renewal of the human being through justifying grace, for the sake of acknowledging God's newly creating power; although this renewal in faith, hope, and love is certainly nothing but a response to God's unfathomable grace. Only if we observe this distinction can we say—but we can then say in all truth: Catholic doctrine does not overlook what Protestant faith finds so important, and vice versa; and Catholic doctrine does not maintain what Protestant doctrine is afraid of, and vice versa.

6. Just as in the question about the concept of faith, a tenable consensus (or at least a mutual noncondemnation) with regard to *the assurance of salvation* (cf. I.6 above) was made difficult even in the sixteenth century by fatal misunderstandings, which continue to make themselves felt even today. Here it is especially clear, incidentally, how "concerns" that are accepted as such on both sides can give rise to misunderstanding because of different opinions about their urgency and scope.

Luther and the Reformers know just as well as their opponents how weak, how halfhearted, and hence how unreliable the human heart is, when it turns to God; and they know all about the assailments to which faith in the promise of Christ is exposed, even though the whole salvation of the human being depends on that faith. Both Catholics and Reformers know equally well that this can never be altered once and for all. The question is: How can, and how may, human beings live before God in spite of their weakness, and with that weakness? At this point the connection between the interpretation of justification and the understanding of the sacraments is brought out particularly clearly. It is a connection that was already stressed above, as the first principle of interpretation.

Catholic doctrine, already officially represented by Cardinal Cajetan in Augsburg in October 1518, replied to this question as follows: Faith may, and must, be completely certain of the forgiveness of God—that is, certain of the special effect of the sacrament in me—insofar as this is viewed in terms of the sacrament itself (Lutherans would say: in terms of what is *extra me*, "outside myself"). But looked at from the side of the recipient, a doubt is justified, because that recipient can never be sure whether he has laid himself sufficiently open to the efficacy of the sacrament (in Lutheran terms: whether he has believed fully and completely). The Christian should endure this uncertainty with patience.

Luther and his followers go a step farther. They urge that the uncertainty should not merely be endured. We should avert our eyes from it and take seriously, practically, and personally the objective efficacy of the absolution pronounced in the sacrament of penance, which comes "from outside." The Reformers answer the question about how to deal with the believer's uncertainty by underlining the unconditional reliability of the priestly absolution. Since Jesus said, "Whatever you loose on earth shall be loosed in heaven" (Matt. 16:19), the believer, as Luther repeatedly argues, would declare Christ to be a liar and would thereby "reject grace," if he did not rely with a rock-like assurance on the forgiveness of God uttered in the absolution, whatever the quality of his own works may be—or even the quality of his repentance and contrition. Luther knows just as well as his opponents that this reliance can itself be subjectively uncertain—that the assurance of forgiveness is not a security of forgiveness (*securitas*); but this must not be turned into yet another problem, so to speak: the believer should turn his eyes away from it, and should look only to Christ's word of forgiveness.

This indicates the true meaning of the Protestant doctrine of the assurance of salvation: because we can of ourselves never "subjectively" meet the claims of the divine law, which demands our works, faith should rely on "the most objective thing" there is for the church: the Word of God—and this irrespective of the "condition" of the person who relies on it. It is true that this faith is always exposed to trial and temptation. It is therefore *possible* for a person to doubt. But he is *not obliged* to doubt, and should not do so. He is not merely assured of salvation in the sense of a theoretical assurance; he may and should be assured of it, in the sense of a confidence and trust. The person tempted should not look at himself, his sin and his doubt. He should look to Christ and his fellowship with him, founded on baptism and continually promised anew in repentance. If a person believes like this, and inasmuch as he does so, he is in fact assured of his salvation, because it is impossible to rely on God's saving Word and at the same time, in the very act of reliance, hold that Word to be unreliable.

The Reformers' opponents, however—and Cajetan first of all—interpreted this view to mean that the assurance of salvation is founded on the believer's subjective conviction, or even on his subjective feelings. And the Reformers seemed to them to be actually claiming for this subjective assurance the objective certainty of the church's creed (". . . with the certainty of faith which cannot be subject to error": DS 1534). The Reformers for their part understood the rejection of their view to mean that their opponents had a positive interest in keeping believers in a state of uncertainty, and that for these ends they would not even shrink from implying a doubt in the reliability of Christ's promises.

Difficulties of mutual understanding increased once more, from the very beginning, because the dispute flared up in the context of extremist positions, or at least in connection with statements that were misleadingly formulated. These were later more closely defined, if not actually superseded, but this did not make itself fully felt in the condemnations. People on both sides therefore failed to perceive sufficiently how close to one another they really were. Luther attacked the "contritionism" of Gabriel Biel, who saw complete contrition *(contritio)* as the *condition* for absolution, a condition that was therefore *bound* to leave the Christian in uncertainty, since he can never be sure that he is perfectly contrite. Luther reacted against this in the "Resolutiones" (esp. Res. 7 and 38) and in other writings *(Sermo de poenitentia;* the series of theses *Pro veritate).* What he thought he was doing, and his intention in these writings, was *to give increased importance* to the power of the keys and to absolution, with an emphatic stress on faith in the Word of promise. But this occasionally sounds—as it did to Cajetan—as if faith had now become the work which is the condition for forgiveness. The Council of Trent, following the bull *Exsurge Domine,* pinned Luther and his supporters down to these statements (cf. *DS* 1533f., 1563f., with 1460–62). Indeed, the Council rejects the position that—as long as one does not renounce one's faith—anyone who has been baptized can no longer lose grace, even if he wants to, and however much he sins—the Council's target here was a sentence of Luther's in *De captivitate Babylonica* (WA 6, 529, 11–13; cf. *DS* 1540, 1673). But Luther later defined his doctrine more closely, securing it against theological and pastoral misunderstanding. He even retracted the sentence mentioned when, in the Smalcald Articles, he dissociated himself from the "enthusiasts,"

> who hold that once they have received the Spirit or the forgiveness of sins, or once they have become believers, they will persevere in faith even if they sin afterwards, and such sin will not harm them. They cry out, "Do what you will, it matters not as long as you believe, for faith blots out all sins," etc.[41]

As if he wanted from the outset to cut the ground from later misgivings, Luther explicitly rejected from the very beginning an assurance of faith that had its foundation only in subjective conviction, not in Christ.[42]

When these misunderstandings and difficulties of comprehension have once been grasped, however, it emerges that what the Council of Trent rejects is precisely what the Reformers were also concerned to avert: security and self-conceit about one's own condition and a complacent certainty of being in grace, self-deception about one's own weakness, insufficient fear of losing grace, comforting "feelings" as criterion, moral laxness under appeal to the assurance of salvation, and—even more—security of predestination. For its own part, the Council stresses the points which are, for Luther and the Reformers also, the foundation and the point of departure for their own view: the reliability and sufficiency of God's promise, and the power of Christ's death and resurrection; human weakness, and the threat to faith and salvation which that involves.[43]

So even in the sixteenth century, mutual condemnations could be pronounced in a number of cases only because the two sides did not listen carefully enough to each other. And these points can even less provide grounds for mutual objection today—particularly if we start from the foundation of a biblically renewed concept of faith (see 4 above). For a person can certainly lose or renounce faith, and self-commitment to God and his word of promise. But if he believes in this sense, he cannot *at the same time* believe that God is unreliable in his word of promise. In this sense it is true today also that—in Luther's words—faith *is* the assurance of salvation. What has to be asked today is only what had already to be asked at the time of the Reformation: whether—as in the case of the Catholic term "cooperation"—the *phrase* "assurance of salvation" cannot perhaps give rise to the misunderstandings that already showed themselves at that earlier time: the notion of "confidence" in the sense of a "fleshly" security, which really is "vain" (cf. *DS* 1533).

But in substance, and in view of what has just been said, the condemnations found in cans. 13 to 16 of the Decree on Justification (*DS* 1563–66, 1573) may be said no longer to apply. There are no explicit condemnations on this point in the Formula of Concord.[44]

Excursus
JUSTIFICATION, BAPTISM, AND PENANCE

At this point the connections between the doctrine of justification and the doctrine of the sacraments emerge particularly clearly. They have to be considered here in the light of our present subject, even though the doctrine of the sacraments will be discussed separately in chapter 3. For since the Reformers refer to questions about the doctrine of justification and questions about the doctrine of the sacraments in a single breath, as it were (cf. 6 above, and earlier sec. II, 1st principle); and since, conversely, the Decree on Justification also refers several times to baptism[45] and to the sacrament of penance,[46] any unsurmounted antitheses here would have an adverse retroactive effect on any agreement (or non-contradiction) perhaps arrived at with regard to the interpretation of the doctrine of justification.

At all events, here we come up against the problem which is generally defined and discussed under the heading of the "mediation" of grace. Neither Roman Catholic nor Protestant doctrine disputes that the grace of God reaches the sinner *in* the church. For when Protestant doctrine says that justification is "mediated" through Christ in his Word, through the power of his Spirit by means of faith, it is talking about processes in the church—processes that is, which take place *in* the community of faith. It has, however, considerable misgivings when it is a question of talking about justification being "mediated" *through* the church, because this could be understood to mean that the church has its own power of disposal over God's grace—whereas grace can be bestowed on us only through God's own activity in Word and sacrament. At the same time, the Confessions can certainly call the sacraments "means" and "instruments" through which the Holy Spirit is bestowed (CA 5: *BC* 31; HC 65).

Roman Catholic doctrine, however, talks without reserve about the "mediation" of grace *through* the church and *through* the sacraments, because it cannot see how it is "disposing" over God's grace when the church sees itself and what it does as an "instrument" of God's activity; and because, after all, faith in God's forgiving grace in Christ is in actual fact required of the individual person and is made possible "through the mediation" of the Spirit-imbued witness and acts of those who have believed before him.

In considering the background of this problem, it would seem necessary to establish the following general points first of all; and it will perhaps be permissible to offer the following reflections, without fear of glossing over the antitheses.

1. It was not correct when, in the sixteenth century, the Reformers were reproached—as they are occasionally reproached still—with disparagement of the sacraments. In actual fact, the sacraments, together with the proclamation of the Word, were for the Reformers, as they were for the apostle Paul, the concrete form in which the justifying act

of God reaches the sinner. This is particularly true of Luther and the Lutheran Confessions; but it applies also to Reformed doctrine, properly understood (cf. HC 65ff.). The Reformers fought against groups in their own movement who really did disparage the sacraments as "an outward thing," and in this dispute they used almost the same arguments that adherents of the old faith thought must be leveled against all the Reformers: that is, they pointed to God's wise ordinance, which in its wisdom we have to obey.

2. It was not correct either when the Reformers reproached Roman Catholic doctrine (as Protestant theologians not infrequently do even today) with teaching that justifying grace is bound to the sacraments and is in this sense "sacramental grace"; so that by refusing the sacraments, the church would have the authority to exclude men and women from God's grace. Whatever impression may be given—and may have been given in the past—by a frequently unenlightened practice and by undifferentiated theological formulations, Catholic doctrine adhered, as it still does, to Aquinas's statement: "God did not cause his power to be restricted to the sacraments in such a way that he could not bestow the effect of the sacraments without the sacraments themselves" (*STh* IIIa 64, 7). All the "instrumentality" of church and sacraments is limited by the provision that God is free at any time *not* to use his "instruments." If, in spite of this, Roman Catholic doctrine underlines the sacramental "mediation" of justifying grace, it does so for a reason in which it was at one with the Reformers: because no one can long for God's grace and at the same time deliberately despise the ways which God in his wisdom has appointed for the purpose. It is just this that the classic medieval thesis means when it states that all communication of grace outside the real reception of the sacraments is a kind of "anticipatory sacramental efficacy."

3. Nor is it correct to say that Roman Catholic doctrine maintains that grace is communicated through the administration of the sacraments, independent of faith, as if the readiness of the heart to surrender itself were not necessary if a person really wishes to receive God's grace in the sacrament. It must be admitted that medieval formulas could give this impression, if they were misunderstood and misused for pastoral purposes—for example, the formula about *non ponere obicem* (not placing any barrier) or the phrase *ex opere operato* (through the operation of the rite itself), although the precise sense of these formulations can easily be made clear and hence unobjectionable. But over against this it must be remembered that it is also Roman Catholic doctrine that the sacraments are not a way of salvation with easier conditions, which

bypasses personal faith (for a closer exposition see Part II.2 below, on the general doctrine of the sacraments, 2.2).

Up to this point, therefore, differences and antitheses which emerge in the understanding of the sacraments go back to the differences and antitheses that have already been discussed in connection with the interpretation of justification itself; and together with these, they can be overcome today. They at least require no mutual condemnation. This is true, fundamentally speaking, of the Protestant interpretation of *baptism* and its consequences for the Christian life, where this differs from traditional Catholic baptismal doctrine.

Where *the sacrament of penance* is concerned, on the other hand, there are open questions. We must go into these here, at least in principle, for the reason already given: our mutual recognition, or at least noncondemnation, in the doctrine of justification, has to stand up to a countercheck. On the other hand, in view of the endless discussion about the historical, dogmatic, and pastoral problems involved in the sacrament of penance, it is not possible in our present framework to arrive at firm judgments, and to justify them, with the same certainty as in the other points we have considered hitherto (see pp. 9f. above).

The situation is made additionally difficult because the Reformers differed among themselves about the sacrament of penance, and consequently views vary in the Protestant churches too. It is true that Luther actually developed his doctrine of justification in the context of new reflections about the sacrament of penance; but later, in spite of a lifelong regard for private (auricular) confession, he no longer allowed penance to count as a separate sacrament. In the Augsburg Confession, Melanchthon assumes that penance is a sacrament,[47] and in the Apology he explicitly interprets it as a sacrament in the true sense.[48] The Reformed church disputed the sacramental character of penance and ceased to practice private confession from the very beginning. Here the assurance of the forgiveness of sins is given primarily through the sermon, and the newly ordered office of the keys (cf. also HC 83–85), as well as in pastoral dialogue, on which Calvin, for instance, laid particular stress (cf. *Inst.* IV, 1, 22; on the sacramental character, cf. IV, 19, 14ff.). The statements in the Augsburg Confession and the Apology referred to here do not apply to Reformed theology.

In spite of the different Lutheran assumption in the Confessions, however, since the end of the eighteenth century penitential practice in the form of private (auricular) confession has largely ceased in the Lutheran church also. Even in the Roman Catholic Church the sacrament of penance is going through a crisis today. So the question between the churches now is not only their agreement or opposition about the interpretation of the sacrament of penance. The crisis about penitential practice and the sense of sin shows that the question also has to do with the meaning of repentance in general.

All this being so, we cannot always offer solutions; but we should like to show what the real questions are, and to indicate the problems that have not yet been fully talked through. But the direction in which these questions and problems point does not seem to be an entirely hopeless one. It is in this sense that the following hints should be understood.

1. We have to start from a fundamental viewpoint which profoundly stamps spirituality in the Lutheran church and which has therefore influenced the discussion in controversial theology down to the present day; and here we also have to discover how far this fundamental viewpoint involves an inherent antithesis to the Catholic view. How is the sacrament of penance to be understood and accordingly practiced?

• As a *new communication* of justifying grace, *following the loss of baptismal grace* (Roman Catholic doctrine)?[49]

• Or as a *return*, or better: as *God's bringing back* of the sinner in consideration of *the forgiveness of sins which has never been revoked*, since it was promised to the sinner in baptism once and for all, as if in a "covenant," as Luther says (Protestant doctrine).[50]

Roman Catholic doctrine assumes that baptismal grace can be lost. Protestant doctrine assumes that it *cannot* be lost as such, although a person can no doubt "fall out of it" (LC, Baptism, 82: *BC* 446; cf. II.4 above). According to the Catholic view, absolution is efficacious when it is linked with the triad: contrition, confession of sin, and satisfaction; in the Protestant view its efficacy is linked with the duality: contrition *(contritio)* and faith *(fides)* (cf. CA/Apol. 12: *BC* 182ff.). According to Protestant interpretation, good works are certainly the fruit of repentance and the way repentance shows itself; but they are not a satisfaction, for the purpose of attaining a remission of punishment.

Are we bound to establish that there is an antithesis at this point? Earlier reflections (III.4 above) should have made it clear that baptismal grace can be lost only insofar as it is also a gift bestowed on human beings. But the unfathomable forgiving love of God, which never repents of itself, cannot be lost. We explained that biblical testimony requires us to see both dimensions of justifying grace in their context, as we must see the indissoluble connection between "uncreated" and "created" grace, or between "forensic" and "effective" justification. If this is so, then the two contrasting approaches in the interpretation of the sacrament of penance must be seen as complementary ways of expressing a single fundamental fact. And this in itself excludes mutual condemnation.

Moreover, even in the sixteenth century, people perceived quite clearly that a considerable unity in substance was being obscured by a terminology which appeared suspect to the other side. The Protestant concern to maintain the permanently valid assurance of grace is expressed in scholastic terminology through talk about the *character indelebilis* (the indelible mark) bestowed in baptism; but this is obscured by the controversy about the "spiritual condition." Conversely, Catholic concern about the possibility of losing grace (understood as *gratia creata* or "created grace") is expressed in Protestant terminology by phraseology such as "losing faith and the Holy Spirit"[51] or "falling again"[52] and "falling out" of grace.[53]

The background of the controversy about penitence also becomes clear in the "false teachings" listed in the Apology 12.17–27 (*BC* 185), which are aimed at the late scholastic doctrine of penance (forgiveness through *attritio* or *contritio*, "imperfect" or "perfect" contrition, and the corresponding depreciation of absolution). Apart from the question about punishment for sin, agreement was already reached in Augsburg in 1530:

> We do not refuse to assign three parts (to penitence), viz.: firstly, contrition, which is the term for the terrors which attack the conscience after the perception of sin; secondly, confession, but here a man must look to the absolution and believe it (for sin is not remitted unless a man believe that it is remitted through the merits of Christ's sufferings). The third part is satisfaction, namely the worthy fruits of repentance. We are agreed in the opinion that sins are remitted as touching their guilt, not because satisfaction is made. But beyond this we have not yet attained to a common position, as to whether satisfactions are necessary for the forgiveness of sins as touching punishment.[54]

Eck believed that it would "be easy to agree" on CA 12, since here it was a quarrel about words rather than about substance.[55] Spalatin put on record here: "Doctor Eck hath also said that in the matter itself there be no dispute."[56]

Systematic reflection, as well as a clarification of the historical background, provides us with a working basis from which to approach the problems that follow (the historical complexity of which it is no longer easy for us to understand today); and this approach may be accompanied by a hope for more agreement than has hitherto existed or than seemed possible to either side. The same may be said about a further historical point.

2. Historically, penitential practice varies enormously and—as pre-Reformation history shows particularly—it also shows many signs of deterioration and misuse. In addition, developments in the Western church took a different course from those in the churches of the East, although down to the present day the Roman Catholic Church has seen no reason for rejecting and condemning the different practice of the sacrament of penance in the Eastern church or the canon law regulations applying to it. Moreover, the theological interpretation of the canons of the Council of Trent on the sacrament of penance (*DS* 1701–15) is the subject of an open and sometimes controversial discussion in the Roman Catholic Church. This discussion has made one thing at least clear: apart from its judicial and disciplinary definitions, not every one of these canons is also a cogent theological or dogmatic statement. This complex fact makes it considerably more difficult to insist on only a single interpretation of the sacrament of penance, and only a single practice, and to condemn all contrary views—provided only that the common ground discovered in the interpretation of justification is fully and firmly adhered to.

3. Of the questions that cannot be fully discussed in the framework of this excursus, two are particularly important:

a. The interpretation of the "judicial office" of the confessor, and absolution as a "judicial act" *(actus iudicialis)* (can. 9 on the sacrament of penance: DS 1709; NR* 668). The *contrasting position* here, according to the same canon, is an interpretation of absolution as "an empty service of pronouncing and declaring to the one confessing that his sins are forgiven, provided only that he believes that he has been absolved"[57]—that is, the very interpretation of the assurance of salvation based on absolution which we were able to say above (III.6) could be agreed upon, provided that Protestant doctrine and Roman Catholic doctrine are rightly understood in each case, and their special concerns appreciated.

It is a fact, first of all, that according to the explanations in cap. 6 of the Decree on Penance, the *actus iudicialis* is not to be understood in the strict sense, but as an analogy: "in the nature of a judicial act . . . just as a judge pronounces a sentence."[58] According to cap. 8, the sacrament of penance is not "a tribunal of wrath or punishment" *(forum irae vel poenarum, DS* 1692). John Paul II's Apostolic Letter *Reconciliatio et Paenitentia* is referring to cap. 6 when it says that "the nature of the judicial procedure" of the sacrament "is comparable with human tribunals only in an analogous sense" (No. 31.II).

It is a fact, further, that Catholic priests know that their function in the confessional is not merely to "judge" the penitent but to console and encourage and to give pastoral guidance. This is in harmony with tradition,[59] with the practical instructions given to priests,[60] and with the new liturgy.[61] The *actus iudicialis* must therefore always be simultaneously an *actus pastoralis;* for the *actus iudicialis* is actually *the absolution* as well.[62]

The task will be to understand and interpret the *actus iudicialis* in such a way that there is no suggestion that here human jurisdiction, in the form of an ordained minister of the church, decides whether God's grace is to be promised to, and bestowed on, a man or woman. In any case, no such notion finds any place in the liturgical texts, and it would directly contradict the *sola fide* which both sides affirm.

The indispensable *meaning* of the priest's judicial office is this:

• The priest holds the penitent accountable, not merely generally, but—on the basis of his confession—for specific sins, in this way pointing out the seriousness of his responsibility before God. In extreme cases he may even refuse absolution.

• Together with the forgiveness which he promises in Christ's name, the priest also places the penitent under Christ's judgment, which is always the other side of his forgiveness; for without this judgment, the forgiveness would lose its seriousness.

Seen in this way, the priest's *actus iudicialis* expresses the eschatological dimension of justification.

b. The other question has to do with the concept and practice of reparation or satisfaction *(satisfactio)*. The Reformers took grave exception to the use of this concept in the context of the theology of penitence, and this is still the case today (cf. cans. 12–14 on the sacrament of penance: *DS* 1712–14).

The term "satisfaction" also has been much disputed in the history of theology and dogma. How is it related to the period of penance which preceded absolution in the ancient church? How ought we to understand the "punishment" for sin, for which "satisfaction" or reparation still has to be made, even after absolution? Is satisfaction identical, historically and substantially, with the struggle against sin without which—as Protestants agree—there can be no true repentance? In the Reformation period, the clarification of this question was made more difficult by the late scholastic definition of satisfaction as "an external act done to placate the divine displeasure."[63] Another special difficulty was the debased practice of indulgences, which closed the door to any better theological insight and to any renewal of penitential practice. In the Roman Catholic Church today, satisfaction—insofar as it is to be understood as an essential part of the sacrament of penance and hence as necessary for the "validity" of the absolution—is frequently, contrary to doctrine and to both canon law and liturgical instruction, merely a brief prayer, in which the penitent lingers in thanksgiving before God, after he has received absolution. The penitent himself will hardly be aware any more of the dubious practices which were once connected with this act. At the same time, an extremely lively discussion is being carried on today in all the different disciplines of Roman Catholic theology as to how the ancient church's understanding of absolution and "reconciliation with the church" can be regained, under the conditions of modern life. This discussion has found expression in the church's official documents.[64]

For one thing has become clear: it is not the brief prayer that is the true reparation or "satisfaction"; it is the new life lived out of the forgiveness received. This gives back to the idea of satisfaction its proper but forgotten sense. For all penances can only have the function of urging Christians to grasp what Luther also emphatically stressed: that the struggle with sin is not finished with absolution. It begins afresh and has to bring worthy fruits of repentance.

Other questions are still open also. For example, What is the point of obliging the penitent to confess all his mortal sins completely, insofar as he can conscientiously remember them (cf. *DS* 1679f.)? The Council's aim here is not to encourage a scrupulous self-laceration, as the Reformers feared. The purpose, as has already been suggested, is to sharpen the penitent's sense of responsibility before God for his specific sins.

One very important question is, Who has the authority to grant or to refuse absolution? According to the Council of Trent, the answer is: the priest, because on him has been conferred the authority to bind and to loose (*DS* 1684 and 1710, with reference to Matt. 18:18; John 20:23). According to Protestant doctrine, the power of the keys—the power to bind and to loose—is a mandate given by Christ to the church and is as such still valid. This is the reason for the varying statements in the Protestant texts. Every Christian can promise forgiveness to the "brother" who confesses to him (e.g., WA 8, 183, 28 [On Confession, 1521]). Other texts do not distinguish between confession to a priest or minister and to the lay Christian (cf. HC, Confession 13; Tract. 24). Other texts, again, assume that confession will be made before the ordained pastor, as the appointed minister of the church.[65] Finally, there are statements which associate the hearing of confession with the episcopal office (CA 28.5: *BC* 81). Incidentally it emerges unambiguously from many present-day Lutheran ordination formularies that to hear confessions and to give absolution are among the basic functions of the ordained ministry.

Whereas statements about confession vary, Lutheran doctrine reserves church discipline to the ordained minister (CA 28.21f.: *BC* 84). Calvin and Reformed doctrine also stress the inner link between the power of the keys and the ordained ministry.[66] Discipline, on the other hand, is a matter for the presbytery or the synod. In both Lutheran and Reformed doctrine, church discipline is associated with the authority to admit or exclude from the Lord's Supper. In the present Roman Catholic discussion about the sacrament of penance, there is a reminder of the practice of lay confession in special cases, a practice which was alive and undisputed right down to the Middle Ages (cf. Thomas Aquinas, *STh*, Suppl. 8, 1–3). Melanchthon also appealed to this (Tract. 67). If all these things are viewed as a whole, we find ourselves faced imperatively with the question whether in this important sector it would not be possible to recover common theological ground which has meanwhile been silted over and forgotten.

As we have said, these questions, and others, cannot be decided here. But two *interim* conclusions may perhaps be drawn, again in the form of questions rather than postulates.

• Is it not time that we dissociated ourselves from what was pushed into the center of the stage *merely* out of the questionable desire to "distinguish" ourselves from the other side and to preserve our own "identity"? In the Protestant churches, a new awareness of the value of private confession and individual absolution is growing, in the footsteps of Luther and in "the freedom of a Christian."

• Should the Roman Catholic Church not ask itself: Is it really a reason for condemnation if the act of penitence is seen and performed as a graciously effected bringing back to baptism—baptism being from God's side irrevocable? If what was said above about absolution as an *actus iudicialis* is tenable (3.b), then the doctrine of the Council of Trent[67] is also open for just such an understanding of the sacrament of penance in the light of baptism. Is not Luther's doctrine of baptism—which Paul Althaus rightly termed "a precise expression of his doctrine of justification"—an exceedingly important contribution to the understanding of Christian baptism, particularly now that research into the history of the sacrament of penance and its liturgy has shown the extent to which, at this point, Luther was bringing to light submerged treasures of the church's tradition? Is the *Ordo Poenitentiae* not already moving in this direction when it instructs the priest to remind the penitent that through the sacrament of penance the Christian participates in Christ's death and resurrection, and that his life is renewed through the paschal mystery (no. 44)? In the light of what we have said, is it really out of the question for us even to concede a different practice to one another, without condemnation—as, after all, the Roman Catholic Church does where the Eastern Orthodox churches are concerned? And is it really impossible for us to recognize that, since the differences of interpretation are in any case no longer very important, substantially speaking, both practices are valid, or at least by no means stand in contradiction to the witness of the New Testament?

This ends the necessary excursus about the connection between the doctrine of justification and sacramental doctrine. We shall now continue our discussion of the sixteenth-century condemnations where we broke off (cf. p. 56).

7. Finally, strange though it may seem, the dispute about *merit* also rests largely on a misunderstanding (cf. I.7 above; also I.5; and 5 in this section). The Tridentine fathers ask: How can anyone have doubts about the concept of merit, when Jesus himself talks about "reward" and when, moreover, it is only a question here of acts that a Christian performs as member of Christ? The Reformers ask: How can anyone call the works that follow from faith "meritorious," when it is faith alone that justifies, and works remain imperfect and for the most part in need of divine forgiveness?

Yet the Reformers' reproaches are not in fact applicable, in the form in which they are made. The Reformers are afraid of the self-glorification of human beings in their works. But the Council excludes the possibility of earning *grace*—that is, justification—(can. 2: *DS* 1552) and bases the earning or merit of *eternal life* on the gift of grace itself, through membership in Christ (can. 32: *DS* 1582). Good works are "merits" as a *gift*. Although the Reformers attack "Godless trust" in one's own works, the Council explicitly excludes any notion of a claim or any false security (cap. 16: *DS* 1548f.). It is evident—and the genetic history of cap. 16 and can. 32 bears this out—that the Council wishes to establish a link with Augustine, who introduced the concept of merit, in order to express the responsibility of human beings, in spite of the "bestowed" character of good works.

So when the Council defends the concept of merit as a way of expressing the responsibility of human beings and the eschatological structure of grace, while Protestant theology rejects it as a practical, ethical (and pastorally applicable!) idea, the two sides are not saying "yes" and "no" to the same thing. For even *without* the concept of merit, the Reformers uphold the responsibility of human beings just as firmly as they do the eschatological structure of justification. Conversely, the Council of Trent above all is against any trend in theology and spirituality which would encourage the Christian to see his works again as an achievement which he himself has to produce, and from which claims on God can be derived. In substance, the Council could have echoed Luther's assertion: "The sons do not merit the kingdom but the kingdom merits the sons."[68]

Yet Catholic theology must explicitly concede that the term "merit" has often been used in an unbiblical and curtailed form in theology, pastoral care, and spirituality. The Reformers rightly criticized the calculation of rewards, and the thinking in terms of "claim," which were associated with the concept of merit and the practice of reparation or "satisfaction" *(satisfactio)* (cf. Excursus 3.b above). Not least because of this criticism, Catholic theology, religious instruction, and, above all, the official documents of the church[69] make only a restrained use of the concept of merit and express what it really intends to say in another way. Conversely, Protestant theology also stresses the importance of good works, since God has commanded us to exercise faith and because such works are a testimony and thanksgiving (Apol. 4, 189: *BC* 133). These works are to be performed for our fellows. They do not make us sons, but they do make us better sons.[70]

Many antitheses could be overcome if the misleading word "merit" were simply to be viewed and thought about in connection with the true sense of the biblical term "wage" or reward (cf., among other passages, Matt. 20:1–16; 5:12; John 4:36; 1 Cor. 3:8, 14; Col. 3:24). There are strong indications, incidentally—and a linguistic analysis could provide the evidence—that the language of the liturgy does not merely reflect the true meaning of the concept of merit stressed here, but—quite contrary to the Reformers' fears—prefers to explain what was meant through the word *meritum* rather than through the term *merces* (reward), for the very reason that merit sounds less "materialistic" than reward.

We may therefore arrive at the verdict that, in the face of all these assumptions and clarifications, the relevant condemnatory pronouncements no longer apply to our partner today—that is, the pronouncements found in cans. 2, 24, and 32 of the Decree on Justification (*DS*

1552, 1574, and 1582) and those in the Formula of Concord (SD IV.3: *BC* 551; cf. Epit. IV.16–18).

IV. A SUMMING UP, AND ITS SCOPE

How far has the path brought us, the way which began with the traditional antitheses and condemnations and which led us to a reexamination in the light of the growth of ecumenical conversations between theologians and the churches in our century?

1. Fundamentally, we may undoubtedly, and without any reservation, sum up as follows. Where the interpretation of the justification of the sinner is concerned, the mutual sixteenth-century condemnations which we have discussed no longer apply to our partner today in any sense that could divide the churches. This result has all the more weight, since historical investigation into the dispute of the time shows that in many individual points the rejections did not, even at that time, meet the target of the opponent's real intention in what he said (although this is not intended as adverse criticism of "the fathers"!). Today, at all events, both partners have learned to listen self-critically to each other. Consequently, each understands better what the other means. We no longer fight against bogus adversaries, and we are careful to express ourselves in such a way that our partner does not misunderstand us—indeed, can respect our particular "concern," even if he is not himself able to adopt our way of thinking and speaking.

2. The ending of the rejections does not mean that there are no longer any differences of interpretation about the justification of the sinner, or that these are *confined* to mere misunderstandings or different modes of expression. There continue to be differences (cf. esp. III.4, 5, and 7 above, as well as the excursus on the sacrament of penance). But, if our previous reflections are correct, these are not decisive questions of such a kind that the answer to them would decide about the true and false church. In other words they are not such that with them "the church stands and falls." At the same time, they do certainly present us with theological tasks which have to be taken seriously and pursued further, even in legitimate theological dispute—*within* the one church, which must not be allowed to founder on them.

3. The experiences of history, and especially Reformation history, teach us that there really can be an interpretation of the justification of the sinner on which the unity of the church will founder, as it foundered once before. This would be an interpretation that truly maintained, and really meant, the positions we encountered in the antitheses and common prejudices listed at the beginning. For that reason, the doctrine of justification—and, above all, its biblical foundation—will always retain a special function in the church. That function is continually to remind Christians that we sinners live solely from the forgiving love of God, which we merely allow to be bestowed on us, but which we in no way—in however modified a form—"earn" or are able to tie down to any preconditions or postconditions. The doctrine of justification therefore becomes the touchstone for testing at all times whether a particular interpretation of our relationship to God can claim the name of "Christian." At the same time, it becomes the touchstone for the church, for testing at all times whether its proclamation and its praxis correspond to what has been given to it by its Lord.

3

THE SACRAMENTS

I. THE DOCTRINE OF THE SACRAMENTS
IN GENERAL

Rejections of Catholic positions in the doctrine of the sacraments are to be found in the Augsburg Confession, Art. 13 *(Ed. pr.)*, and the Apology, Art. 13 *(De numero et usu sacramentorum,* On the Number and Use of the Sacraments), as well as in various Reformed confessional writings. The rejections of Protestant positions are to be found in cans. 1–13 of Sessio VII of the Council of Trent *(De sacramentis in genere,* On the Sacraments in General: *DS* 1601–13). These rejections are summed up below under five headings: (1) The Constitutive Marks of the Sacraments; (2) The Effect of the Sacraments by virtue of their performance *(ex opere operato),* and the importance of faith *(sole fide);* (3) The Unrepeatability of Certain Sacraments, because of the permanent character they confer (their *character indelebilis);* (4) The Priesthood of All the Baptized, and the authority to administer the sacraments; and (5) The Alterability of Forms of Celebration or Worship. The aim of the investigation is to determine whether the sixteenth-century condemnations still apply to our partner today. In clarifying this question, it is helpful to realize that, seen retrospectively, the respective positions did not deviate as widely even in the sixteenth century as it seemed at the time. Nonetheless, fundamental problems certainly exist in the differing understanding of the nature and communication of grace; and therefore in the interpretation of the relation between Word and Sacrament, faith and Word/Sacrament, and church and sacrament. These aspects will be touched on here only insofar as they are important for a consideration of the texts mentioned above. They are discussed in more detail in the working paper on Justification.

1. The Constitutive Marks

The differing view about the nature of the sacraments emerges first of all in the differing opinion about their number. Whereas Apol. 13.1–7 *(BC* 211f.) rejects the traditional seven (though without condemnation), and the Confessions only allow the validity of two (or sometimes three) sacraments (baptism, the Lord's Supper, sometimes confession), Trent emphasizes the traditional number and in can. 1 *(DS* 1601) rejects the position that is not prepared to allow all seven to be true sacraments. However, this antithesis does not have the rigor initially suggested by the external fact of the different number. For the differentiated discussions in Apol. 13 show that the Protestant concept of the sacraments is not clearly fixed in the Lutheran Confessions; while on the other hand the Council of Trent, can. 3 (*DS* 1603), makes it clear that varying importance was ascribed to the different sacraments, this implying a stress on Baptism and the Eucharist, as being what the Middle Ages called *sacramenta maiora* or *principalia*, the greater or principal sacraments. Both sides undoubtedly proceed equally from the three essential definitions of a sacrament, but behind the two positions is *a differentiating interpretation* of (1) the institution by Jesus Christ, (2) the meaning of the sacramental sign, and (3) the relation between the communication of grace and the performance of a sacrament.

1.1 The historical process in which the number of the sacraments was fixed shows that there was considerable openness in this matter. Since for both the Catholic and the Protestant churches *the institution by Jesus Christ* is a constitutive aspect of the concept of sacrament, the weight of disagreement has shifted from the varying number of the sacraments to the question about their authorization and their ecclesial foundation.

The medieval interpretation of what is meant by Christ's institution is broader than the modern one, which is shaped by historical thinking. According to the medieval viewpoint, the sacraments were brought into being through Jesus' salvific work—his cross and resurrection, his bestowal of the Spirit, and his commissioning of the apostles. In this sense, therefore, *institutio* includes the development of sacramental life in the church after Easter, no difference of principle being seen between Christ's institution and the action of the Holy Spirit in the church. This way of expressing the matter is behind can. 1 of the *Council of Trent's Decree on the Sacraments* (*DS* 1601).

The Protestant understanding is different. In the Protestant view, *institutio* means the directly demonstrable institution through Jesus Christ himself, or through an explicit divine mandate *(mandatum Dei);* although here too the essential element is to be found in the relation of the sacrament to Christ and in the divine charge (the command for repetition).

However, the force of the biblical evidence has been relativized by modern biblical scholarship—and especially in view of the fact that the sacrament of Baptism was not simply instituted by the earthly Jesus. Even where Matt. 28:19 is concerned, "dominical institution" means a saying of the risen Jesus, as well as the relation of the sacrament to Jesus' acts, and its foundation in the Christ event as a whole—before Easter and afterward. The dogmatic relevance of the reference to the risen and exalted Lord accordingly brings the Protestant viewpoint quite close, fundamentally speaking, to the medieval understanding of what is meant by institution. On the other hand, the weight of the exegetical findings makes certain attempts on the part of traditional Catholic theology appear problematical, when they try to provide a scriptural foundation for each of the seven sacraments in the same way.

Ultimately speaking, therefore, the question as to which acts of the church can and should count as sacraments is a decision that has to be made on substantial grounds. Here Protestant doctrinal tradition points to an institutional command by Christ himself, to which Scripture testifies. According to Catholic doctrine, "dominical institution" is shown particularly in the aspect that a sacrament contains a particular divine promise and act of grace; it is a concrete form of the promise of salvation that is bound up with the Christ event. This is important for the Protestant interpretation of the sacraments also, because the significance of Christ's instituting command is not isolated from the corresponding promise of salvation and the corresponding grace conferred. In this respect the positions are clearly beginning to converge.

1.2 The number of the sacraments also depends on whether the point of departure is a strict *interpretation of the sacramental sign* or a broader one. Luther bases his view on a strict definition of sign and does not include confession among the sacraments, since for him the visible element is lacking; although he stresses Christ's promise (Matt. 16:19; 18:18; John 20:23). In the Apology, Melanchthon presupposes a broader definition, which identifies sign and ceremony; and he includes confession among the sacraments in the strict sense (Apol. 13.3–4: *BC* 211). The same view emerges indirectly from the Augsburg Confession (which places Arts. 11–12 between Arts. 9 and 13) and from Luther's Small Catechism, where Confession appears between Baptism and Lord's Supper. This was not rescinded later, but the view nonetheless came to prevail in the Lutheran church that ordination, confirmation, matrimony, and extreme unction (the anointing of the sick) cannot be allowed to count as sacraments, either because they lack an explicit word of institution by Jesus or because the visible element is lacking or "was not instituted by God." At the same time, it is stressed that all of them are linked with special divine promises. In the light of the Confessions, this exclusion is not dogmatically fixed.

On the Catholic side the problem has been felt and thought about only to a limited extent, although the scholastic distinctions between *materia* (happening, act, together with the element, where applicable) and *forma* (the constitutive Word, or administrative formula) do not offer generally satisfactory solutions. The different definition of sign (strict or broad, as the case may be) cannot in itself provide a sufficient foundation for mutual rejection. The real issue is, rather, whether a convergence is possible in our general understanding of sacramental symbolism.

In regard to this question, the point should be considered that, fundamentally speaking, both sides stress the constitutive importance of the Word in the sacrament and accordingly the connection between the Word and the *nonverbal* sign in the sacramental act. The Protestant churches understand the sacramental act as proclamation;[1] but at the same time, they stress—though certainly in varying ways—that the promissory character which belongs to the sacraments is not expressed merely in the word, as *forma sacramenti*. Because the promise (the *pro me* reference) applies to the whole person, it also manifests itself in the nonverbal happening, since it is related to the bodily character of human beings, and hence to the deeper layers of the personality, which are not fully accessible to reason. Moreover, in the light of Protestant practice, the question as to which of the acts in question can count as "sacramental" should be thought through afresh, if due weight is given to the symbolic character inherent in them.

There is historical evidence to show that earlier on, confession was given considerable importance in the Protestant churches. The Lutheran churches (unlike the Reformed) retained (private) confession, preserving the traditional form in its fundamental elements, right down to the nineteenth century—to the present day in the form of "public confession" (which was constitutive for Reformed confessional practice). In the twentieth century, the value of (private) confession has been newly appreciated, taught, and—to a limited degree—practiced in Protestant churches. Marriage, confirmation, and ordination have also retained elements of sacramental practice (blessing and the promise of God's grace for a particular "state"; the laying on of hands and the prayer for the Holy Spirit; on Ordination, cf. pp. 150ff. below).

1.3 In relating the performance of a sacrament to the *communication* of salvific grace, the Catholic position assumes that the sacrament in question also possesses a specific inner reality, which is called sacramental grace (cf. Justification, pp. 30ff. above). According to the Protestant view, the essential content of the sacraments rests in the assurance of the forgiveness of sins (*promissio*) as the acceptance of the believer into fellowship with God (*fides*). Grace is understood accordingly.[2] In this sense the forgiveness of sins includes a comprehensive healing and

reorientation of human existence (cf. SmC 6.6: *BC* 352). The Tridentine condemnations in can. 5 *De sacramentis in genere* (On the Sacraments in General)[3] and can. 5 *De eucharistia* (On the Eucharist)[4] were
understood on the Protestant side as a condemnation of this personal
concentration. But according to today's Catholic view also, grace is
primarily a personal category and means God's gracious commitment to
human beings, although this means that he turns to them in each case in
a concrete and specific way. For this reason, the consequences for an
understanding of the sacraments which emerge from a convergence in
the understanding of grace must be considered afresh.

Modern Catholic doctrine especially stresses the tie with Jesus
Christ, the primal sacrament; and this averts an unduly marked differentiation (of such a kind as to suggest that every sacrament confers an
isolated grace). On the other hand, Protestant doctrine certainly takes
account of differentiations and varying efficacies, when in Baptism it
refers to the condition of being a child of God, and when it describes the
communion given in the Lord's Supper. Even the nonsacramental acts
which take place in confirmation, marriage, and ordination effect a
specific assurance of the divine promise of grace, according to Protestant interpretation, since—together with the obligation laid on the
recipient in each given case—they promise God's blessing for a particular situation in life. It is very important for mutual understanding to see
that the central terms "the forgiveness of sins" and "grace" both mean
in the comprehensive sense the salvation which God offers human life.

Catholic and Protestant churches alike stress that sacraments and
ministrations have to do with community or fellowship. In addition,
modern reflections about the ministrations of the church for special
occasions are a reason to ask whether the Protestant churches could not
learn from the Catholic idea about the specific efficacy of grace and
whether—in discussing the number of the sacraments—they should
not take more fully into account the aspect that particular acts of
blessing carried out by the church are a specific and practical promise of
God's grace. On the other hand, Catholic doctrine should bring out
more strongly the promissory character of the sacraments. It may
therefore be said that important convergences between the Protestant
and the Catholic positions also emerge from the question about the
specific communication of grace through the sacraments. This being so,
the Tridentine condemnation can apply today only within certain limits.
But the Protestant rejection of the seven sacraments must also be
reconsidered in the light of contemporary practice.

2. The Effect of the Sacraments by Virtue of Their Performance (*ex opere operato*), and the Importance of Faith (*sole fide*)

The Protestant Confessions utter their sharpest condemnations against the doctrine that the mass is "a work which by its performance [*ex opere operato*] takes away the sins of the living and the dead" (CA 24.22, 29: *BC* 58f.; Apol. 24.9–12: *BC* 250f.).[5] The Confessions set over against this the importance of faith for the proper performance of the sacraments. On the other hand, the Council of Trent condemned the assertion that sacramental grace is not communicated through the performance of the sacraments but solely through faith in the promise (can. 8: *DS* 1608). The condemnations in cans. 2, 4–7, and 12 are linked in substance with this fundamental rejection in can. 8, which the Reformers saw as including a rejection of their theology of the Word.

2.1 In this confrontation, *different perspectives* in the understanding of the formula are at work; and these must be taken into account in today's consideration of the rejections. The Protestant side looks at *the reception* of the sacrament and denies that it "justifies" *ex opere operato* (CA 13.3, *Ed. pr.*: *BC* 36; Apol. 13.18: *BC* 213). The Catholic side looks at *the dispensation* of the sacraments, and says that this is an efficacious sign "containing" and "conferring" grace (cans. 6 and 8). If these different perspectives are ignored, the Protestant side views the Catholic affirmation of the *ex opere operato* as the affirmation of an automatic, salvific sacramental efficacy; and the Catholic side, conversely, sees the Protestant denial of the *ex opere operato* ("through the performance itself") as a denial of the efficacy of sacraments in general.

Both sides reject the other side's interpretation of what they mean. For Catholic doctrine too, believing reception is required, if the sacrament is to be "for salvation." The formula about the efficacy of the sacrament *ex opere operato* is actually intended to stress the fact that the divine offer of grace is in principle independent of the worthiness of the one administering the sacrament and the one receiving it. By defining Christ as the active subject of the sacrament, the tendency of the formula is to contradict any view which interprets the sacraments in the sense of a righteousness of works. Conversely, for Protestant doctrine also the sacraments depend for their existence on Christ's institution and are independent of the worthiness of the one administering them (cf. CA 8.2: *BC* 33) or the one receiving (cf. LC V.17, 61, 69: *BC* 448, 453f.). But they effect salvation only through faith.

To say this, however, does not make the controversy null and void; for considerable *differences* do nevertheless exist about the relation between the performance of the sacrament, and faith. These differences show that here two varying approaches stand over against each other, approaches which it was hard to reconcile under the controversial theological conditions of the time.

2.2 In the Protestant rejection, the *ex opere operato* is more closely defined by the additional phrase "without a good disposition in the one using them ... without faith" (Apol. 13.18: *BC* 213). What is in the background here is not the official doctrine; it is the Scotist view of the doctrine of the sacraments, mediated through Gabriel Biel. In addition, the *abuses* in pre-Reformation eucharistic practice moved the Reformers to inveigh against any understanding of the Eucharist which separates its efficacy from participation by believers, so that in the popular view reception of the sacrament had an automatic, magically ritual effect. This interpretation was not in accordance with official Catholic doctrine. It was at that time largely associated with a one-sided and incomplete interpretation of sacrifice, which in the opinion of the Reformers made the eucharistic celebration "an affair of works." Criticism of this kind was also nourished by late scholastic discussions about the limited value of the mass and the use of especially effective masses. This meant that the phrase *ex opere operato* was "loaded" from the outset and invested with a different meaning, which makes it understandable that the Protestant Confessions should have rejected it in so sharp a form.

2.3 The Catholic condemnations underestimate the *ecclesial and soteriological importance* which the sacraments have for the Protestant churches as *means of salvation;* for they base these condemnations on statements made by the young Luther, which are too limited and one-sided. Moreover, the Council interpreted these statements in a Zwinglian sense. This influenced cans. 4 and 6 (*DS* 1604, 1606), which therefore did not really meet the opponent's position even at that time. For the Reformers, the sacraments (which of course for them meant Baptism and the Lord's Supper, and to a limited extent penance) are necessary for salvation. The dispute with the Anabaptists and the Enthusiasts makes this plain. They did not play off justification by faith alone *(sole fide)* against the celebration of the sacraments, as they were accused of doing. To say that the sacraments do not contain the grace to which they point, but are mere signs (thus can. 6), is not a true representation of the Lutheran viewpoint. It applies at most to the

Zwinglian position, which in this crass form was not accepted by the later Reformed church either.[6] At the same time, it must be noted that the phrase *continere gratiam* ("contain grace") does not accord with the Protestant interpretation of the relation between sacrament and the promise of grace.

2.4 In the sixteenth century, understanding was also made difficult by the fact that—in the context of the respective doctrinal systems—no agreement could be reached about the interpretation of what *faith* means. To this extent differences about the doctrine of justification strongly influenced the condemnations with regard to the doctrine of the sacraments. Mutual understanding today about the doctrine of justification (cf. Justification, pp. 50ff. and 68f. above) therefore surely ought to have consequences here too. Even in the sixteenth-century discussions it became evident that the Reformers maintained a concept of *fides* according to which its acceptance includes the transformation of existence, a notion to which Catholic tradition gave a name of its own: *gratia gratum faciens*, sanctifying grace (cf. Apol. 4.116: *BC* 123; cf. pp. 51f. above). In this respect, can. 5 (*DS* 1605), which starts from a narrow concept of faith, and from that standpoint condemns the view that the sacraments are "for the nourishing of faith alone," does not really touch the Protestant position; because for the Reformers *fides* includes, or stresses, everything that the sacraments effect according to the Catholic view.

3. The Unrepeatability of Certain Sacraments, because of the Permanent Mark They Bestow (*Character Indelebilis*)

Trent can. 9 (*DS* 1609) condemns the rejection of the teaching that baptism, confirmation, and ordination imprint an indelible mark (*character indelebilis*) on the recipient of the sacrament. The Confessions do not treat this subject separately, but the writings of the Reformers show that this view is rejected where ordination is concerned. The scholastic term *character* (mark, impress) refers first of all to the unique character of baptism, and is related to terms such as *sphragis* (seal), *signaculum* (identifying stamp), or *consignatio* (sealing or ratification), all of which were used in the ancient church for baptism as a whole or for individual rites (e.g., the laying on of hands) and which signify the belonging to Christ and the gift of the Spirit. This *Christological and pneumatological reference* (which implies both the permanent gift and the permanent obligation) must be taken into account, if we wish to arrive at a proper understanding of the term *character indelebilis*, which was attacked by the Protestant churches and for which the Catholic Church frequently put forward a misleading interpretation.

The reason for using ontological terminology to describe the effect of baptism, confirmation, and ordination, according to the Catholic view, is to stress the precedence of everything that Christ does for those who are baptized, confirmed, and ordained, compared with everything that the baptized and confirmed can do in the life they live as Christians, or anything that the person who has been ordained can do in the exercise of this special ministry. The new "being" which proceeds from God's sole creative efficacy is not the result of human activity. It is the precondition for all the activity to which those baptized, confirmed, and ordained are called; and over this precondition human beings cannot dispose. The "indelibility" of the sacramental "mark" rests on this precedence of the being effected by God before all human activity. And this also explains the unrepeatable nature of the dispensation of baptism, confirmation, and ordination.

3.1 It is common Christian doctrine that through *baptism* the Christian is accepted by God in a unique and fundamental way. And through baptism God makes an irrevocable claim on the whole of the Christian's life. Baptism can therefore never be repeated, either in the Catholic Church or in the Protestant churches. *Confirmation* links on to baptism and is not repeated either. Even though confirmation is not prescribed in the Confessions, the Lutheran churches have practiced it for sound reasons ever since the sixteenth century (Martin Bucer, Martin Chemnitz)—generally, since the eighteenth. The theological reason why confirmation cannot be repeated has not been clarified, but its dogmatic center is promise (blessing and the communication of the Spirit) and obligation (personal appropriation of the baptismal vow). Catholic teaching about confirmation expresses similar ideas in different language (relation to baptism, sealing through the Holy Spirit). The rejection in can. 9 (*DS* 1609) is therefore not applicable to the Protestant views of baptism and confirmation, since according to the Protestant view both involve a permanent claim.

The idea of a special individual bestowal of the Spirit in *ordination* also (which is supported by scriptural and patristic testimony) was expressed by high scholasticism in the doctrine of the *character indelebilis* (permanent mark) of the consecrated priest. The intention here was to deduce the unrepeatability of ordination from the fact that *the divine claim* could never be lost. Protestant criticism is directed less against this idea than against the associated notion of a special ministerial grace, which separates the priest or minister qualitatively from other Christians (cf. here pp. 152f. below on Ordination). In the sixteenth century the Protestant churches sometimes saw ordination as one with induction (installation) and therefore repeated it; but in the succeeding period the principle that ordination is not repeated generally came to prevail. The Tridentine condemnation therefore no longer applies to today's partner.

According to the Protestant view, Catholic doctrine is in danger of laying an illegitimate stress on some special quality in the priest. If the use of ontological categories is understood as an expression of the fact that God's irrevocable act of grace in the ordained person takes absolute precedence before all human action on the priest's part, then this way of expressing things does not contradict a "personal" understanding, which sees the consecrated priest as permanently claimed by God for a particular ministry, the divine promise endorsing the validity of the priest's ministerial acts, quite apart from his own subjective quality as a person. The Reformers agreed with this in principle, as the Augsburg Confession shows in what it says about the validity of the sacraments (CA 8: *BC* 33; cf. Calvin, *Inst.* IV, 19, 31; IV, 3, 16). Understood in this way, the doctrines of the two partners no longer contradict one another today in any sense that would justify a continuance of the mutual condemnation or rejection in its hitherto existing form.

4. The Priesthood of All the Baptized and the Authority to Administer the Sacraments

Trent can. 10 (*DS* 1610) rejects an interpretation of the priesthood of all the baptized which the Reformers never taught in that form. According to the agreed doctrine of the Lutheran and Reformed churches, *the public proclamation of the Word and the administration of the sacraments* are reserved for ordained ministers. But if the implications of the condemnation are to be properly understood, the differing interpretation of the term "authority" (*potestas*) must be noted, a difference which derives from the divergent understanding of priestly consecration/ordination and spiritual authority. According to Catholic doctrine, the *potestas* is a qualification, given in grace, which is linked with the priestly commission. For that reason, a Eucharist celebrated by one of the laity, for example, is not valid.

When Protestant doctrine speaks of its ministers, it does not talk about their enjoying any special *potestas*. Nevertheless, the special call to proclaim the gospel and administer the sacraments which finds expression in ordination is not merely a measure of external order. It expresses the fact that the Christian church does not live from itself, but rather from a counterpart: *God's* Word and the sacraments, which are *God's* sacraments. Only in an emergency situation in the church can a lay person fulfill the ministerial function, in the Protestant view, and then only provided that that person is explicitly appointed to do so. The connection between dogmatic and "judicial" questions is not satisfactorily clarified at present in the [Lutheran] Protestant church. The Tridentine condemnation in can. 10, however, must be held not to apply to the Augsburg Confession 5 and 14 (*BC* 13 and 14) or to the Apology 13.7–13 (*BC* 212f.): cf. Ministry, pp. 149f. below). It emerges from these passages that the idea of order is not merely external but is substantially linked with the sacrament, since the call and authorization to the divinely instituted ministry of Word and Sacrament, and to administer the sacraments "in Christ's stead" (Apol. 7.28: *BC* 173), is given with God's command and promise in ordination.

5. The Alterability of Forms of Celebration or Worship

According to the Protestant view, specific liturgical forms belong to the adiaphora ("indifferent matters"), as long as the central parts of worship are not affected. In the changes it has made to the Catholic cult the Lutheran church is much more conservative than the Reformed. Generally speaking, the Reformers wished to restore the simplicity of the ceremonies used, in accordance with the biblical form. In the dispute about the adiaphora, the relation between "good order" and evangelical liberty was clarified, so that the Formula of Concord rejects the teaching "that human precepts . . . are to be regarded as in themselves divine worship" (FC Epit. X: *BC* 494; SD X: *BC* 610ff.). Trent can. 13 (*DS* 1613) is directed against the contempt, omission, or new introduction "at pleasure" of ceremonies in respect of the traditional, approved order for administering the sacraments. It must be asked whether this superficial sense of the condemnation still applies to the Protestant churches today, in view of the factual division which has now existed for centuries. The liturgical reform of Vatican II, and the differences about it in the Catholic Church, show that there too can. 13 can be interpreted flexibly. Fundamentally speaking, can. 13 is directed against subjectivist caprice in altering the liturgy laid down by the church. That the liturgy is a matter for the church, and is not at the mercy of the subjective caprice of the individual minister, accords with the view of Protestant churches also. Moreover, it must be established that there has always been a basic stock of liturgical elements and ceremonies which for various reasons have never been surrendered (because of their catholicity, the continuity of development since the ancient church, etc.). This common stock should be consciously cultivated.

6. Conclusions

6.1 Seen in retrospect, the mutual condemnations relating to the doctrine of the sacraments did not in all cases exactly apply to the real substance of the opponent's position, even in the sixteenth century (cf. 2.3–4 and 4 above).

6.2 In other cases, more modern developments on both sides mean that the rejections have been relativized or even superseded, and no longer apply, or no longer apply precisely, to today's partner, because considerable doctrinal convergences have meanwhile emerged.

6.3 Nonetheless, because of different language and different practice in this complex, considerable differences still remain (cf. esp. 1.2–3 above). Both sides take as fundamental starting point the following essential marks of the sacrament: dominical institution, the external sign, the specific promise or communication of grace. But in particular instances they draw different conclusions from these things. The result is that there are two different "systems," in which the same statements take on different meaning, and apparently different statements mean something analogous.

6.4 Clarification through further discussion is required, especially with regard to the still open questions of substance which are connected with the different approaches of Protestant and Catholic doctrine and devotional practice. The fundamental importance of the sacraments for the praxis of the churches means that a thorough discussion is required about their interpretation of the connection between God's Word, the sacraments, and the church.

6.5 All in all, the condemnations on both sides may be viewed as not ecclesially insignificant; but largely speaking, the lines of division which they draw still obtain in their traditional rigor only if their formulations are viewed superficially. As soon as the way in which the sacraments are understood is considered, as well as the theological reasoning about the mode of their efficacy, a considerable measure of agreement emerges. This mitigates the ecclesial importance of the rejections that still remain.[7]

II. THE EUCHARIST/THE LORD'S SUPPER

The Tridentine canons that have to do with eucharistic theory and practice are subdivided into three complexes: *Canones de ss. Eucharistiae sacramento* (Canons on the Most Holy Sacrament of the Eucharist): *DS* 1651–61; *Canones de communione sub utraque specie et parvulorum* (Canons on Communion Under Both Species and That of Little Children): *DS* 1731–34; and *Canones de ss. Missae sacrificio* (Canons on the Most Holy Sacrifice of the Mass): *DS* 1751–59.

This division also designates the *three thematic sectors* to which the relevant rejections in the Protestant Confessions chiefly refer. They are directed against "the sophistry" of the doctrine of transubstantiation, against the denial of the cup to the laity, and against the doctrine that the mass is a good work and a sacrifice.

The criticism of the mass as sacrifice is especially important here, because it is extremely closely connected with the fundamental Protestant viewpoint, which is expressed in the doctrine of justification through faith, not through meritorious works on the part of men and women.

1. The Sacrifice of Jesus Christ in the Lord's Supper

1.1 The fundamental Protestant reproach (to which all particular objections can be traced back) was that the sacrifice of the mass is a work of human self-justification.[8] This view undoubtedly found support in *the theory and practice of the mass* at that time.

The struggle of the Reformers against the mass as a "work," satisfaction *(satisfactio)*, sacrifice *(sacrificium)*, and ceremony efficacious through the performance itself *(ceremonia ex opere operato)* can be rightly judged only if we take into account the opinion maintained by leading scholastic theologians in the late Middle Ages about the particular and finite value of the mass, as well as the views that were widespread in popular piety about the mass's efficacy. We must also remember the effects of these views on the practice of the religious life.[9]

On the other hand, the Reformers' criticism does not do justice to the

Catholic side inasmuch as it identifies the views against which they fought with the Catholic position in general. They did not take sufficient cognizance of more differentiated statements by such Catholic theologians as Silvester Prierias, Schatzgeyer, and others.

1.2 The Reformers bring their criticism to a point in the thesis that the Roman doctrine about the sacrifice of the mass contradicts *the full sufficiency of Christ's sacrifice on the cross, which was once and for all.* The atoning act of Jesus Christ on the cross, accomplished once and for all, requires neither multiple repetition nor any addition or complement.[10] But this acknowledgment of the uniqueness and the full sufficiency of the atoning event in Jesus Christ is clearly shared by the Council of Trent, since it defines the sacrifice of the mass as a making present *(repraesentatio)* of Jesus Christ's once-for-all sacrifice of himself on the cross.[11]

The Eucharist is a true and actual sacrifice, not "in itself," not parallel to or in addition to the cross, but as an actualization and application of the one, atoning, universal sacrifice for the church.[12]

Both Protestants and Roman Catholics are accordingly agreed in stressing that Christ's sacrifice on the cross "can be neither continued, nor repeated, nor replaced, nor complemented."[13]

On the basis of this agreement, the reproach in can. 4 is essentially not applicable today, and the same may be said of the sharp criticism of the Roman mass in the Smalcald Articles and the Heidelberg Catechism; for the facts are not as they are there represented.

In the sixteenth-century disputes, different concepts—apparently irreconcilable at the time—meant that the one side saw the other in an unendurably one-sided way. The Reformers interpreted Christ's command "Do this in remembrance of me" to mean solely and exclusively the proclamation of Christ's saving act on the cross, and the believing reception and public acknowledgment of its salvific effect. They saw the Roman mass as a repetition of the sacrifice of the cross through the mere operation of the act which the priest performed *(opus operatum).* The Council of Trent, on the other hand, stressed the sacramental representation of Christ's sacrifice on the cross in the performance of the sacrifice of the mass, and viewed the Protestant position as a mere verbal remembrance *(nuda commemoratio:* can. 3). Yet the Reformers were concerned to make it clear that the reality of the saving event itself becomes present in the Word, since it is Christ himself who says, "This is my body—this is my blood." But they were unable to state sufficiently clearly that in *the celebration* of the

Lord's Supper with the person of the crucified and risen Jesus Christ, *the event* of his unique sacrifice on the cross is also itself truly present, sacramentally— that is, in the sign of the Supper.[14]

On the other hand, the discussions in Trent, and certain formulations in the Decree on the Sacrifice of the Mass, show what difficulty the conciliar fathers had in describing theologically the mystery of the unity between the sacrifice of the cross and the mass. It was for them important neither to allow the Eucharist to evaporate into a mere remembrance (*nuda[m]* *commemoratio[nem]*: *DS* 1753; NR 608) nor to endanger the once-for-all character of Christ's sacrifice on the cross, by assuming another, even if bloodless, sacrifice (*DS* 1740).[15]

Today these disagreements can be clarified through a profounder understanding of "remembrance" in the sense in which it is used in the Old and New Testaments. Through the remembrance in worship of God's saving acts, these acts themselves become present in the power of the Spirit, and the celebrating congregation is linked with the men and women who earlier experienced the saving acts themselves. This is the sense in which Christ's command at the Lord's Supper is meant: in the proclamation, in his own words, of his saving death, and in the repetition of his own acts at the Supper, the "remembrance" comes into being in which Jesus' Word and saving work themselves become present. (In this sense, Word and element—*verbum* and *elementum*—belong essentially together.) So in this sense it is possible for both sides today to understand the relationship between the sacrifice on the cross, which took place once and for all, and the eucharistic celebration, as a single yet inwardly differentiated complex. In this way the danger of an equivalence without difference, and the pitfall of a division into an alternative—an "either-or"—can be avoided. It cannot be denied that here different ways of thinking have to be taken into account; but this is not a reason for necessarily condemning one another, especially since the form of both the Reformers' and the Tridentine theory shows obvious deficits.

1.3 In spite of its intention to adhere to the uniqueness and full sufficiency of Christ's sacrifice on the cross, the Council of Trent emphatically rejects any separation between the Lord's Supper (or the account of its institution) and *the priestly ministry* (*DS* 1752). This view intends to maintain that the priestly act in the "commemorative event" of the Eucharist is christologically anchored, while the priestly ministry of human beings is at the same time debarred from being founded and described other than christologically; and in this respect, the viewpoint does not have to conflict with the Protestant conviction that Christ himself is the priest who represents his work, performed once and for all, so that it is he who is and remains the reality of reconciliation in person.[16]

In this context too there has to be one fundamental insight behind all individual theological definitions: the insight that the atoning history of God in Jesus Christ overcomes every form of the antagonism that is characteristic of "worldly powers." Anything in the nature of participation in the sacrifice of Jesus Christ can be appropriately expressed only if God's activity and the response of human beings are not thought of in terms of mutually exclusive competition, but if *God's unique saving efficacy* in Jesus Christ is so described that it does not merely require, and result in, *the response of human beings*, but actually *first makes that response possible, and sustains it*. This response, above all, takes the form of the church's grateful reception, assent, and discipleship.[17] Accordingly, the catabatic aspect of the sacrament of the altar (the movement from above to below), the one-sidedness of which Trent resisted, and the anabatic aspect (from below upward) describe a reciprocal relationship (although the direction of the two movements is irreversible). The Christian existence issuing from the performance of the sacrament is never a "parallel" event, in the sense of an independent "complement." It is participation in the sacrifice of Jesus Christ, which possesses saving power for all peoples and times.[18] It is a curtailment of the biblical statements and of theological inquiry if the description of the Eucharist as sacrifice mentions (only) the descending line (God's act in Jesus Christ) and (only) the ascending line (the act of the church).[19]

The ecclesiological use of the concept of sacrifice must always be in accord with this, if the "ambiguity,"[20] of which the Reformers rightly complained, is to be averted. Even the new eucharistic prayers still show considerable tension in the sacrificial terminology, although the statements about sacrifice have undeniably been deepened.

1.4 The many differences of interpretation between the churches in this sector can ultimately only be convincingly eliminated if the liturgical and conceptual *distinction between* sacrificium *(sacrifice) on the one hand and* sacramentum *(sacrament) on the other* can count as having been surmounted in eucharistic doctrine and practice. This distinction was customary in late medieval and Reformation theology, even if it was only after the Council of Trent that it was carried through as a general principle.[21]

If the sacramental act of the making present of the offering of the cross in the sacrificial offering appears separate from the performance of the offering of this gift, then the performance of the sacrifice of the mass can no longer be properly and harmoniously conceived as sacramental actualization of the once-for-all offering on the cross. Once the sacramental presence of the offering on the cross and the church's performance of its sacrifice are separated from each other, the cogent conclusion will rather be that the offering of the mass, if not a complementary act, is at least a true repetition of Christ's sacrifice on the cross, in which it is the church, and no longer Christ, that acts as the agent of reconciliation.

This being so, Protestant criticism of the sacrificial aspect of the canon of the Roman mass is comprehensible. But the intention is by no means to set the canon aside altogether. All that is required is a formulation and an interpretation that are open to no misunderstanding. To the degree in which the identification between the canon and a (false) theology of sacrifice is broken down, traditional elements of the eucharistic prayer can be preserved in the Protestant churches also.[22]

At the same time, Protestant criticism of the alternative between *sacrificium* and *sacramentum* remains—or at least applies to the presuppositions that led to this alternative.

In Protestant theology a distinction is made between two kinds of sacrifice: the propitiatory sacrifice (*sacrificium propitiatorium*) and the thankoffering (*sacrificium εὐχαριστικόν*). Here the term expiatory or propitiatory sacrifice is restricted to the death of Jesus Christ alone. When the word "sacrifice" is used in connection with the celebration of the Eucharist, the word is used to mean solely the congregation's offering of praise or thanksgiving.[23] This argument is explicitly rejected by the Council of Trent (*DS* 1753; cf. already 1751). And an obvious difficulty is in fact implicit here. For under the presupposition (never disputed by the Reformers) that Christ is really present in the sacrament of the altar—irrespective of its verbal, promissory character—it is difficult to see why this presence should not at the same time mean the true making present of the event on the cross, defined as expiatory sacrifice. This conclusion could only be avoided *either* by thinking of the presence of the exalted One as not being mediated through participation in the earthly Jesus on the cross, but as a direct becoming present from heaven, in the elements; *or* by seeing in the offering of the Lord's Supper only the fruit of the sacrifice of the cross, the *applicatio* of what was gained there, but no longer the presence of the crucified One himself and as such. Both solutions contradict the fundamental concerns of Protestant theology, if we take seriously, in its key importance for the Protestant understanding of the Eucharist, the insistence on the words of institution (which is intended to testify particularly to the historical contingency of revelation and to the identity of the One present in the Lord's Supper and the One crucified) and the concern that in the celebration of the Eucharist also, Christ in the power of his Spirit is the sole and personal agent (which can only be conceived of as a making present of himself).

The strict Protestant distinction between the sacrifice on the cross and the congregation's offering of praise and thanksgiving becomes understandable only against the background of the severance between *sacrificium* and *sacramentum*. If this can be considered as having been surmounted, there is no longer any reason for the Protestant churches to distinguish fundamentally between the sacrifice of the cross and the sacrifice of praise and thanksgiving.

But in this case the first Tridentine canon (*DS* 1751) no longer has to be viewed as antithesis to Protestant doctrine. For its condemnation is directed against a severance between cross and mass—that is, the complete separation of the sacrament of Jesus' body and blood from Jesus' sacrifice—and against the description of the relationship of the two as a mere distribution and bestowal of something fundamentally past. But it leaves open here that the very distribution as food, both as liturgical sign and in the substance itself, has directly to do with the sacrifice of Jesus Christ.[24]

The canon itself does not speak of this, but the Doctrine suggests the connection in cap. 1, in the *ut sumerent* ("that they might partake"). In this respect, when can. 3 condemns those who say that the sacrifice of the mass is of use only to the one who communicates, this must not be interpreted as making an antithesis between the food offered and received and the sacrifice. What is being rejected here is merely an incomplete view of the universal dimension of the sacramental presence of Jesus Christ. "The body of Christ" comprises more than the congregation celebrating here and now, or those who are actually taking Communion. The Reformers never denied this universal dimension of the Eucharist. In this respect, Lutheran doctrinal definitions, for example, appear quite open for a church practice which—in the direction of the biblical concept of *koinōnia* (community)—strives to include symbolically the dead as well in the bodily fellowship of Jesus Christ manifested in the sacrament of the altar. At the same time, any idea of something achieved by human works for the benefit of the dead must be excluded without any reservation (cf. 4.3 below).

2. The Presence of Jesus Christ in the Sacrament of the Eucharist

2.1 The Struggle for an Understanding of the "Real Presence"

Canon 1 of the Tridentine Decree on the Eucharist condemns those who deny "that in the sacrament of the most holy Eucharist there are truly, really, and substantially contained the body and blood together with the soul and divinity of our Lord Jesus Christ, and therefore the whole Christ, but shall say that He is in it as by a sign or figure, or force (*ut in signo vel figura, aut virtute*)" (*DS* 1651; NR 577).

The history of the genesis of this canon shows that this condemnation is directed, not against the Lutheran position, but against "Zwingli, Oecolampadius and the Sacramentarians."[25] In the draft of the article, the phrase "not truly . . . but as by a sign" is explained as follows: "Just as one says the wine is in the ivy-bush hanging in front of the tavern"[26] [the ivy-bush indicating an inn—TRANS.] What is being rejected, therefore, is a way of thinking which understands a sign in the sense of a merely external label that draws attention to something.

The *Lutheran* doctrine of the Real Presence is certainly not touched by this. For it must be said that, in spite of differences of viewpoint about the mode of the Real Presence, the Lutheran Reformers— explicitly dissociating themselves from the "Enthusiasts" and the Zwinglians, and in fundamental agreement with the Roman Catholic Church—stressed that in the Lord's Supper Jesus Christ is "truly" (*vere et substantialiter*, truly and substantially) present in his body and blood, and permits himself to be received by us under the species of bread and wine.[27]

What is *Calvin's position*, and what is the position of the Reformed theology on which he put his impress? Calvin does indeed stress the distinction between *signum* and *res* (the sign and the thing represented), frequently using terms such as *figura, imago,* and *symbolum;* and he interprets the bread and the wine accordingly. But he stresses that the *signa* (signs) are "as it were joined . . . to the mysteries."[28] Calvin always and consistently rejected a purely external symbolism, such as was occasionally maintained by Zwingli.[29] He also talks about the efficacy or force (*virtus*) which proceeds from Christ; but he does not do so in the sense condemned by the canon: in Calvin the *virtus* is nothing other than the unrestricted efficacy of the Holy Spirit (*virtus Spiritus sancti*). This is by no means properly represented by *tantummodo . . . virtute* ("merely as by a . . . force").

On the other hand, this does not mean that Calvin and Reformed theology could simply assent to the positive assertions of can. 1 as they are worded. In order to make this clear the matter must be subjected to a more differentiated analysis than the canon itself offers.

Calvin distinguishes between the living presence of "the whole Christ" (*totus Christus*) and the bodily or physical presence of his human nature,[30] which is part of "the whole Christ." He rejects any spatial or bodily presence of Christ's human nature "in" or "under" bread and wine, for two reasons: it would be unworthy of Christ's divine glory; and it is also incompatible with the essence of his true humanity, which is now exalted to the right hand of the Father and there makes intercession for us. Accordingly, Calvin will not—starting from a "real presence" of the body and blood—arrive at the presence of the *totus Christus* by way of a doctrine of concomitance.

Such a "perverted" way of looking at things, he declares, tries to maintain the truly fundamental point—the Lord's presence, and his communication of himself by virtue of the Holy Spirit—by way of a deduction from a disputable and biblically unjustifiable metaphysical and theological thesis. Calvin himself, on the other hand, concentrated on the acknowledgment of the personal presence of Jesus Christ in the sense found in the Bible, and set aside the over-subtle questions of the medieval West about the mode of connection between the bread and the body of Christ.

In the light of Calvin's ideas, therefore, we are presented with the "alternative" (a somewhat curious one, for today's way of thinking) as to whether it is "Christ's body and blood" that is present or "Christ as person." Here we can also see the limitations of Calvin's eucharistic theology. Calvin takes issue with the notion of a "somatic" presence of Christ's body and blood, a presence conceived of as joined to the elements, whether this is explained by way of transubstantiation or through the ubiquity of Christ's human nature. Instead, he emphasizes that the presence of Jesus Christ comes about *vere, realiter et substantialiter* ("in truth, reality and substance") by virtue of his promise, through the efficacy of the Holy Spirit.

Calvin was thus able to assent without any difficulty to the formulation in the Augsburg Confession, Variata 10: "With bread and wine the body and blood of Christ are truly shown *(exhibeantur)* in the Lord's Supper to those who partake of it."[31] Christ himself in his wholeness is the active subject who so unites us to himself by virtue of the Holy Spirit that we are truly fed with his body and blood. In saying this, Calvin also rejects a *manducatio impiorum*, a partaking by the unworthy, or unbelievers. The sacrament is offered to all, but unbelievers receive only the sign; they are not united with the life-giving body of Christ by the Holy Spirit. For "those who are without the Spirit of Christ are unable to eat the flesh of Christ."[32]

As we know, this whole question was hotly disputed in the sixteenth century, not merely between Trent and the Reformers in general, but between Lutherans and Reformed as well. The new ecumenical conversations of recent years, however, have led to an understanding which the Leuenberg Concord expresses in the following words: "In the Lord's Supper the risen Jesus Christ imparts himself in his body and blood, given up for all, through his word of promise with bread and wine. He thus gives himself unreservedly to all who receive the bread and wine; faith receives the Lord's Supper for salvation, unfaith for judgement."[33] This formulation clearly goes beyond Calvin, but at the same time tries to preserve his concern.

The report of the dialogue between the Secretariat for Promoting

Christian Unity and the World Alliance of Reformed Churches also explicitly maintains that in the biblical testimony "the emphasis is on the fact of the personal presence of the living Lord in the event of the memorial and fellowship meal, not on the question as to how this real presence (the word 'is' in the words of institution) comes about and is to be explained." Accordingly, the report stresses that "both traditions, Reformed and Roman Catholic, hold to the belief in the Real Presence of Christ in the Eucharist. . . . In the Eucharist he communicates himself to us in the whole reality of his divinity and humanity."[34]

Finally, in the Lima convergence declaration, Lutheran, Reformed, and Catholic theologians together arrived at the following formulation: "The Spirit makes the crucified and risen Christ really present to us in the eucharistic meal, fulfilling the promise contained in the words of institution. . . . Being assured by Jesus' promise in the words of institution that it will be answered, the Church prays to the Father for the gift of the Holy Spirit in order that the eucharistic event may be a reality: the real presence of the crucified and risen Christ giving his life for all humanity."[35]

It may therefore be said in conclusion that in view of the doctrinal statements and convergence declarations of today, and in spite of diverging terminology, the condemnation of the Tridentine can. 1 (*DS* 1651) does not apply to the present Reformed understanding of the eucharistic presence of Christ.

2.2 The Dispute About Transubstantiation

In Sessio XIII (1551), in can. 2 *de ss. Eucharistiae sacramento* (On the Most Holy Sacrament of the Eucharist), the Council of Trent endorsed as the doctrine of the church a "wonderful and singular conversion" *(mirabilem . . . et singularem conversionem)*, a transformation "of the whole substance of the bread into the body, and of the entire substance of the wine into the blood, the species of the bread and wine only remaining." And it added that the Catholic Church "most fittingly" *(aptissima)* calls this transformation *(conversio)* a transformation of essence *(transsubstantiatio)* (*DS* 1652; NR 578).

The Protestant Confessions reject the doctrine of transubstantiation, giving various different reasons. The Formula of Concord actually "rejects" and "condemns" the doctrine as "false, erroneous, and deceiving."[36]

In order to arrive at a proper evaluation of this controversy, it is of fundamental importance that we see it in its historical context.

Excursus
THE HISTORICAL BACKGROUND

1. Antiquity

It is very important, first, to establish the fact that for the first whole thousand years Christians were able to celebrate the Eucharist, and to think about it in faith, without using this terminology, even though from early times they were guided by the conviction that in the Lord's Supper there was a "transformation" *(metabole, conversio)* of the bread and the wine and of those holding the feast.[37] The Reformers were also familiar with this idea.[38] But among the fathers of the church the concept of reality (and hence real "transformation") had a largely dynamic character; that is to say, reality was chiefly defined in the light of the relationship of ownership, lordship, or influence existing between the mighty God and the eucharistic celebration.

2. The Early Medieval "Crisis"

The value and limitations of the doctrine of transubstantiation must be seen against the background of a century-long development which has been called "the crisis of the sacramental idea." What is meant by this is the process of early medieval, and medieval, speculation in which sign and the thing signified, symbol and reality, became more and more sharply divided from one another, so that the ancient Christian concept of "mystery" increasingly broke down. The roots of this crisis reach back far into the prescholastic period.

For example, Ratramnus of Corbie begins his treatise *De corpore et sanguine Domini liber* (written in 860) with the curious alternative: Does what happens in the Eucharist take place in the mystery *(in Mysterio)* or in truth *(in veritate)*? This question in itself suggests an understanding of sacrament which feels that there is an antithesis between what is symbolic and what is real, an understanding which shakes the unity between the sacramental *figura*, or symbol, and the *veritas* or truth signified. And by introducing a cleavage of this kind into the sacramental concept, this viewpoint very soon became a genuine threat to the Eucharist. For the theological positions of the medieval eucharistic disputes swing between the extremes of a heavily materialistic misunderstanding and an equally mistaken spiritualization.

At the same time, research into the history of dogma in recent decades has been able to make it clear that it is nonsense to suspect of an objective, materialist understanding of the eucharistic Real Presence those high scholastic theologians who (after a protracted and complicated reception process)[39] brought the concept of transubstantiation into the tractate on the Eucharist.

For if we look at the matter more clearly, it becomes clear that this was in fact a reaction in a diametrically opposite direction: because of the dispute about the spiritualistic standpoint of Berengarius of Tours (d. 1088), an almost "mythical," and definitely sensualist, view of the Real Presence had become widespread. This viewpoint must have been common on the level of scholarly reflection as well, for it very strongly colors the text drawn up by the Roman synod, for example, to which Berengarius had to swear in 1059.[40]

3. High Scholasticism

The theologians of the high scholastic period turned against this impoverishment of the sacramental concept, in the process drawing on the (then new) potentialities offered by an Aristotelian philosophy of nature. The metaphysical concept of *substantia* (substance, or essential nature) seemed precisely designed to overcome both a crass "materialism" in the understanding of the Real Presence and a purely intellectualist interpretation of "sign" (*signum*), in this way throwing open once more for a comprehension of the Eucharist the spiritual and personal dimension, the dimension of faith. It is in this context that the concept of "transubstantiation" has to be seen.

For the concept of substance as metaphysical component of reality meant precisely the levels of understanding, that is, that which denotes or reflects the unified intelligibility of sensory data.[41] To take over the terminological distinction between accident and substance was therefore a way of retaining and stating simultaneously the reality of the transformation on the one hand (the substance) and the still-remaining reality of the sign (the accidents) on the other. This made it possible to retrieve the real point of the sacramental concept, at least where the eucharistic offerings were concerned (reality *in* the sign: *signum efficax; efficit quod significat*, effectual sign, a sign effecting that which it signifies).

But even apart from all controversy about the theological utility or nonutility of Aristotelian philosophy, the use of the concept of substance can contribute to an understanding of the Eucharist by bringing out two aspects: on the one hand the identity of the one Lord who "then, in the past" encountered his disciples visibly in the flesh and who "now, today" bestows his presence in a completely different way on the worshiping congregation; and on the other hand the independence of this presence of the Lord of the response which men and women give to it, be it in faith or in disbelief.

4. The Problem Posed by the Doctrine
of Transubstantiation

Tying inquiry down to the question of the "somatic Real Presence" narrowed the perspective very considerably. But even apart from that, the limitations of this conceptual pattern very soon made themselves felt.

How can the "new substance" (of the body of Christ) sustain the *quantitas dimensiva* ("spatial dimension")—which counted as "accident"!—of the "previous substance" of the bread, which was different in kind? Does the "transformation of the substance" mean that it disappears or is destroyed? Without postulating an additional miracle, is it possible to explain how the accidents remain without the substance that really supports them? Questions such as these, which were discussed at the greatest length, show that the very conceptuality which helped to solve one fundamental problem, itself created new difficulties—difficulties which did not arise out of the mystery of faith in its reality, but were the result of a particular philosophical system.

It is therefore not surprising that soon after Aquinas himself, the unified interpretation of this "classic" solution broke up. The division between the metaphysical and the physical levels was not sustained and, almost unnoticeably, the understanding of "substance" shifted in the direction of a "physical" concept of quantity and mass.

5. *The Reformers' Rejection*

For the Lutherans,[42] the scholastic doctrine could at most count as one theoretical variation among others. It could certainly not be declared binding for faith. The formulation in the Smalcald Articles shows the extent to which the conceptual details of the theory were felt to be a hindrance to an appropriate description of the *signum sacramentale* (the sacramental sign): "We have no regard for the subtle sophistry of those who teach that bread and wine surrender or lose their natural substance *(naturalem suam substantiam)* and retain only the appearance and shape of bread without any longer being real bread."[43] But otherwise the question had not as yet for Luther the dogmatic importance which the Formula of Concord assigns to it.[44]

The Formula of Concord "rejects and condemns" the doctrine of transubstantiation, when it maintains that the bread and wine are transformed into Christ's body and blood in the sense of an annihilation *(annihilatio)* of the substance of the bread and wine, so that "only the exterior appearance remains" *(accidentia sine subiecto)*.[45] In considering this condemnation one should remember that the viewpoint of both Luther and the fathers of the Formula of Concord was largely influenced by the nominalist school of thought. Like the nominalists, Luther rejects "any permanent quantity separate from the substance" as sustainer of the accidents remaining after transubstantiation, because the quantity cannot be divided from the substance.[46] On the other hand, it was precisely the nominalist form of the doctrine of transubstantiation which he (and with him the Formula of Concord) combated; for, unlike Aquinas, the nominalists assumed that the substance of the bread ceased to be altogether, or was annihilated. Consequently, the result of taking over the empirical concept of substance from late scholasticism was a misinterpretation of transubstantiation, which saw it as meaning a physical transformation (*conversio physica*) or a spatial encapsulation of Christ's body and blood.[47]

The Formula of Concord, for its part, in defining more closely the relationship between Christ's body and blood and the bread and wine, is concerned not to distract attention from the unambiguous character of the *verba testamenti* (the words of [Christ's] testament), but to emphasize it.

For it adds to the statements in CA 10, Apol. 10, and SmC (*BC* 34, 179f., 352) the explanation: "that, even though they also [i.e., Luther and his followers] use these different formulas, 'in the bread, under the bread, with the bread,' they still accept the words of Christ in their strict sense and as they read, and they do not consider that in the proposition (that is, the words of Christ's testament), 'This is my body,' we have to do with a figurative predication, but with an unusual one (that is, it is not to be understood as a figurative, flowery formula or quibble about words)."[48]

6. The Ubiquity, or Omnipresence, of Jesus Christ

The reflections which are designed to make the Real Presence of Christ's human nature "in, with, and under" the elements comprehensible, and which offer the Lutheran alternative to the doctrine of transubstantiation, are Christological in kind: according to the Lutheran view, the sacramental Real Presence is based on Christ's "ubiquity." Here, however, it is extremely important that this presence should not be thought of in "spatially local" terms. It accords with the mode of God's ubiquity; for God is indeed present "in" created things, but in such a way that they do not include him, but that, on the contrary, he comprehends them.[49]

Christ, "since [he] is one person with God, [can be somewhere in] the divine, heavenly mode."[50] Here it is not a matter of the essential properties (*proprietates essentiales*) of Christ's human nature, which remain unchanged in eternity, just like the natural properties (*proprietates naturales*) of his divinity.[51] It is a matter of Christ's majesty (*maiestas Christi*), which is grounded in his assumption of human nature (*assumptio humanae naturae*), and of his exaltation to the right hand of the Father (*exaltatio ad dextram patris*).[52]

This Christological approach must in principle be judged positively. But it is impossible to overlook the fact that the ubiquity doctrine of the Lutheran Reformation poses its own problems. At a number of important points it goes beyond what is said in Holy Scripture, and it stands in considerable tension to the way of thinking and speaking found in the Christology of early times. Moreover, it raises several difficulties in the doctrine of God.

7. Analogy with the Incarnation

The Lutheran starting point was the assumption that bread coexists with Christ's body, and wine with his blood, in sacramental unity. Following Luther, and pointing to the example of antiquity, this could be related to the unity of the divine and human nature in the person of the God/man Jesus Christ: "For as in Christ two distinct and untransformed natures are indivisibly united, so in the Holy Supper the two essences, the natural bread and the true, natural body of Christ, are present together here on earth in the ordered action of the sacrament."[53]

It must be noted that this is not intended to be a direct equation; it simply indicates a correspondence. The abiding difference between the personal unity of the two natures in the person of Jesus Christ and the sacramental unity of the bread and the body of Christ is in no way abrogated; it is explicitly retained.[54] The suspicion that the said structural parallelism between Christology and the doctrine of the Lord's Supper *necessarily* leads to the notion of an impanation, or to a eucharistic reincarnation, or to a duplicated hypostatic union, is hence unjustified. The meaning and purpose of the comparison between the *unio personalis* and the *unio sacramentalis* is on the one hand to emphasize that the *verba testamenti*—the words of Christ's own testament—are to be taken literally, that is, that the food blessed really is the true body and true blood of Christ. In addition, the aim is to relate the reality promised in the words of institution, and present in the elements of the feast, to the whole of Christology, so as to prevent the Lutheran doctrine of the Lord's Supper from falling victim to a rigid biblicism.

This idea must certainly not be permitted to lead to a unilinear deduction of the doctrine of the Lord's Supper from Christology; it is essential to preserve quite unequivocally the special character of the Lord's Supper, as distinct from the incarnation, and vice versa. At the same time, however, and notwithstanding the contingency of its institution, if the Lord's Supper is to be identifiable as such, it must not be removed from its context in the revelatory history of the crucified One who is now risen.

8. Three Forms of Doctrine

The Lutheran doctrine of the Real Presence would seem to approach very closely to the Catholic doctrine of transubstantiation, both differing from Reformed doctrine in this respect. Yet on closer inspection it becomes clear that in one central point the Lutheran doctrine takes up a special position which would be similarly rejected by both Aquinas and Calvin.

Both Aquinas and Calvin held that the transfigured human nature of Jesus Christ is enthroned at the right hand of the Father and is hence not as such omnipresent (not even by way of the hypostatic union—that is, through participation in the divine omnipresence).

According to the doctrine of transubstantiation, the *substance* of the bread and wine is transformed into the *substance* of Christ's body and blood; that is to say, the "accidents" of Christ's human body, including the *quantitas dimensiva* (spatial extension), are *not* present in the sacramental mode of his presence. Calvin sees the matter similarly, only he formulates it pneumatologically: the statements about the Holy Spirit as "surmounter of all distances" fulfill for Calvin a function similar to the statements about transubstantiation in Aquinas or the the ubiquity doctrine in Luther.

In this respect, the three positions form a triangle, in which a group of two always stands over against a third opinion in one or the other point: Luther and Calvin have in common their rejection of transubstantiation; Aquinas and Calvin are at one in denying the ubiquity of Christ's humanity; Aquinas and Luther both maintain the presence of the true body "in" the elements, or *sub specie panis* ("under the form of the bread"), as the case may be.

The concern and fundamental intention of the other position in each given case can be better understood in retrospect. All three doctrinal forms were trying to express the mystery of Christ's presence in the Eucharist, but by way of different theoretical approaches which were apparently irreconcilable under the conditions of the sixteenth century.

In *judging the sixteenth-century controversy,* it is important first of all to observe that the Council of Trent itself already held aloof quite noticeably from the traditional concepts and terminology still employed: that which is possible to God alone and which can be perceived by our reason, enlightened in faith—that is to say, the sacramental presence of the exalted Lord—is such that "we can scarcely express it in words" (cap. 1: *DS* 1636; NR* 568).

Together with the ancient church, the mystery of the *conversio* is acknowledged in faith, the doctrine of transubstantiation being seen as an attempt to find an explanation; and the solution is termed "appropriate" (*convenienter et proprie: DS* 1642) and "most fitting" (*aptissime: DS* 1652). It emerges from the conciliar documents that in can. 2 the fathers were not concerned to tie the matter down to a particular kind of philosophical thinking.[55] Their purpose was a theological one. They wished to reconcile the once-for-all nature of the incarnation with the presence of Christ "in many other places sacramentally" (*DS* 1636), thereby resisting the view of a hypostatic union between the human nature of Christ and the substance of bread and wine (a view ascribed to Luther in the conciliar drafts of this article[56]). The idea of the *conversio*, or transformation (explained with the help of the doctrine of transubstantiation), also tries to preserve the idea of "sacramentality" from a falsification which it was feared could arise through notions in the direction of reincarnation, impanation, or a repeated hypostatic union.[57]

In addition, a consideration of the complicated controversy has made the following fact plain: once the metaphysical concept of substance has been taken into account (a concept which belongs to the Thomist tradition), the Lutheran rejection of transubstantiation cannot be said to apply to the Catholic doctrine. On the other hand, when the Council of Trent condemns the view that "in the sacred and holy sacrament of the Eucharist there remains the substance of bread and wine" (can. 2: *DS* 1652; NR* 578), this condemnation has to be judged in the light of the Lutheran doctrine of the Lord's Supper outlined above (a doctrine which people have sometimes tried to explain by the term "consubstantiation"). This rejection too fails to apply to the Lutheran position, since " 'transubstantiation' does not signify an antithesis to 'consubstantiation,' if the latter is simply intended to mean that the bread and wine continue to exist unaltered, as physical and chemical entities."[58]

The state of the theological discussion is meanwhile such that the essential preconditions exist for avoiding false alternatives drawn from controversial theology, and for expressing afresh and together our common faith with regard to the eucharistic presence of Jesus Christ also.

In the context of these attempts, the ideas that have come to be known under the term "*trans-signification*" could also take on ecumenical importance.[59]

This idea was initiated by the Reformed theologian F. J. Leenhardt and was developed on the Catholic side by Piet Schoonenberg especially. It starts from the recognition, central to human experience of reality, that whatever is encountered in any given situation has to be grasped as an element in a web of relationships. It is this complex which fundamentally lends meaning to the experience. Once we take seriously the fact that the "essence" of a thing or an event emerges from the complex of relationships to which it belongs, and in which we encounter it, then the concept of "substance" will have to be newly defined in the light of the concept of "meaning" and relationship. But if essence, substance, and meaning belong together in this way, then "substance" is not simply something that always remains the same, something belonging-within-itself, something that unalterably precedes and underlies all change. Even the natural conditions with which we have to do frequently take on new meaning in the changed context of human behavior into which they enter. For every event and every object is by nature open and capable of entering into new relationships of meaning, out of which its own, primal reality is newly defined, so that there is a "transformation of essence."

An essential *transformation of meaning* of this kind takes place when the meal to which Jesus invites us becomes the efficacious sign of communion with him, and thus also with the divine eschatological future. *Through Jesus Christ himself,* the crucified One who is exalted, and in the power of his Holy Spirit, the gifts of bread and wine are set in a completely new relationship to us. They receive a new meaning, and take on a new function as sign, a function instituted and effected by him and which we perceive and accept in faith. By being taken into God's service in this way, the gifts lose the poverty of being in relation only to themselves, and receive a *definitive* transformation of significance which brings with it a transformation of "the thing itself."

It is obvious that here a *relational ontology* plays an essential role, relational ontology signifying the philosophical determination of being by way of rela-tionship and meaning. For if relationship is viewed as the decisive level of being (because the "reality" of the spirit, of knowledge, personhood, commitment, and communication is more intense than the "reality" of mere existence and tangibility), then in talking about the Eucharist (and since the Eucharist is the essential process of personal communion) we have to talk about a trans-signification, in the sense of a true, essential transformation "of being," a transformation of the event of the feast and the elements offered there, a transformation which is, on the one hand, constituted through the celebration of the feast and, on the other hand, gives the feast itself its specific quality.

This viewpoint can open up a new helpful way of access to the total sacramental reality of the eucharistic celebration. For trans-signification talks about a "transformation of the essence," not of the elements alone, but of the whole symbolic, faith-imbued event of the eucharistic gathering: the assembled people, the preparation of the meal, the words of institution, the bread and wine, the distribution of the food, the eating and drinking, the whole communicating community are "trans-signified." They take on a new meaning, a new "being," bestowed by the Spirit.

It must be stressed here that Vatican II (cf. *SC* 7 and elsewhere) and the postconciliar texts refer several times to an actual presence of Christ in the congregation gathered together in his name (in accordance with Matt. 18:20); in the Word of God; in praise; and in the sacraments, especially the Eucharist. The purpose here is to surmount an isolated fixation on a "substantial" presence, different from these, under the eucharistic "species."[60]

Summing up, we may therefore say the following:

The sixteenth-century controversy about the presence of Jesus Christ in the Lord's Supper is surmountable to the extent in which the following principles are jointly recognized:

1. Through their sacramental use, the eucharistic offerings of bread and wine undergo that change which has from ancient times been termed *conversio* or *mutatio* ("transformation" or "change"). The "transformation of essence" which takes place in this feast and its offerings of bread and wine, in the power of the Holy Spirit, through the Word, cannot be revoked. It has an eschatological significance and designates the ultimate essence of this "food for eternal life."

2. The clear and unambiguous acknowledgment of the true presence of Jesus Christ is not necessarily tied to the explanatory models offered by the doctrines of transubstantiation and ubiquity. But it is important that the danger of either falsifying or attenuating this acknowledgment should be averted by together agreeing that the presence is not spatial or natural in kind and that the sacrament should not be understood in a merely commemorative or figurative sense.[61]

3. "The eucharistic meal is the sacrament of the body and blood of Christ, the sacrament of his real presence. Christ fulfills in a variety of ways his promise to be always with his own even to the end of the world. But Christ's mode of presence in the eucharist is unique. Jesus said over the bread and wine of the eucharist: 'This is my body . . . this is my blood . . .' What Christ declared is true, and is fulfilled every time the eucharist is celebrated. The Church confesses Christ's real, living and active presence in the eucharist."[62]

4. All the conceptual efforts of *fides quaerens intellectum* (faith seeking understanding) are not attempts to eliminate the mysterious character of the eucharistic presence. They presuppose the mystery and express it; for the promised reality (the real presence of Jesus Christ) is far beyond and ahead of all attempts at reflection in retrospect.

2.3 The Usus, or Practice, of the Sacraments

In the light of these reflections, the justice and defects of the Lutheran polemic against Roman Catholic devotion to the reserved sacrament can be defined afresh.

The criticism is based on the "useful rule and norm . . . derived from the words of institution: *Nihil habet rationem sacramenti extra usum a Christo institutum* (Nothing has the character of a sacrament apart from the use instituted by Christ). That is, if one does not observe Christ's institution as he ordained it, it is no sacrament."[63]

This by no means restricts the *usus*, or use, to "tasting with the mouth" *(sumptio)*. It is the term used for "the entire external and visible action of the supper as ordained by Christ: the consecration or words of institution, the distribution and reception, or the oral eating of the blessed bread and wine, the body and blood of Christ." Apart from this use, however, "it is not to be deemed a sacrament, as when in the papistic Mass the bread is not distributed but is offered up, or locked up, or carried about, or exposed for adoration" (FC SD VII.86f.: *BC* 584f.).

According to these stipulations, the criterion for the Lutheran understanding of *usus* is the institutionary intention—that is, the sacrament of the altar must be directed toward the specific act of bodily eating and drinking in an actually present eucharistic fellowship, in accordance with the words of institution. In saying this, Lutheran doctrine defines "use" in such a way that Christ's sacramental presence is not restricted to the moment of reception but embraces the whole celebration of the feast, which in its inner intention is directed toward the "communion," because this "communion" in the meal is the meaning and essence of the eucharistic act (cf. 1 Cor. 10:16f.).

The rejection uttered in the relevant Tridentine can. 4 condemns all those who say that the true presence of the Lord's body and blood is in the sacrament "only in use *(in usu)*, while it is taken *(dum sumitur)*, not however before or after" *(DS* 1654; NR* 580). It therefore does not apply to the Lutheran doctrine in its understanding of "use" but only to a view which directly identifies "use" with "reception."

In addition, it must be realized when cap. 2 says of the *ratio institutionis* (the reason for the institution) of this sacrament: "He wished that this sacrament be received . . . *(sumi autem voluit DS* 1638; NR* 570), that this description is fully in accord with the fundamental Protestant conviction about "use," and could easily be summed up as: *ad usum, ut sumatur* (for use, so that it may be received). The Council of Trent, however, also defends the remaining *(remanere)* presence of the Lord in the wafers that have been left (can. 4: *DS* 1654); it justifies the adoration of Christ in the sacramental species, when they are carried in procession also (can. 6: *DS* 1656); it supports the reservation of the sacrament and the solemn carrying of the sacrament to the sick (can. 7: *DS* 1657); and in defending these practices it rejects the opposing Protestant assertions.[64] These assertions were for their part bound up with rejections of the relevant Catholic practices, being determined by the conviction that certain forms of piety that had developed in the Middle Ages were contrary to the intention of the institution of the sacrament, which was directed toward believing reception (FC Epit. VII. 40: *BC* 486; and SD VII.126: *BC* 591: adoration of the elements; FC SD VII, 87: *BC* 585: reservation, adoration, procession).

The theological and practical liturgical development in our churches up to now must not remain unnoticed in a *present evaluation* of this controversy.

Thus the liturgical reform of the Second Vatican Council introduces what was practically a new form for the eucharistic celebration (see, e.g., the position of the priest and the placing of the tabernacle), and with its theological description and justification of these changes made it clear that the feast itself stands at the center of eucharistic devotion;[65] according to the Council, the ancient practice of reserving consecrated wafers is kept primarily for the sake of the sick, although meditation and prayer before the tabernacle are still recommended.[66]

This development makes it plain that according to the Roman Catholic view, reverent reservation does not take away from the essential trend of the sacrament, which is toward bodily reception; in fact, this is the very presupposition of reservation. In this context, devotion to the reserved sacrament is given an ancillary and indicative function, which in the actual praxis of the church's life requires an interpretation that is open to no misunderstanding.

This assignment of relative theological importance and this practical elucidation take account of the Protestant concern at its essential point, so that there is no further occasion for condemnation. Both sides are united in teaching that the adoration is given to the Lord present in the feast, not to "the visible forms of the elements of bread and wine."[67] Consequently, the reproach of adoration of the elements, and hence idolatry, does not apply to Catholic doctrine.

Once this new reflection and emphasis has been communicated to the general awareness of Catholic believers, it should surely be possible for them to understand in retrospect the difficulty that Protestant Christians still have about medieval forms of piety which are still retained (e.g., the Corpus Christi procession). On the other hand, Protestant Christians have grasped how much

Catholics are hurt by the way of handling the remaining elements which is still practiced among them in certain places—a practice by no means required by the theological premises, and one that offends Catholics, because it contravenes their devotion to the eucharistic sacrament.

The Lima declaration rightly stresses that the handling of the elements calls for particular attention and that "the best way of showing respect for the elements served in the eucharistic celebration is by their consumption, without excluding their use for communion of the sick."[68]

All practical regulations about the *communion of the sick* have to be justified in the light of the *communio* structure which, as both sides stress, is fundamental to the eucharistic celebration. The (full) celebration of the Eucharist at the sick person's bedside was explicitly recommended following the Second Vatican Council;[69] and this meets the usual Protestant concern with regard to the communion of the sick. On the other hand, it should be possible, at least in principle, for Protestant theology and spirituality to find a new approach to the church's ancient practice of reserving the eucharistic bread for reception at home, on days without a eucharistic celebration, and for distribution to those absent, especially the sick.[70] Protestants should find it possible to recognize once more the legitimacy of this early church form of house communion and the communion of the sick, the more so since it is not explicitly condemned in the relevant passages in the Confessions. For the fundamental intention of Protestant eucharistic theology, where the duration of the sacramental presence is concerned, proves to be reconcilable with the practice used in the church since early times. This has always, among other things, had the purpose of including the sick in the worshiping koinonia of the eucharistic feast, even though at a distance in space and time. The stipulation here is that the institutional character of the Lord's Supper, including the indissoluble connection between Word and Sacrament, should be taken into account in an appropriate way in the liturgical form given to the feast.

Summing up, we must therefore say that considerable *theological clarification* has meanwhile been arrived at in the question about the duration of the eucharistic presence. We share the conviction that "the eucharistic presence of the Lord Jesus Christ is directed towards believing reception, that it nevertheless is not confined only to the moment of reception, and that it does not depend on the faith of the receiver, however closely related to this it might be."[71]

Of course—as has already been said—considerable efforts will be required if this theological clarification is to bear fruit *in the praxis of the churches*, in an ecumenically appropriate way. Catholic spirituality is strongly marked by the conviction that the Lord who is really present in the form of bread is—as the center of all Christian life—always "available" in the actual area of the church for the prayers of those who believe in him. For Protestant devotion, on the other hand, adoration of the Lord in the Host outside the celebration of the Lord's Supper itself is alien. This will no doubt only become comprehensible for Protestants, if at all, if the relation to the eucharistic celebration is clearly evident—that is, if the connection between *conversio* (transformation) and *sumptio* (reception) is preserved. Protestant Christians, on the other hand, are accustomed to be conscious of the sacramental Real Presence of the Lord (only) during the celebration of the Lord's Supper. They must, however, realize that they are confronted by this question of the lasting sacramental presence in the context of their handling of the elements remaining at the end of the celebration; this must make it clearly perceptible to Catholic Christians that the Real Presence of Christ's body and blood in, or with, the offerings of the meal during the celebration of the Lord's Supper is taken seriously.

No clear solutions emerge out of this situation in the sense of practical results; but *the following questions* present themselves.

• How do *Protestant Christians* see reservation for the purpose of the communion of the sick and house communion, and its presupposition in the theology of the sacraments, since to set aside the sacrament for this purpose was common practice from antiquity—that is, in the long period of our shared history?

• Can a temporal limit be laid down for the sacramental duration of the presence, if the Word brings about a definitive transformation, and if reception as the purpose of the celebration is in tendency maintained, even if—because of external circumstances—a gap in space and time has to be bridged before believers can receive?

• Is a fundamental recognition of the Catholic practice of the communion of the sick conceivable, even if in Protestant quarters the full Lord's Supper, celebrated together with the sick person, remains the usual practice?

• On the basis of the theological understanding achieved, would it be possible for Protestant Christians to respect Catholic *forms* of eucharistic devotion, without adopting them for themselves, but also without declaring them to be divisive of the churches, or even condemning them as "idolatry"?

• Would Protestant theology be prepared to admit that in the elimination of abuses by the Reformers, forms of eucharistic devotion worth preserving were surrendered?

• Is *Catholic theology*, on the other hand, prepared to concede that there have been, and are, practices connected with the sacrament which distort rather than illuminate the intention of its institution?

• Is it so unquestionably a matter of course that forms of eucharistic devotion which developed at the height of the Middle Ages and in modern times, and which are still recommended in the Roman Catholic Church (prayer before the tabernacle, eucharistic procession, the benediction of the sacrament, perpetual prayer, etc.), are really in line with the full use of this sacrament, according to its institution?

• Did the link between the tabernacle and the "high" altar (which became usual only in the nineteenth century), together with the undue emphasis on "the presence of Jesus Christ in the tabernacle," not after all lead at an unconscious level to a spatial fixation of the eucharistic Real Presence, which— although it is contradicted by all the classic statements of Catholic theology— is still deep-seated among clergy and faithful, because of actual devotional practice?

• Must all those who cannot themselves adopt these forms, and all who avoid them, or are suspicious of them, still be anathematized?

These questions vary in importance; but they aim to make it clear that further conversation and mutual reflection are needed in this sector of liturgical practice, in which theological conviction, the devotional practice that has grown up over the years, and the actual performance of the sacrament are linked and come to a head.

3. Communion Under Both Kinds

The withholding of the cup from the laity is unanimously condemned by the Protestant Confessions.[72]

In the Augsburg Confession this problem is put at the head of the "abuses" listed, but its fundamental theological implication is dealt with directly: to distribute the bread only, counts as *consuetudo contra mandata Dei introducta* (CA 22.9: *BC* 50: "introduced contrary to the commands of God"). It is contrary to the testament of Christ, "For Christ instituted both kinds, and he did not do so only for part of the church, but for all of the church," and his ordinances (*ordinationes*) are not matters of indifference (*res indifferentes*). Consequently, this abuse is unanimously condemned and rejected as sacrilege.

The Tridentine *Canones de communione sub utraque specie* (canons on communion under both kinds) are evidently explicitly directed against those assertions in the Confessions.

They anathematize, first, the assertion "that each and every one of the faithful of Christ ought by a precept of God, or by necessity for salvation to receive both species of the most holy sacrament" (*DS* 1731; NR 592; Deferrari 114); second, the view "that the holy Catholic church has not been influenced by just causes and reasons to give communion under the form of bread only to laymen and even to clerics when not consecrating" (*DS* 1732; NR* 593: Deferrari 114); and, third, condemn the thesis that it is not "Christ whole and entire, who is the fountain and author of all graces, [who] is received under the one species of bread, because . . . he is not received according to the institution of Christ himself under both species *(sub utraque specie)*" (*DS* 1733; NR* 594; Deferrari 114; cf. *DS* 1653).

The Council of Trent is manifestly defending the existing practice but without making this absolute. For the canon itself reminds readers that the original form was different, and that the general practice of withholding the cup from the laity only grew up in the course of history for grave reasons *(gravibus et iustis causis)*.

How little theological antitheses were at work here is shown by the fact that—in accordance with the wish of German participants in the Council—communion under both kinds was permitted for decades.[73] The doctrine of concomitance, to which the Council pointed in this connection, could be accepted in substance by the Reformers too (even if it is criticized in AS III.6 [*BC* 311]) as "the specious learning of the sophists"). To this extent, the condemnation in can. 3 (*DS* 1653) does not apply to the Protestant position.

The controversy took on theological acrimony, however, at the point where the opinion was maintained, or rejected, that the curtailment of the sign also meant a diminution of grace (cf. *DS* 1729 and *DS* 1733).

Luther himself was certainly not among the supporters of the theological opinion which was termed false *(quidam falso asserunt,* "some falsely assert": *DS* 1733). This is shown by AS III.6 (*BC* 311 [altered]): "Even though it be true that as much is included under one form as under both, yet administration in one form is not the whole order and institution as it was established and commanded by Christ." The Reformers' stress in the dispute therefore clearly lies on the attempt to restore the integrity of the sign as given in the institution, out of faithfulness to its biblical origin and the tradition of the early church. The church's insistence on a custom *(consuetudo)* deviating from the institution, and one that generally prevailed only from the thirteenth century onward, was felt to be arbitrary and an act of clerical arrogance (cf. Apol. 22.9: "that the priestlings might seem holier than the laity"; cf. *BC* 237). But that those who pleaded for the restoration of the full, original form should now be disciplined and condemned, could only be interpreted as provocation: ". . . those who not only omit both forms but even go so far as autocratically to prohibit, condemn, and slander the use of both as heresy and thus set themselves against and over Christ, our Lord and God" (AS III.6: *BC* 311).

The powerful emotions that were evoked certainly did not prevent the connection between divine institution and ecclesiastical authority from being raised, but they did make it difficult for both sides to treat this fundamental theological problem with the necessary objectivity.

That the bishops in Trent should have stressed more emphatically the authority of the church with regard to the practical form given to the sacrament was the inevitable result of their position in this conflict. But it is noticeable that they too tried to find support in the New Testament and to regulate the authority of the church (*potestas ecclesiae*) and the administration of the sacraments in accordance with the time (*salva illorum substantia*, "preserving their substance"!), anchoring them in the practice of the apostles themselves (cf. *DS* 1728). In the arguments of the Council, therefore, the church's authority is not viewed as an additional—let alone a superfluous—element, parallel to Scripture and the patristic tradition; it is presented as something already implicit in, and given with, these. For even Scripture, the Council maintains, does not regulate the eucharistic celebration in every detail but concedes a certain liberty to apostolic competence in the shaping of the form given to it (cf. the reference to 1 Cor. 11:24 in *DS* 1728).

In this question also, the *dialogue situation* has *changed* considerably in the meantime. In the light of the common endeavor for a strong and convincing biblical foundation, the following *exegetical recognition* is worth mentioning first of all.

By body and blood the early eucharistic tradition certainly did not mean two different, complementary "components" of Jesus Christ. It meant the one Lord in the one, single act of his self-surrender. Irrespective of the different wording of the "interpretative words," the acts of blessing over bread and cup are not separate acts of consecration performed over different sacred objects. They are a double proclamation of one and the same event. This fact makes it clear on the one hand how much the intensity of the sign emerges from the integrity of the specific form of the feast; but on the other hand it also indicates the theological possibility that in the communion of believers—in exceptional cases or in case of need—one of the signs can stand for the whole. When the Book of Acts calls the celebration of the Eucharist "the breaking of bread," this points in the same direction.

The Catholic side has meanwhile also regained a sense of the value of the full eucharistic sign, and this has also been officially stated (as *SC* 55 already shows).

The Holy Communion becomes a clearer sign if it is received under both kinds. For in this form the sign of the eucharistic feast can be more easily recognized, and clearer expression is given to the intention that the new and eternal covenant is to be sealed in the Lord's blood, and to the relationship between the eucharistic feast and the End-time banquet in the Father's kingdom (Matt. 26:27–29).[74]

Accordingly, it is recommended that the cup be offered on many occasions, and this is increasingly practiced. The Reformers' concern has therefore been in principle taken up and affirmed.

On the Protestant side, it is clearly stated that to withdraw the cup from the laity must be seen as an abuse because to do so is a departure from Christ's institutionary acts, not because Protestants deny that Christ is wholly present under each of the two species.

Both sides are at one in their concern to restore the institutional completeness and wholeness of the sacramental sign, and they agree in their conviction that bread and wine belong to the Eucharist in its full form. Even with respect to the church's authority to regulate this question practically, a basic convergence has emerged, since on the Protestant side too it is agreed that for grave pastoral reasons it is possible to modify and adapt the practice of Communion (e.g., only wine, or only bread, in the case of the sick; unfermented wine [grape juice] in the case of those who might be endangered by alcohol).

It has to be said that considerable differences still exist at the present time with regard to the practice of Communion under both kinds. But in view of the agreement about the theological principles, these differences "no longer have a church-dividing character."[75]

4. Remaining Condemnatory Pronouncements with Regard to the Eucharist

4.1 Rites and Ceremonies

Canon 7 (*DS* 1757) desires to assert the fundamental justification of outward ceremonies, signs, and vestments in the eucharistic celebration.

Apology 24.52 (*BC* 259) also refers to this matter, laying weight on the difference between the Old and the New Testament and rightly warning against the adoption of Old Testament cultic and sacrificial notions together with the Old Testament signs and ceremonies. The general principle is that "such outward ceremonies, though they may be necessary for the upbringing of children, should be used discreetly" (*BSLK* 365.17f.). Their value is clearly not considered to be very high, but their justification is not denied in principle.

This question was already considered above (pp. 82f.) in sec. 1 of the Doctrine of the Sacraments in General (can. 13: *DS* 1613). What was said there applies here also. The emphases certainly vary, but even in the sixteenth century there was no disagreement about the ancillary character of outward ceremonies.

After the new theological reflection and the practical renewal in the liturgical sphere which came about through Vatican II, it is surely even easier today than formerly to express the *agreement in principle* which does not exclude differences of specific practice but includes them. "Ritualizations" are anthropologically indispensable, for the "embodiment" of human behavior is necessary, human nature being what it is. But since the external forms of expression can also distort what is to be expressed, these forms must continually be newly interpreted and also critically reexamined. In making practical changes, however, we do well to resist together the danger of a one-sided "didacticism." The deeper dimension of symbolic actions reaches far beyond the catechetical intention.

Canons 8 and 9[76] deal with individual questions about the specific form of the liturgy in terms that are strongly marked by the dispute. These have been quite simply "superseded" by the historical development. The active participation of all the faithful, the use of the vernacular, the audible pronunciation of the eucharistic prayer, including the words of institution, have become a matter of course in the Catholic Church. But even the Council of Trent says explicitly and repeatedly that the communion of all the faithful belongs to the celebration of the Eucharist (cf. *DS* 1747, 1638, 1648, 1649) and urgently demands regular vernacular instruction in the liturgy, especially on Sundays and feast days (*DS* 1749). The one-sidedness of the "exclusive" statements in cans. 8 and 9 was therefore, even at that time, comprehensible only as resistance against an exaggerated formulation or an extreme stress on points of view that were in themselves correct (and that were elsewhere affirmed by the Council itself).

A fundamental theological controversy was bound up with the rejection by the one side and the defense by the other of the custom of mixing water with the eucharistic wine (cf. can. 9: *DS* 1759; cap. 7: *DS* 1748).

Against the background of the varying interpretations of this ancient rite of the church's tradition, the parties to the discussion were concerned about the fundamental questions of accordance with Scripture, and the church's authority in questions of worship, as well as the interpretation of the sacrament as a "pure" and undeserved gift of God.[77] To the extent to which agreement has been reached about these fundamental questions, the controversy about this special eucharistic rite has lost its explosive quality and importance.

4.2 The Forgiveness of Sins as Fruit of the Eucharist

Canon 5 of the Decree on the Eucharist (*DS* 1655) condemns the view that the special fruit of the Eucharist is the remission of sins. But it is precisely this which both Luther's writings on the Lord's Supper and the Apology stress: "Surely the Lord's Supper was instituted for the sake of forgiving guilt."[78] The area of this problem and controversy was already pegged out in the text about the Doctrine of the Sacraments in General, I 1.3.

It ought to be possible to establish clarity about the fact that the way the Reformers think and talk about the forgiveness of sins is determined by the comprehensive aspect of the fellowship with God that has once more been bestowed (cf. SmC. *BC* 352, "For where there is forgiveness of sins, there are also life and salvation"). Since the forgiveness of sins means the raising up, through the power of God's love, of the sinner who has been turned in upon himself, forgiveness cannot be supplemented or intensified. We must, however, ask whether it would not be less misleading to give another name to just this all-embracing aspect of the divine salvation bestowed on the sinner: if it should not be called (with equally clear New Testament justification!) the dawn of the rule of God (Mark 1:15, and frequently), the love of God (Romans 5), koinonia (1 Cor. 10:16f.)—especially since this would be a way of averting the danger of separating the individual aspect from the social one. Incidentally, it should not remain unnoticed in this connection that in the different biblical versions of the *verba testamenti* (the words of Christ's testament), it is *only* Matt. 26:28 that explicitly mentions the forgiveness of sins. It was common conviction even in the sixteenth century (cf. *DS* 1638) that the forgiveness of sins was an aspect that ought certainly to be mentioned in describing the Eucharist. On the other hand, the practice of examination and confession which was supported by the Reformers ("The sacrament [should not be administered] except to those who have previously been examined and absolved," CA 25.2: *BC* 61) makes it explicitly clear that there too the forgiveness of sins was understood and given concrete form in different ways (cf. 1 Cor. 11:27f.). And in this light it also becomes evident that the above-mentioned comprehensive interpretation of *remissio pec-*

catorum (the remission of sins) as the fruit of the Eucharist was simply not unequivocally clear in the controversial discussion.

Without at this point attempting a fundamental theological determination of how faith and love stand to one another (although the definition of this relationship certainly also underlies this problem; cf. pp. 50f. above), we may nonetheless *sum up* by saying:

Where a narrow interpretation of the forgiveness of sins was involved (or still is), can. 5 (*DS* 1655)—which itself starts from an incomplete way of speaking—still applies. But where "the forgiveness of sins" is seen as being one with the new fellowship (*communio*) with God conferred through grace, the canon is null and void.

4.3 Masses for the Dead

The Formula of Concord condemns as an abuse and an abomination "the sacrifice of the Mass for the living and for the dead."[79] Precisely this formulation (*"missae sacrificium . . . pro vivis et defunctis . . . offerri debere"*) is defended by the Council of Trent, which defines it more closely by saying that those who are meant are "the dead in Christ who are not yet fully purged," appealing to "apostolic tradition" (*DS* 1743; NR* 599). This reciprocal condemnation touches an *elemental difference* in the devotional practice of the different churches. The Reformers turned against abuses of the mass which also resulted from particular ideas about purgatory.

Today, in the light of the changed dialogue situation on both sides, it is possible to come to an agreement over the eschatological utterances about judgment and purification. This being so, what is of essential importance for working through the difference we are considering here is what has been worked out together about our understanding of the sacrificial character of the Eucharist: the Eucharist does not add any "merits" or expiatory power to the sacrifice made once and for all on the cross. It merely desires to make this sacrifice present, and apply it, in its once-for-all salvific function. Any interpretation of the (certainly highly misleading) formulations of the Council of Trent which fails to accord with this common principle must therefore be excluded; or, if and insofar as it is present at all, must be corrected. If "the mass for the dead" was, or is, ever understood as an independent or complementary expiation for the dead, the verdict of the Confessions is justified. It should be noted here that Trent already corrected the view, widespread in popular piety, that particular forms of the mass, and "series of masses," could not fail in their effect for the redemption of "poor souls" in purgatory.[80]

Yet the question remains as to how the expiatory power of Jesus Christ's sacrifice on the cross, which was once and for all, can be evoked in sacramental remembrance *(memoria)* without contracting its universal dimension. How can the *fellowship (koinonia) with the dead* to which we have already referred, find appropriate expression in the feast commemorating the body given for us (cf. here pp. 87f. above)? Modern anthropology recognizes that the individual, the way he personally lives, and the conduct for which he is personally responsible are also essentially interwoven and bound up with the community. They are part of the warp and weft of the individual's relationship with other people, who are in this way part of his existence. This therefore brings to a point the fundamental question: How can the perfecting of such a humanity, in its corporeality, historicity, and sociality—a perfecting for which we hope from God's power and faithfulness—be stated? How, that is, can it be expressed without falsifying the Christian hope, through forward inquisitiveness, into unsubstantiated embroidered description? *Intercessory remembrance* is probably the best way of "recollecting" the link beyond death that joins the living and the dead in the eschatological community of salvation instituted by God in Jesus' destiny; for the possibility of intercession for the dead is an idea familiar to a number of Christian traditions.[81] The communion of believers, the church, is not broken by death. In death as in life, the Christian is dependent on the community. In prayer, the congregation intercedes before God for the dead, praying that their sins be forgiven, that they may be accepted by God and receive eternal life.[82] Lutherans too view this prayer of intercession for the dead as legitimate and meaningful. This is shown by "official" liturgical practice (cf. the burial service and the announcement of a death, with a prayer for the one who has died). There is no theological dispute about the point that such intercession for the dead finds a special place in connection with the Lord who is present at his Supper and who intercedes for us with the Father.

If there is unity about the fact that God's gracious dealings with us find no final limits in death, it should also be possible to understand the real concern of *the Council of Trent's statements about purgatory*. Figurative biblical language about the fire of the divine judgment which annihilates, cleanses, and purifies[83] has certainly degenerated in the course of history into fantastic notions and inappropriate forms of piety. In response to the necessary protest by the Reformers, Trent itself attempted to do away with "curiosity or superstition," practices that "savor of filthy lucre" or that are "stumbling blocks to the faithful" (*DS* 1820; NR 908) in this sector, although without surrendering the biblical idea of "purification." Trent makes no binding statements here about the "how" of a "perfecting suffering" of this kind, in which the person who comes before God's face in all his sinful resistance experiences God himself as the painful and releasing purification for the final community of love. This believing hope for a final purification for love is at the same time a decisive appeal for conversion and discipleship of Jesus now, in our present life. Because guilt must always be understood at the same time as the inward abyss of death, intercession for the dead—the prayer that their guilt may be forgiven—can also belong within this context, as living solidarity with our dead, as a joining in Christ's own intercession that God may prepare them for the fullness of his life.

5. A Summing Up

The result of our investigation of the condemnations touching on "the sacrifice of the Mass/the Eucharist/the Lord's Supper" may be summed up as follows:

1. Important controversies of the past can from today's standpoint count as having been *theologically surmounted, at least to a point* where the reasons for mutual condemnation no longer apply.

a. This is true, first, of *the controversy about "the sacrifice of the mass"* in the narrower sense. It has been found possible to state in common our believing conviction about the uniqueness and full sufficiency of Jesus Christ's sacrifice on the cross, as well as the bearing and scope of the *anamnesis* in the eucharistic celebration of the church.

This jointly worked out interpretation of sacrifice is presented in the contributions, and above all in the Closing Report of the volume published by our working party under the title *Das Opfer Jesus Christi und seine Gegenwart in der Kirche* ("The Sacrifice of Jesus Christ and His Presence in the Church"). This common interpretation is briefly repeated here under 1.1—1.4, in the context of the condemnations. On its basis, the following may be said. The sharp criticism of the Smalcald Articles and the Heidelberg Catechism, on the one hand, and the condemnatory rejections of Protestant positions by the Council of Trent, on the other, were both in part unjustified, even in the sixteenth century; at all events they do not apply to our partner in the dialogue today. The controversy about "the sacrifice of the mass" and its church-dividing character has therefore been superseded. The suspicion earlier was that to understand the Eucharist as sacrifice means seeing it as a "work." Since this suspicion has proved to be unfounded, this may also be said to be true of "masses for the dead," whether or not there is detailed agreement about the question of how to articulate more precisely the eucharistic koinonia with the dead.

b. The controversies of the past about *faith in the Real Presence* of Jesus Christ in the Lord's Supper have also been theologically superseded, because, and insofar as, there can be joint assent to the following principles.

• Today's understanding of faith is not bound to express itself in binding terms exclusively in the same intellectual terms and the same language as the sixteenth century. As history shows, it was never enough simply to compare mere wording, in the language of faith. For it is only when *there is awareness of the historical context* that the real statement of faith made in the controversial positions can be elucidated, compared, and, it may be, reconciled. And to the extent to which this historicity of the condemnations is taken seriously, and in the degree to which we above all discern the common endeavor to pass on the apostolic heritage already given to us as norm in Holy Scripture, the positions that were once in confrontation can either come closer to one another in substance or can be understood as expressing a complementary concern.

• Historical investigation shows that in the doctrines of transubstantiation and ubiquity, and as regards the theory about the mediation of the Spirit, *a common basic concern* was pursued from three different theoretical approaches— this concern being to express the mystery of the Real Presence of Jesus Christ in the Eucharist. These different theories were deliberately defined over against one another, and under the conditions of the sixteenth century they were apparently irreconcilable. But they lose their antithetical (and mutually exclusive) character inasmuch as it has to be admitted that each of them has its obvious strengths and weaknesses, and that none of them can claim exclusive validity of such a kind that in each given case the other form of doctrine would have to be judged heretical.

• Even without directly adopting the conceptual terminology of one of the mutually conflicting sixteenth-century doctrinal systems, it is possible to express *all the essential elements of faith* in the eucharistic presence of Jesus Christ, as has already been done in a number of consensus and convergence texts:

> The exalted Lord is present in the Lord's Supper
> in the body and blood he gave
> with his divinity and his humanity
> through the word of promise
> in the gifts of bread and wine
> in the power of the Holy Spirit
> for reception through the congregation.

The unique "sacramental" nature of the Real Presence is jointly guarded by both partners against, on the one hand, the misunderstanding that "the body of the Lord" is present in a natural or spatially limited sense and, on the other hand, against a remembrance and a symbolism founded solely on the thinking of the believer.

In view of our common conviction in faith about the true and real presence of the Lord in the Eucharist, the remaining different emphases in the eucharistic theology and spirituality (differences stamped by denominational traditions) need no longer be termed divisive of the churches. The condemnations which are directed at the theology of the Real Presence no longer apply to today's partner and have become null and void.

c. The dispute about *the forgiveness of sins as fruit of the Eucharist* may also count as having been clarified and theologically settled: the "incomplete" language of the Council of Trent applied, and applies, only to a narrow interpretation of the forgiveness of sins. It does not apply to its more comprehensive aspect: the new fellowship with God, bestowed once more through grace; and it was this which was generally meant by the Reformers.

d. The matters of dispute which were concerned rather with *the outward forms* given to the celebration of the mass in word and sign may even more be regarded as superseded. Differences still remain, even after the endeavors of both sides toward liturgical reform; but these differences no longer mean division with regard to the matter itself.

2. The condemnations relating to the considerable *differences about the practice of the eucharistic celebration* and eucharistic devotion require a special note. These differences certainly derived from theological premises, but they continue to exist at the present day.

a. The dispute about *communio sub utraque* (communion under both kinds) is the easiest of all to sum up here. There has meanwhile come to be full and explicit fundamental agreement that the offering of the cup belongs to the wholeness and intensity of the sign of the meal as God intended it to be, and that the restriction (which is in itself theologically conceivable) should be confined to a form of the feast adapted for emergencies or cases of special need.

In Catholic practice this principle has certainly as yet by no means generally come to prevail; but in view of the unity about the theological principle, it no longer has a church-dividing character. A development is taking place here similar to that on the Protestant side, where there is a trend toward reintroducing the celebration of the Lord's Supper every Sunday.

b. Important approaches to one another have also emerged in the controversy about the enduring nature of the sacrament (a controversy pursued under the heading "*usus*").[84] Both sides agree that the eucharistic sacrament points toward the *communio* of the congregation—

that is, toward its believing reception. At the same time, the sacrament is not restricted to this element, because *usus* means the whole eucharistic act, not merely the instant of reception *(sumptio)*.

c. The theological premises or implications of the handling of the eucharistic offerings following the celebration (where practice still varies very greatly) are less clear as a whole. At this point the weight of century-old custom seems to a great extent to have taken the place of explicit reflection and reasoning.

Here a number of questions have still not as yet been clearly answered on either side.

III. CONFIRMATION

1. The Augsburg Confession never mentions a separate sacrament of confirmation (cf. pp. 123f. below on the anointing of the sick). The Apology defends this omission by pointing out that although confirmation is certainly a traditional rite, the church has never viewed it as being necessary for salvation, since it lacks God's appointment and commandment. It is therefore useful to distinguish this rite from the sacraments, which have a direct divine mandate and carry an explicit promise of grace.[85] Luther himself, without wishing to repudiate the church's practice of the laying on of hands in blessing, already disputed the sacramental character of confirmation in 1520, in *The Babylonian Captivity of the Church* (cf. WA 6, 549f.). Calvin (cf. *Inst.* IV, 19, 4ff.) and the Reformed tradition (cf., e.g., the *Confessio Helvetica Posterior,* chap. 19) come to the same conclusion, even if the individual emphases are different—as they also are in the rejection of the sacramental character of extreme unction. Moreover, the Reformers criticize especially the claim that only a bishop may confirm (a claim which is put down to clerical arrogance and presumption) as well as the assertion that the chrism has a particular spiritual power. In addition, the Reformers complain of the complete lack of instruction about the real meaning of the rite. If the custom of confirmation is to be permitted as a "rite of the church" or "a sacramental ceremony," then it is only to be so coupled with a decisive rejection of any idea that confirmation complements baptism, in the sense of completing its gift of grace, or supplementing its bestowal of the Spirit. Any assertion that confirmation is necessary for salvation was also felt to be a devaluation and disparagement of baptism. In liturgical history the rite of confirmation belongs to the whole "ceremonial complex" of baptism; but this does not seem to have been known at that time.

In spite of the Reformers' reservations about the medieval theory and practice of confirmation, basic elements of a Protestant confirmation ceremony already developed in the sixteenth century and in the first half of the seventeenth, even though it was not until the era of Pietism and the Enlightenment that confirmation became general practice, and even though a unified theology of confirmation was not developed. The element common to the various different forms was that confirmation was interpreted as part of the church's order; it was not seen as a sacrament. A determinative element in this development was, above all, the renewal of the catechumenate, as well as the practice of a doctrinal examination, in which the children or young people were supposed to give an account of their faith before the church (cf. Calvin, *Inst.* IV, 19, 13). A doctrinal examination of this kind was often made the condition for admission to the Lord's Supper. In addition, in some places the laying on of hands was also given new importance, as an act of blessing communicating the gift of the Spirit, and as a confirmatory act of ecclesial incorporation. This is shown by Bucer's influential program for confirmation, for example. The German term *Einsegnung*—literally, "being blessed *into*"—should be seen in this context. Today's situation is marked by a wide variety of confirmation theory and practice.

2. The Council of Trent first turned its attention to the Reformers' attacks on confirmation in the General Congregation of 17 Jan., 1547, in which lists of the relevant errors were read (cf. *CT* V, 835–38). In the sources cited for these, reference is made to Luther's *De captivitate Babylonica*, to the Apology of the Augsburg Confession, to Melanchthon's *Loci communes,* and to the so-called *Kölner Reformation,* the reform document of the Archbishop of Cologne, Hermann von Wied, which was largely drawn up by Bucer. On 26 Feb., 1547, thirty canons on the sacraments in general, baptism, and confirmation were then distributed to the prelates (cf. *CT* V, 984–85). These canons were debated in two General Congregations only, on the morning and afternoon of 1 March, 1547.

The doctrinal utterances of the Council on confirmation (3 March, 1547) are finally contained in three canons (*DS* 1628–30; NR 555–57). *The first canon* states: "If anyone shall say that the confirmation of those baptized is an empty ceremony and not rather a true and proper sacrament, or that in former times it was nothing more than a kind of catechism, by which those approaching adolescence gave an account of their faith before the Church: let him be anathema."[86] *The second canon* condemns the assertion that it is "an outrage to the Holy Spirit . . . [to ascribe] any power to the sacred chrism of confirmation." *The third canon* anathematizes those who say that "the ordinary minister of holy confirmation is not the bishop alone, but any simple priest."

3. Irrespective of the strong stress in the Protestant tradition on catechizing, or on the doctrinal examination for the purpose of admission to the Lord's Supper, the ecumenical understanding of confirmation has to start from the close ties between confirmation and baptism, as the foundation for the whole of Christian life. From the very beginning, and for many centuries, anointing with chrism (consecrated oil), signing with the cross, and (in the Roman as well as in the Coptic and Ethiopian rites) the laying on of hands were rites genuinely belonging to the baptismal liturgy. They should be judged, not as secondary ingredients added to an original, authentic Christian rite of baptism (baptism with water), but as early—probably already New Testament—interpretative ritual acts which express a fundamental difference between the baptism into Christ, which is once and for all, and the many lustrations and immersions of Old Testament and Jewish tradition. According to Western tradition, these acts include the laying on of hands, Acts 8:14–20; for the chrismation or anointing, cf. 1 John 2:20, 27; for the signation, 2 Cor. 1:21f.; Eph. 1:13). The baptism into Christ bestows the Holy Spirit as pledge and seal of the consummation. Even if the ritual complex of baptism—water, and the rite of the Spirit—has two distinct emphases, yet the whole is seen as the one baptism and is taught as such; and this is the case still in the Eastern churches.[87]

We therefore have to start from the presupposition that the different aspects of the Christian rite of initiation reflect an inward theological unity. Historically, this is shown by the fact that the act which later took on independence as confirmation was originally administered at the same time as baptism; and to some extent this practice continued right down to the late Middle Ages. It is anyway still the general rule in the case of adult baptism.[88]

Roman Catholic confirmation theology today also emphatically stresses the close connection between confirmation and baptism. The Second Vatican Council demands the restoration of a catechumenate consisting of distinct steps marked by liturgical rites, leading up to the final celebration of the sacraments of initiation;[89] the mission of the Christian (the lay apostolate) is traced back to baptism and confirmation.[90] Today's practice of adult baptism is in accordance with this.[91] It is also Roman Catholic opinion that confirmation must endorse baptism and succeed it as a second sacrament of the initiation which finds its consummation in participation in the Eucharist for the first time.[92] As Christian initiation and incorporation into the church, baptism and confirmation belong closely together and are similar in their effect. Confirmation is designed to consolidate and develop the inclusion in the whole salvific structure, an inclusion initiated through baptism. "Incorporated into the Church by Baptism, the faithful are appointed by their baptismal character to Christian religious worship; reborn as sons of God, they must profess before men the faith they have received from God through the Church. By the sacrament of Confirmation they are more perfectly bound to the Church and are endowed with the special strength of Holy Spirit. Hence they are, as true witnesses of Christ, more strictly obliged to spread the faith by word and deed" (*LG* 11; cf. *AG* 11, 36).[93]

The Protestant churches will have to respect the clear determination of Roman Catholic theology to avoid any division in principle between baptism and confirmation, even though the difference between the two is emphasized. The distinction between the rite establishing the state of faith and the rite that strengthens that state, through obvious, not least in the light of a Christian's "biography," should not lead to an illegitimate divorce between these two rites; nor should it in any way detract from the character of baptismal grace, which establishes and embraces the whole of Christian life.

On the other hand, the Roman Catholic Church will have to recognize that the Protestant stress on the unity of the Christian initiatory event, which is expressed in the retroactive tie binding catechesis and confirmation to baptism, is not a denial of the inner differentiation; and that stress on the completeness of baptism is not intended to call into question its dynamic character, which reaches out to the whole of life. With regard to the link between baptism and repentance, Luther particularly stressed the need for baptism to be "appropriated" by the person baptized in day-to-day life.[94]

In view of the inner cohesion of baptism and the rite of confirmation, it would seem the obvious course to give this aspect an appropriate application. Just as God's gift has to be followed by commitment on the part of the human being, so the event of baptism ought to be the beginning of a process of growth in faith, "to mature manhood, to the measure of the stature of the fulness of Christ" (Eph. 4:13). Accordingly, baptism "is related not only to momentary experience, but to lifelong growth into Christ. Those baptized are called upon to reflect the glory of the Lord as they are transformed by the power of the Holy Spirit, into his likeness, with ever increasing splendor (II Cor. 3:18)"

(Lima, Baptism 9: cf. 8ff. as a whole). Since according to the Protestant view the fullness of baptismal grace is received only through faith, from which the fruits of love proceed, the churches of the Reformation consider it possible to separate baptism and confirmation into two acts, divided by a greater or lesser gap in time. This is not least a result of the church's custom of baptizing children or infants, and is of special importance as showing the close connection between baptism and personal faith, which is continually and strongly emphasized (cf. Lima, Baptism 1 ff.; esp. also 14 ff.). On the other hand, it is worth noting that in recent years orders for initiation have been authorized by some Protestant churches in which baptism with water is followed by the laying on of hands, accompanied if desired by anointing with consecrated oil (confirmation); and these are orders not only for adults but also for infants and children, the orders for adults including the receiving of the Eucharist.[95]

4. In the framework of the present state of the discussion as we have described it, it is possible to arrive at an agreed judgment about the disputes of the Reformation period and also at a factually appropriate harmonization with regard to the theory and practice of the church at the present day.

The sixteenth-century controversies had as their precondition the separation of confirmation into an independent sacramental rite, a separation that came about in the West during the Middle Ages. With the firm establishment of the seven sacraments, confirmation being the second of these, the process leading to independent status reached completion. However, medieval confirmation theology (as expressed in the *Decretum Gratiani* and in the *Sentences* of Peter Lombard) did not satisfactorily succeed in expressing the particular character of confirmation without diminishing the importance of baptism. The Reformers, in contrast, stressed the full sufficiency of baptism and rejected the assumption that it needs any addition. An act of blessing following baptism can therefore, in the Protestant view, do no more than endorse the reception of the gifts which God's gracious act has conferred in that sacrament itself—endorsement meaning not an act of completion but the concentrated actualization of what has already taken place in the Christian once and for all in baptism. Here—in accordance with the link between baptism and faith—weight is laid on an act of confession on the part of the Christian who has now "come of age." At the same time, the main subject in a Protestant confirmation must not be seen as the confirmation candidate, with his or her act of decision. The subject is the triune God, whose gracious will is proclaimed to those who are to be confirmed by the person appointed to the preaching office, with the accompaniment of the congregation's intercession. This proclamation takes the form of a confirmation of the promise given in baptism; and it may be, and often is, accompanied by symbolic acts (such as the laying on of hands and the signing with the cross).

The view taken of the catechumenate—which according to the Protestant view necessarily belongs to confirmation as an ordered whole— has to correspond to this: the confession of faith of the confirmation candidate, in the structure of the catechumenate, can be nothing other than the response of faith to the divine promise that has already been uttered. In this sense the instruction itself must be presented as one element in that event of grace which finds expression and representation in the act of blessing. The still frequent practice of making admission to the Lord's Supper dependent on a doctrinal examination before confirmation, or in conjunction with it, should be reexamined in the light of this insight and, at the least, should not run counter to it (cf. Lima, Baptism 14, Commentary b).

Whether this view of confirmation falls under the condemnations pronounced in the first Tridentine canon on the subject (*DS* 1628) seems more than doubtful, at least if we may assume that the dispute about the sacramental nature of confirmation can be settled in the context of the general doctrine of the sacraments (cf. pp. 72ff., 80f. above). On the other side, Protestant theology no longer maintains that confirmation is "an empty ceremony" (*otiosa caeremonia*) or that it "is an outrage to the Holy Spirit" to ascribe any power to the chrism used at confirmation, provided only that the sign is framed in words and is directed toward faith—which *SC* 59 explicitly requires of all sacraments (cf. *CIC* 1983, can. 840), and which the Praen. 3, 4, 11, and 13 of the *Ordo Confirmationis* require for confirmation (cf. *CIC* 1983, can. 889 §2; can. 890; 1917, can. 786), which is administered either during a celebration of the mass or during a special service without the celebration of the Eucharist (cf. *CIC* 1983, can. 881). Consequently, the rejections in the Tridentine cans. 1 and 2 no longer apply to today's Protestant view.

5. The problem implicit in can. 3 can be adequately discussed only in connection with the subject of the ministry or, to be more exact, in the light of the different definitions in Roman Catholic and Protestant theology of the relationship between priest and bishop. It is worth noting that according to Vatican II the bishop is called "the original

minister of Confirmation" (*originarius minister*, not *ordinarius*), but not its sole dispenser (cf. *LG* 26 [3]). Its administration by priests on the basis of general law, or with the special permission of the apostolic see (*CIC* 1917, can. 782), has meanwhile been considerably extended.[96]

Whatever opinions may be about those aspects of confirmation which touch on the theology of the ministry (cf. pp. 154–57 below), there is agreement among the churches that confirmation represents an act on the part of the church signifying that the person confirmed is taken into Christ's service within the living context of the church. In confirmation, the church is officially present, through the act of its officeholder, in the framework of the worship of the whole congregation—indeed, as a rule it is already present in the instruction preceding confirmation. In Roman Catholic and Protestant theology, therefore, confirmation, like the preaching of the Word, baptism, and the Lord's Supper, has a clearly ecclesial character. According to Catholic doctrine, confirmation binds believers more closely to the church and furnishes them with a special power of the Holy Spirit, so that they are even more strictly obliged to spread and defend the faith, both in word and deed, as true witnesses of Christ (cf. *LG* 11 [1]). If we heed the differentiated unity of baptism and confirmation, this view stands in no contradiction that could be termed church-dividing to the Protestant view; for according to this, confirmation is an act of the church, performed on those who have already received full membership of the church of Jesus Christ through baptism, and who in the catechumenate have been guided toward the full implementation of that membership.

IV. THE ANOINTING OF THE SICK

1. A separate sacrament for the anointing of the sick is nowhere mentioned in the Augsburg Confession. In the Apology of the Confession, Melanchthon explains this omission in the same words with which he explains the lack of a sacrament of confirmation: both are "rites received from the Fathers which even the church never required as necessary for salvation since they do not have the command of God. Hence it is useful to distinguish these from the earlier ones which have an express command from God and a clear promise of grace."[97]

Luther vehemently denied the sacramental character of extreme unction (*extrema unctio*) in his *De captivitate Babylonica ecclesiae praeludium* of 1520 (cf. WA 6, 567 ff.)—thus departing from the recommendation in his 1519 sermon on the preparation for death (WA 2, 685–97, esp. secs. 4 and 15). He criticizes two things: first, that the custom of anointing the sick is called a sacrament; and second, that this custom has been turned into a "last" anointing, which may not be given to anyone unless he is at the point of death (567, 34ff.). As far as the sacramental character of the anointing of the sick is concerned, Luther holds that it is no doubt possible to read into James 5:14f. the two constitutive elements of a sacrament: promise (the forgiveness of sins) and sign (oil). But no apostle has the right to institute a sacrament on his own authority, that is, to issue a divine promise in association with a sign; for this only Christ may do[98]—quite apart from the fact, says Luther, that the Epistle of James was not written by the apostle James and that it is not worthy of an apostolic spirit. Moreover, if proper attention is paid to the content of James 5:14f., it emerges, according to Luther, that what the passage is talking about is by no means a final anointing, reserved for the dying. What is recommended here is a general anointing of the sick, with prayer, the purpose being their recovery. Not only does the practice of extreme unction fail in this purpose, the purpose is positively distorted (cf. 569, 13ff.); and that provides further proof that this cannot be a sacrament, since a sacrament effects what it signifies.

It follows for Luther that the rite of the anointing of the sick, as it is correspondingly described in Mark 6:13, and in analogy to other miraculous signs in the early church (Mark 16:17f.), no longer applies at the present day. He does, however, leave open the possibility of continuing the custom in particular cases, although he stresses not so much the anointing itself as the prayer to be pronounced over the sick person by the elders (*a senioribus, gravioribus et sanctis viris*, by elder, dignified, and holy men), about whose promised efficacy for those who believe, Luther incidentally allows there to be no doubt. He then concludes: "I therefore do not condemn this our sacrament of extreme unction; but that it be that which is described by the apostle James, that I do most obstinately deny, since that neither its form, its use, its efficacy nor its purpose agreeth with our (sacrament)."[99]

Calvin (cf. *Inst.* IV, c. 19 n 18–21) and the Reformed tradition (cf., e.g., Confessio Helvetica Posterior, chap. 19) argue similarly, substantially speaking, even if the emphases are occasionally different. Thus it is stressed that even the anointing with oil which was customary in the ancient church (such as is described in James 5:14f., following Mark 6:13) was not intended to be an *instrument* of healing but merely a *symbol* of that healing ("non . . . curationis organum, sed symbolum" [19, 18]). Through the liberty of the Lord and the apostles in their choice of outward signs (cf. John 9:6; Matt. 9:29; Luke 18:42; Acts 3:6;

5:16; 19:12), this fact is confirmed in connection with miracles of healing. Accordingly, the oil must in no circumstances be equated with the gift of the Holy Spirit, with which it is usually associated. But as far as the gracious gift of healing itself is concerned, according to Calvin this has ceased to operate in the church. "Therefore, even if we grant to the full that anointing was a sacrament of those powers which were then administered by the hands of the apostles, it now has nothing to do with us, to whom the administering of such powers has not been committed."[100] It is true that at all times the Lord supports those who are his, healing their weaknesses as often as it is required, now no less than in times of old; but he does not permit those manifest efficacies ("manifestas . . . virtutes") to appear in the same way; nor does he any longer dispense miracles through the hands of the apostles (19, 19).

From this, Calvin concludes that anointing cannot be a sacrament, "for neither is it a ceremony instituted by God, nor has it any promise. Indeed, when we require these two things in a sacrament—that it be a ceremony instituted by God, and that it have God's promise—at the same time we demand that that ceremony be delivered to us, and the promise apply to us."[101]

Incidentally, Calvin points out, James 5:14 is not talking about an *extrema unctio*, the anointing of half-dead corpses (*semimortua cadavera*). He is talking about an anointing of all those who are sick, an anointing which is to be carried out by the elders of the church (*a senioribus ecclesiae*) and is not reserved for the priest. Nor can the requirement that the anointing oil be consecrated by the bishop find any justification in James 5:14. And indeed in this passage the prayer of believers is considered to be the really efficacious means of healing, not the oil (19, 20).

2. Twelve articles about the anointing of the sick, consecration, and marriage were put forward in Bologna on 26 April, 1547 (cf. *CT* VI/1, 96–99), and of these, two deal with extreme unction. In the sources given, reference is made to Luther's *De captivitate Babylonica* and the *"Testament"* (= *Vom Abendmahl Christi. Bekenntnis*), to Melanchthon's *Loci communes* and the Apology of the Augsburg Confession, to Calvin's *Institutio*, and to Bucer (i.e., *Die Kölner Reformation*). The canons on supreme unction which were formulated in July and August 1547 no longer came before the plenary session in Bologna and were not promulgated. "Apparently they influenced particular formulations in the four canons passed during the second period of the Council (*Sessio* XIV), but they were not simply taken over" (Jedin III, 75).

On 15 October, 1551, four articles about the sacrament of extreme unction were presented (cf. *CT* VII/1, 239–40). The sources were the same as those cited in 1547. On 15 November, 1551, the four canons on extreme unction were passed (cf. *DS* 1716–19; NR 700–703). The first canon defends its sacramental character: "If anyone says that extreme unction is not truly and properly a sacrament instituted by our Lord Jesus Christ (cf. Mark 6:13) and promulgated by blessed James the apostle (James 5:14), but is only a rite accepted by the Fathers, or a human fiction: let him be anathema" (cf. *DS* 1695, 1699). The second canon has to do with the effect: "If anyone says that the sacred anointing of the sick does not confer grace nor remit sins, nor alleviate the sick, but that it has already ceased, as if it had at one time only been a [merely bodily] healing grace: let him be anathema" (cf. *DS* 1699, 1696). The third canon has to do with the practice of the dispensation: "If anyone says that the rite of extreme unction and its practice *(ritus et usus)*, which the holy Roman church observes, is opposed to the statement of the blessed Apostle James, and that it is therefore to be changed, and can be contemned without sin by Christians: let him be anathema" (cf. *DS* 1699). The fourth canon, finally defines the administrator of extreme unction: "If anyone says that the priests of the Church *(presbyteri Ecclesiae)*, whom blessed James exhorts to be brought to anoint the sick, are not the priests ordained by a bishop, but the elders by age in each community, and that for this reason a priest alone is not the proper minister of extreme unction: let him be anathema" (cf. *DS* 1697).

The Doctrine (*DS* 1694–1700; NR 696–99) teaches that Christ himself instituted extreme unction, as is indicated in Mark 6:13, and that it is recommended and proclaimed to the faithful by James, the Lord's brother (James 5:14f.). The matter of the sacrament is the oil consecrated by the bishop; its form is the words: "By this anointing . . ." (cap. 1). Through this the grace of the Holy Spirit takes effect, whose anointing gives the forgiveness of sins, strengthens the soul of the sick person, and sometimes helps him to regain bodily health (cap. 2). The bishop and the priest are named as the dispensers of the sacrament. The sacrament is to be administered to the sick, "but especially to those who are so dangerously ill that they seem to be facing the end of life, for which reason it is also called the sacrament of the dying. But if the sick should recover after the reception of this sacrament of extreme unction, they can with the aid of this sacrament be strengthened again, when they fall into another similar crisis of life."[102]

3. The disputes carried on about extreme unction in the sixteenth century appear to us today in a new light. For the history of the anointing of the sick has meanwhile been made the subject of more precise research. In addition, there is a new recognition of the significance of charismata, and among them the gift of healing. But above all, the theology and the practice of anointing the sick were renewed by the Second Vatican Council and by Paul VI (*Ordo unctionis infirmorum eorumque pastoralis curae*, 1972). The result was renewed reflection about the biblical and early Christian view of the anointing of the sick.

In the Constitution on the Liturgy we accordingly read the following: " 'Extreme Unction,' which may also and more fittingly be called 'Anointing of the Sick,' is not a sacrament for those only who are at the point of death. Hence, as soon as anyone of the faithful begins to be in danger of death from sickness or old age, the fitting time for him to receive this sacrament has certainly already arrived."[103]

Article 75 then says about the new order of the actual dispensation: "The number of the anointings is to be adapted to the occasion, and the prayers which belong to the rite of Anointing are to be revised so as to correspond to the varying conditions of the sick who receive the sacrament."[104]

The new order which Vatican II wished for was published and came into force in 1974.[105] Prefaced to the ritual is Paul VI's Apostolic Constitution of 1972. Where the *forma sacramenti* is concerned, the following regulations are to apply in the Latin rite: "The sacrament of anointing of the sick is administered to those who are dangerously ill. They are to be anointed on the forehead and hands with blessed olive oil or, as circumstances suggest, with another oil extracted from plants, the following words being spoken: 'Per istam sanctam unctionem et suam piissimam misericordiam adiuvet te Dominus gratia Spiritus Sancti ut a peccatis liberatum te salvet atque propitius allevet' " ("Through this holy unction may the Lord in his rich mercy help thee, may he support thee in the power of the Holy Spirit: The Lord who saves thee from sins save thee, may he in his grace raise thee up").

Three leading themes may be detected in general in the new order initiated by Vatican II. (1) The communal and ceremonial character is stressed. Neither the sick person nor the priest is seen merely and exclusively as an individual. Both act as members and servants of the church. (2) The symbolic action in the anointing of the sick takes its bearings in a new way from the biblical pattern. "The prayer of faith" moves into the center of attention, parallel to the laying on of hands and the anointing. The purpose is that the sick person should "stand the test" of his illness, and that the person who is seriously hindered and incapacitated in his opportunities for living, and in his self-realization, and who knows what is taking place, should receive help and support in his unhappy situation, so that he can make his own personal contribution to it in an appropriate way.

4. Through this reorientation, Roman Catholic doctrine and praxis have taken account of an essential point of Protestant criticism. There is therefore no need for the Protestant churches to maintain that the way of dispensing extreme unction practiced by the church of Rome today is in contradiction to the exhortation of the holy apostle James and must therefore be changed. But if this assertion is no longer maintained, then can. 3 no longer applies today either, especially since all that this canon maintains is that Roman practice does not contradict James 5:14f.; the canon does not assert that contemporary practice is identical with what is put forward in the Epistle of James. In a similar way, the chapter in the Doctrine (cf. *DS* 1699) says that in its practice of extreme unction the church observes the injunctions of James in substance. This shows that the Council did not wish to utter a dogmatic definition. Its aim was to safeguard the practice of the time, by way of an anathema.

After the Second Vatican Council, the church was not content with the apologetic assertion of the Council of Trent. It sought greater agreement with the relevant text in James, above all with regard to the question of who was to receive the sacrament. It accordingly changed the rite for the anointing of the sick. In so doing, it at the same time provided an example of an ecumenically supported reform. For the Reformers had rightly criticized the fact that the anointing of the sick had been turned into a sacrament for the dying. The Council of Trent felt the weight of this objection, and declared in the Doctrine (cf. *DS* 1698) that the anointing is to be dispensed to the sick. But it was not really able to surmount the medieval development which had turned the sacrament for the sick into a sacrament for the dying; for it added that the sacrament should be dispensed especially to all those who were so dangerously ill that their lives seemed to be in danger. In the period that followed, the anointing remained, both in pastoral practice and in the awareness of the faithful, a sacrament for the dying. It was only the Second Vatican Council and the postconciliar renewal of the anointing of the sick that brought about a change in this respect.

5. When a Protestant pastor visits the sick, his visit also includes essential elements belonging to James's instruction. The minister prays with the sick person and for him, asking God's support and help in all his necessities of body and soul. Trusting in the promise given to prayer, he consoles him with the assurance of the divine salvation prepared in Jesus Christ and made available through the Holy Spirit. According to Roman Catholic practice, the reason for the prayer-accompanied anointing is help for the sick person through the grace of the Holy Spirit, the effects being named as the saving and raising up of the sick person and, it may be, the forgiveness of sins. The Protestant churches are also firmly convinced that—apart from the Lord's Supper celebrated with the sick person—the pastoral assurance, given under prayer—which may be, and often is, linked with a visible sign of blessing (the laying on of hands, the signing with the cross[106])—can effectively communicate to the sick person the trusting assurance of faith that God, the Lord over sickness and death, has in Jesus Christ given us a physician who is himself life[107] and whose life-giving Spirit can give us health of body and soul.

According to the Protestant view, every Christian has in principle the authority to give this assurance; yet at the same time the presence of the ordained minister at the sickbed means that through him, as representative of the church in its public character, the church's support and sympathy are given expression. Conversely, the Roman Catholic Church is aware that during the first thousand years, until well into the ninth century, the anointing of the sick by the laity was known and recommended, the oil being consecrated by the bishop or the priest. The frequently expressed desire that the authority for dispensation should be extended (e.g., to deacons) is accordingly for present-day Roman Catholic theology quite open to discussion; for even the Council of Trent does not exclude the possibility that, although the priest is the "proper minister" (*proprius minister*), others are called to dispense the anointing of the sick. Canon 4 does not therefore have to provide the basis for a permanent antithesis in this point.

The same may be said in a different way of can. 2, since this is directed against positions whose exegetical presuppositions are no longer shared in this form. On the other hand, a definitive decision about the external and historical facts was not within the competence and intention of the Council. Although can. 2 insists on the distinction between the charism of healing in the primitive church and the anointing of the sick, the formulation it chose (*tantum*) shows that it by no means excludes a connection and relationship between the two. The passage in the Epistle of James therefore does not have to be viewed in isolation; it can, rather, be seen together with the gift of healing which existed in the early church. The churches of the Reformation do not maintain that this gift of healing originally consisted solely of physical healing. "Saving" and "raising up" (James 5:15) can also mean that the sick person is encouraged to endure his suffering in fellowship with the crucified and risen Lord, and with him to arrive at the glory of the resurrection (Phil. 3:10). According to our common conviction, it is and remains the gift and task of the church at all times to proclaim Jesus Christ as the savior of the soul *and* the body of men and women, and as the one who overcomes sin *and* death. The manner in which the church perceives this gift and performs this task may very well vary, although the form to which Holy Scripture testifies in James 5:14f. offers itself in a special way.

Finally, with regard to the problem of the sacramental character of an act of blessing carried out by the church on the sick person: this has no dogmatic importance of its own, and can be appropriately treated only in connection with the question about the nature and number of the sacraments. This is confirmed by the Council of Trent: since the sacramental character of extreme unction was already dogmatically defined in Sessio VII, on 3 March, 1547 (DS 1601), can. 1 is not offering a new definition. The biblical foundation for the anointing of the sick, which was a matter of dispute in Trent down to the final session, is here not the subject of a separate conciliar decision.

V. MARRIAGE

The function of the following account cannot and should not be to put forward a joint theology of marriage. For that, a number of convergence documents already offer notable approaches. Attention should be especially drawn to the final report of the Roman Catholic/ Lutheran/Reformed Study Commission on "The Theology of Marriage and the Problem of Mixed Marriages," published in 1976. Here we shall consider only the mutual condemnations of the sixteenth century, or rather the differences stemming from the varying doctrines of marriage which have put their stamp on the practice of the churches. Here it is a question, above all, of two aspects which, although they are related, nevertheless have to be discussed separately: (1) the question of the *sacramental character* of marriage; and (2) the question whether *divorce* is a legitimate possibility for Christians. A third aspect, the disputed evalution of the relationship between marriage and celibacy, will be treated only as an appendix.

The Council of Trent inveighs against the "impious men of this age" who, "madly raging against this teaching, have not only formed false judgments concerning this venerable sacrament, but according to their custom, introducing under the pretext of the Gospel a carnal liberty, have in writing and in word asserted many things foreign to the mind of the Catholic Church and to the general opinion approved from the time of the apostles, not without great loss of the faithful of Christ." With its anathemas against the heretics and their errors, the Council "has decided, lest their pernicious contagion attract more, that the more prominent heresies and errors of the aforesaid schismatics are to be destroyed, declaring anathemas against these heretics and their errors" (*DS* 1800; NR* 734). This sharp rejection must be judged against the background of the picture of Protestant opinion which the conciliar fathers had formed on the basis of collections of heretical Protestant statements. These distorted or falsified the Protestant positions in a number of important points.[108]

In the canons passed on 11 Nov., 1563, at the 24th Session of the Council (*DS* 1801–12), the following individual positions were rejected: the denial of the sacramental character of marriage (can. 1); the denial of the lawfulness of canon law rulings (as a general principle: can. 12; with regard to impediments; cans. 3, 4, 6); the rejection of separation from bed and board (can. 8); and of the prohibition of marriage ceremonies at certain times of the year (can. 11). Rejected also is the assertion that it is lawful to have several wives at the same time (can. 2); that dissolution and remarriage is possible on the grounds of heresy, grievous cohabitation, or voluntary absence (can. 5), or adultery (can. 7); and that clerics can contract marriage and that such marriage is valid (can. 9). Rejected further is the assertion that marriage is superior to virginity (can. 10). The reform decree *Tametsi* anathematized any who deny the validity of clandestine marriages (marriages concluded without the consent of the parents) (*DS* 1813).

The Protestant Confessions contain no explicit rejection of the Catholic doctrine of marriage, but in the course of detailed discussions about the marriage of priests, certain dividing lines are drawn. The prohibition of clerical marriages is called a work of Antichrist (AS XI: *BC* 314) and is described as conflicting "with divine and natural law" (Apol. 23.6: *BC* 240). The Apology also refuses to admit that the state of celibacy merits justification more than marriage (ibid., 23.36ff.: *BC* 244f.). The dissolution of the marriage of priests and monks on the grounds of a vow of celibacy is criticized (CA 23.13, 18–25: *BC* 53, 55; CA 27.18–37: *BC* 73–77).

Where marriage itself is concerned, the following is described as "unjust" (*iniusta tradito, lex*): that spiritual relationships are an impediment to marriage; the prohibition of the remarriage of the innocent party in a divorce; and the recognition of clandestine marriages contracted against the will of the parents (Treatise 78: *BC* 333). In the controversy of that time, theological and legal questions were closely connected; and even today they cannot be separated from one another. We may hope that an approach to one another in theological questions will create favorable preconditions for an understanding with regard to the legal questions also.

1. Marriage as a Worldly Order and as a Sacrament

a. The Doctrine of the Council of Trent

The fundamental assertion of the sacramental character of marriage is essential for the Catholic position, according to the Tridentine canons: marriage is truly and properly one of the seven sacraments of the evangelical law, instituted by Christ, and it confers grace (*DS* 1801). The justification for this doctrine, which is presupposed as a defined statement of faith, is briefly called to mind in the Doctrine (cf. *DS* 1797–1800); it is not in itself the main theme. The doctrinal statement in can. 1 rather provides a self-evident basis of argument for the solution of the problems that are then treated in cans. 2 to 12 (= *DS* 1802–12). Since the sacramental character of marriage was not discussed in any detail at the Council of Trent, we may here first of all look briefly at its background in the history of dogma.

Until the Council of Trent, whenever the concept of sacrament was used in connection with marriage, it could have three different meanings: it could mean a sacred obligation (cf. the original meaning of the word *sacramentum*); it could mean a mere sign (*signum figurativum*); and it could mean an effective sign (*signum gratiam efficiens*). Augustine interpreted the *sacramentum* to be the sacred obligation resting on marriage, meaning by that its indissolubility. Together with children (*proles*) and faith (*fides*), he counted the *sacramentum* in this sense as one of the "treasures" of marriage. But Augustine also used *sacramentum* in connection with marriage to mean "the sign of a holy thing," since he saw marriage as an image of Christ's bond with his church. Both doctrinal opinions had a long-lasting influence and were often repeated in the Middle Ages. On the other hand, the doctrine that marriage is a true and proper sacrament, in the sense of a sign that effects grace, is not found anywhere until the twelfth century; and for a long time it remained a matter of dispute.

Marriage was therefore admitted into the catalogue of the seven sacraments (for the first time by the Second Council of Lyons, 1274; cf. *DS* 860), without the question about the mediation of grace having been finally clarified. However, in the fourteenth and fifteenth centuries only few voices protested against the positive answer that had been emphatically maintained by Albertus Magnus and Thomas Aquinas; so here Trent claims that it is supporting a clear and unequivocal doctrine.

The priority of the practical questions that were before the Council allowed the *interpretation* of the sacramental character of marriage to recede into second place. The Doctrine is accordingly brief and permits considerable openness, relatively speaking, for theological development, provided only that the following basic conviction is maintained: through Christ's grace, marriage as it is lived by Christians surpasses marriage under the old covenant, since the natural love between man and woman (which is founded on God's will in creation) is now completed and cemented into an indissoluble unity. *That* is why marriage is numbered among the seven sacraments and may not be dismissed as a human invention. The term "sacrament" indicates what really happens when Christians enter into a marriage and live it out: through the grace of the suffering Christ (cf. *DS* 1799), who is the head, the Christian believer is given anew the opportunity—an opportunity bestowed on him in an efficacious promise—of realizing this specific and fundamental form of human community; that is to say, he is to be made capable of true self-surrender. The prototype and model is the loving self-giving of the Redeemer to his bride, the church.

The fathers of the Council of Trent saw this last complex of reasoning (only) "intimated" in Eph. 5:25 and 32.

Neither v. 32 nor even the word *sacramentum* (which was the word generally used in the Latin Bible to translate the Greek *mystērion*) contributed to the direct and formal deduction of the sacramental character of marriage.

According to today's Catholic doctrine also, Holy Scripture provides no direct evidence for the true and proper sacramentality of marriage. At the same time, Scripture does offer points of reference for the later description of marriage as a sacrament. The texts drawn upon here are primarily those New Testament passages which testify to the relationship to Christ and to the indissolubility of marriage, which Christ endorsed or emphasized anew: 1 Cor. 7:12–16; Matt. 5:31, 32 (cf. also 20); Eph. 5:21–32. It emerges from 1 Cor. 7:14 that the unbelieving marriage partner is "sanctified" through the partner who believes (and has been baptized). The new quality given to marriage through Christian faith points clearly to the relationship of married Christians to Christ—and also to the workings of Christ in married Christians and in their marriage. This is shown especially in the absolute faithfulness which only those understand to whom it is given (cf. Matt. 19:11)—those, that is, to whom it is given in Christian discipleship.

Ephesians 5:21–32 now closely links the unity of love between Christ and the church with the unity of love between husband and wife. The bond between husband and wife is a living reflection of the mystery of the unity between Christ and his church. Consequently, marriage participates in this great mystery and is then in that sense a mystery itself. Marriage appears as the community in which, through the promise of two of its members, the church as the bride of Christ, who is joined with him in a single body, presents itself—makes itself present—in concrete form. Thus marriage, which is a primal condition of human beings in creation, is drawn into the redemption and is sanctified. The power of Christ's grace lays hold of present-day life in all its spheres, in the sphere of marriage also. But medieval theology and the Council of Trent (cf. *DS* 1603) stress at the same time that marriage is a sacrament in a different way from the main sacraments, Baptism and the Lord's Supper/the Eucharist (cf. *DS* 1603).

b. The Doctrine of the Protestant Confessions

Although the Confessions contain no separate article on the subject of marriage, what they have to say about the marriage of priests includes a number of fundamental aspects.

The general Protestant doctrine of marriage is essentially molded by Luther's standpoint; and in his polemic against the abuses of the time, Luther wishes to stress particularly the importance of this institution for Christian existence and for Christianity in general. This viewpoint is summed up in his *Traubüchlein*, or "Marriage Booklet," of 1529, which was appended to the Small Catechism, and from 1580 onward generally counted as part of the *Book of Concord* and hence as belonging to the Lutheran Confessions (*BSLK* 528–34; it is not included in *BC*). This same viewpoint determines the formulations in the Lutheran marriage service to the present day. For a full statement of the Lutheran standpoint, the relevant pronouncements on the fourth and sixth commandments in the Large Catechism, Apol. 13, 14f., and CA 23/Apol. 23 must be drawn upon in addition; and for the Reformed position, Calvin *Inst.* IV, 12, 23ff.; IV, 19, 34ff., and Confessio Helvetica Posterior 29.

Marriage belongs, not to the order of salvation, but to God's gracious order of creation and preservation. It can therefore be called "a worldly matter" and a "secular order" (*BSLK* 528, 6; 529, 32). This is a way of stressing that it belongs to the sector of civil law and is a protest against the dominance of canon law in marital matters. It does not mean that it is a purely profane sphere. On the contrary, as a work related to the world, the kingdom of God "on his left hand," it is a divine institution and hence a "holy estate" or condition (530, 33). Because it is not a human institution but is based on the Word of God, it can be put forward polemically as the true spiritual estate, over against the monastic life (529, 32–38). This accords with the approach of the Lutheran doctrine of justification, according to which the Christian has to live out his sanctification in the conditions of the world.

The marriage of Christians is constituted by the declaration of consensus made by the bridal pair before the pastor (as a public acknowledgment before God and the world), as well as by the pastor's pronouncement that the two are now joined together (531, 1–21). But the promise of God's command and blessing, given through the pastor (532, 25–534, 16), is an essential part of the marriage ceremony. According to the Lutheran interpretation from the sixteenth and seventeenth centuries until 1874/75, when civil marriage was made obligatory in Prussia and the German empire, the church's wedding ceremony in its totality counted as the real act in which a marriage was contracted. Contrary to the decree of the state, many Lutheran pastors tried in 1874/75—though in vain—to preserve the character of the church wedding as *the* act through which the two persons were declared one. When, in accordance with medieval practice, Luther's Marriage Booklet has the declaration of consensus take place outside the church door, this is intended to express the fact that marriage belongs to the secular sector; so that here the pastor appears initially in his role as "registrar," or "magistrate." But the fact that this legal act belongs to the divine order, not to the secular sphere, is made clear by the pronouncements that the consensus is declared "before God and the world" and by the fact that the two are joined together "in the name of the Father and of the Son and of the Holy Spirit" (*BSLK* 531, 17, 20f.).

The blessing prayer refers to "the sacramental union . . . of Jesus Christ and the Church, his bride," which is reflected in the state of marriage (a reference to Eph. 5:32; *BSLK* 534, 9–11). This gives the state of marriage a Christological reference, over and above its quality as an order of creation and preservation, although it cannot have a sacramental character in the medieval sense.

This viewpoint is supported by the present-day exegetical opinion that in Eph. 5:32 the term *mystērion/sacramentum* is not supposed to be related directly to marriage, but ascribes a hidden spiritual sense to the scriptural text Gen. 2:24: Christ leaves the Father and gives himself up for those who are his. The Christological reference of marriage means that the loving self-giving of the married partners can ultimately be lived only in the light of Christ, in faith.

Fellowship in Christ makes husband and wife subject to the divine promise endorsed in him, as well as to the order and divine commandment which he confirmed. Love, harmony, and faithfulness are to determine marriage, according to God's will (cf. LC, Sixth Commandment: *BC* 392ff.). Its purpose is the community which embraces the whole of life and all its sectors, a community which takes practical form in the fulfillment of the manifold tasks of a married couple. A marriage between Christians is sustained by the blessing bound up with the divine institution and the grace of God, which must therefore continually be sought anew. Stress on the worldly reference of marriage therefore does not contradict its Christological reference, as found in Eph. 5:32. For God's grace and blessing have finally appeared in the person of Jesus; his relationship to redeemed humanity depicts God's fellowship with human beings, and his mission to the world is a mission into which the people of God is drawn. According to Protestant doctrine, marriage as a natural order can certainly be fulfilled by non-Christians too; yet the special character of "Christian marriage" cannot be denied. The divine reference which belongs to marriage can become fully evident only to Christian faith.

This special character is not defined by the application of the concept of sacrament, however (cf. Apol. 13.14–15: *BC* 213). This is considered not inadmissible, but marriage cannot count as a sacrament in the strict sense, because—unlike the sacraments of the new covenant (which are testimonies of grace and the forgiveness of sins)—it is instituted with creation, not first in the New Testament; and also because the divine promise *(promissio)* which belongs to it is related, not to the salvation of the new covenant, but to the mastering of earthly life *(ad vitam corporalem)*. Melanchthon's other argument (ibid., 15–20: *BC* 213) is that if we were to term marriage a sacrament, other "states or offices" could also be called sacraments. But this does not take the special character of marriage into account, for marriage is the basic form and paradigm of all human community (cf. Gen. 2:18); it means in a special way the whole person, including his bodily nature, and is distinguished from all other forms of human community through its intensity and exclusiveness.

Whether the Tridentine condemnation (Sessio XXIV, can. 1: *DS* 1801) applies to the Protestant doctrine of marriage so outlined depends on the meaning given to the term "sacrament." In substance, at all events, there are clearly points of agreement. (Cf. also the report "The Theology of Marriage and the Problem of Mixed Marriages," 12–23: III. The Relation of Christ to Marriage.)

c. Possibilities of Agreement

Provided that questions about the institution of marriage and its emblematic character are not in dispute, agreement as to whether marriage can count as a sacrament depends especially on a more precise understanding of what is meant by the joint assertion that God's promise, assurance, blessing, and grace are associated with marriage. It is agreed (by Catholic doctrine also) that the sacrament of marriage does not confer the justifying grace that provides the foundation for Christian existence; and it is agreed (by Protestant doctrine also) that being a Christian has an essential importance for married life.

Catholic theology adheres firmly to the sacramental character of marriage, while at the same time recognizing that there may be openness about the practical form given to this basic conviction, which is supported at the present time by a number of different forms of reasoning, which take "given" anthropological conditions into account, while giving these varying weight. It may be said generally that the juridical and institutional viewpoint is increasingly giving way to a perspective based on salvation history. For present-day dogmatics too, "covenant" is again becoming the key term in biblical theology;[109] and this lends Eph. 5:21–32 its special dignity as "scriptural evidence."

This is a starting point from which *the traditional misgivings of Protestant theology* about calling marriage a sacrament could be met: the relationship between the order of creation and the order of redemption must not be understood in terms of an alternative. For, after all, it belongs to the basic structure of a sacrament that there what is "creaturely," everyday, "normal," and necessary for living becomes the sign of God's nearness and his saving commitment to men and women.[110] Where the institution of marriage is concerned, Thomas Aquinas, taking up earlier traditions, expounded a helpful, differentiating train of thought.[111]

As our reflections on the general doctrine of the sacraments made plain, *the Catholic doctrine* of *opus operatum* means neither that human beings dispose over grace nor that grace is automatic. Not marriage as such, but only marriage between Christians can be called a sacrament (in the sense of a *signum gratiam efficiens*, a sign effecting grace)—on the basis of the prevenient grace and promise of Christ which has always to be promised anew. The married couple who "mutually dispense the sacrament to one another,"[112] to the extent in which the one is taken into service by Christ for the other, themselves remain receivers of grace in every respect. The interpretation of Christian marriage as a sacrament presupposes a permanent reference to the two fundamental sacraments of Baptism and the Lord's Supper/the Eucharist; and in this way it actually underlines the preeminence of the major sacraments *(sacramental maiora)*. The primary subject of the event of grace in the sacrament of marriage remains Jesus Christ; this is also true of marriage viewed as "the sacrament of married life." This stress in modern Catholic theology is in line with an almost unanimous patristic and medieval tradition, according to which the sacrament is not the marriage rite but the marriage itself. Could the resistance which can be sensed in this context not be influenced to some extent by an all too actualistic understanding of the promise of salvation? Stress on the "worldly character" of marriage retains its critical justifiability, over against certain specific forms of canon law (and marital morality); but on the other hand it should not be overlooked that in clinging to the indissolubility of marriage, the Roman Catholic Church is ultimately expressing the fact that this provision of the order of creation and redemption is outside the (juridical) power of the church.

In view of the particular obligation of the married couple, their intensive life together, and their dependence on the divine blessing, *the Protestant side* too could (with Apol. 13, 14f.) talk about the "sacrament" of marriage, as long as the fundamental difference between marriage and the sacraments of Baptism and the Lord's Supper is observed and as long as the sacramental character of marriage is described in reference to this fellowship with Christ mediated through proclamation, baptism, and Lord's Supper: the married couple enact the gift and obligation of Jesus Christ which applies to all Christians, but they enact them in a specific way, which is related to their relationship to one another and to their shared tasks.

A pneumatological interpretation could help us to express the sacramental character jointly in the following way. A sacrament is in general a pledge of the fact that the Holy Spirit as the Spirit of Christ is given to Christians and desires to determine them as a whole, together with their bodily existence: the fruits of the Spirit (cf. Gal. 5:22: love, joy, peace, patience, kindness, goodness, faithfulness, gentleness, self-control) take on a particular form in marriage. In this respect, the description "sacramental" agrees with the Protestant description of marriage as a holy and divine state. For the holiness of Christians is effected by the Holy Spirit. What still has to be clarified is whether, in the light of this pneumatological interpretation, we can arrive at agreement about what is meant by the Catholic formulation about "conferring grace" (*DS* 1801). The Old Testament comparison between marriage and the relationship of God to his people—seen as "covenant"—also suggests a way of arriving at an agreement.

Catholic theology takes this up affirmatively, and understands marraige as a sign of God's love and faithfulness to his people. In this framework, it attempts to work out an inward relationship of essence between the sign and the thing signified: as a creative force, marriage is the sign best suited to represent the living, efficacious presence of God in human life and activity, the workings of the Holy Spirit in human community. The intertwining of creation and covenant which finds expression in Christian marriage, and is its characteristic mark, is therefore inherent in the nature of human beings. God's inclination toward men and women reveals itself finally and unsurpassably in Jesus Christ; and the marriage that knows and recognizes this divine revelation acquires in the same measure an emblematic quality of new intensity and becomes a sacrament of the new covenant. Modern Catholic theology finds biblical justification for this viewpoint, not in individual verses or terms, but in the total context of Eph. 5:21–32. Here it follows the author of the epistle, who relates the "great mystery" suggested in Gen. 2:24 to the love relationship between Christ and the church, and—in the framework of a parenesis (duty code)—presents this relationship as a model for Christian marriage. This being so, the following connections emerge: the "physical" bond between husband and wife laid down in the order of creation is the prefiguration for the union of Christ the Redeemer with his body the church. This union in its turn becomes the prototype and model for Christian marriage. The argumentation linking the relation between Christ and the church, on the one hand, and marriage (husband and wife), on the other, goes beyond the moral relationship of example or model/copy. It has to be described as a relationship between prototype and reflection, a relationship that is a relationship of being and that is given in grace. This characterization is designed to accord with the indicative-imperative structure of Christian existence in the Pauline epistles.

Further discussions will have to show whether it will be possible to draw together the systematic interpretations on each side, with their preassumptions (which are still conditioned by the different traditions), so that—on the basis of a common interpretation of Eph. 5:21–32—we can formulate a doctrine of Christian marriage, with its moral and legal implications, which can be responsibly accepted by both sides. The final report of the Roman Catholic/Lutheran/Reformed Study Commission (1976) already took a good step forward along this common path:

"(17) If we are ready to step out of our conventional formulations of one form or another, we shall see that this relationship of Christ to the conjugal life of Christians is nothing other than what we all of us refer to as grace. In reality grace is the presence of Christ given to men in the Spirit according to the promise. Thus, without being contained in the state of marriage as if it constituted a reality independent of Jesus Christ, or as if marriage were sufficient of itself to produce it, grace is wholly a gift of Christ to the married couple. This grace, which is granted above all as a lasting promise, is as durable as marriage itself is called to be. (18) This relationship of grace between the mystery of Christ and the conjugal state requires a name. We all of us believe that the biblical term 'Covenant' truly characterizes the mystery of marriage. . . . (19) In fact we are all equally convinced that marriage is closely connected with God's promise. . . . (20) This promise, then, holds the initiative from the beginning and maintains it throughout. It has a kind of autonomy in regard to the spouses. It summons them ceaselessly to allow themselves to be formed by it, without the spouses ever being able to take for granted that they have finally succeeded in wholly identifying themselves with the full measure of its demands and its grace. (21) To bring together in this way the initiative of the promise in regard to the spouses and the re-creative experience which the spouses are called to have of its power over them, is to speak of the sacramental power of marriage considered in the light of the Covenant. It also means that marriage is a sign of the Covenant."[113]

2. The Question of Divorce and the Remarriage of Divorced Persons

The difference between the churches with regard to the sacramental character of marriage appears in its full rigor in the question as to whether the indissolubility of marriage in principle means that divorce is generally impossible. In what follows we shall give an account of the particular doctrinal decisions, or theological reasons, underlying the practice of both sides. These must be distinguished from today's reflections in the secular sphere about the "breakdown" principle.

a. Catholic Doctrine

The Council of Trent rejects the view that under particular conditions (NR 739: "because of heresy, or grievous cohabitation or voluntary absence"[114]) a marriage could be dissolved and a remarriage permitted. But—having in mind the ancient church—the Council avoids anathematizing the practice of remarriage in the Eastern Orthodox churches.[115] Only those who maintain that the Tridentine doctrine shows "that the church errs" are condemned (*DS* 1807). Nor does the church err if, for a number of different reasons, it concedes the possibility of a separation *quoad thorum, seu quoad cohabitationem* ("from bed and board") for a limited or unlimited period (*DS* 1808).

b. The Protestant Position

According to the Protestant view, marriage is concluded for life, as is shown by the formulations used in the wedding ceremony: "as long as ye both shall live" and "until death us do part"—formulations which still apply at the present day. The Protestant Confessions treat the subject of divorce only in passing, and then generally in critical dispute with particular canon law regulations and the rulings of ecclesiastical legal practice. In Apol. 23.23, Christ's prohibition of divorce according to Matt. 19:6 is held up against the dissolution of a priest's marriage (*BC* 242). Treatise 78 (*BC* 333) rejects the fundamental ruling forbidding an innocent party to remarry after divorce. Moreover, the validity of secret marriages is denied if they are "clandestine and underhanded betrothals in violation of the right of parents" (ibid.). In the Large Catechism the seizing of a bride by trickery is mentioned as an exception to Christ's fundamental prohibition of divorce (LC 305f.: *BC* 406). Finally, in confutation of the Anabaptists, the Formula of Concord rejects the application of the *privilegium paulinum* (1 Cor. 7:15), which permits the dissolution of a marriage because of differences of faith (SD XII.24: *BC* 634).

More detailed statements, which are then fixed in the Protestant law of marriage, are to be found in the writings of the Reformers.[116] These establish that *divorce* is fundamentally contrary to God's will. Nevertheless, the following reasons for divorce are recognized: adultery (the exception clause of Matt. 5:32; 19:9); also malicious desertion (*desertio malitiosa*); the *privilegium paulinum*, cruelty (*saevitia, insidia vitae*), as well as the definitive refusal of marital duties.

The possibility that *divorced persons may remarry* is permitted in such cases only to the innocent party, under appeal to Rom. 7:1ff. and 1 Cor. 7:8f., the reason given being that here the dissolution of the marriage is the equivalent of death: "for he that committeth adultery hath divorced himself, and may be held to be dead" (WA 10, II, 289, 11f.). Divorce and the punishment of adultery are here a matter for secular law.

The *disruption* or *breakdown* of a marriage because of a deep-seated inability of the married partners to be reconciled is judged differently, however. Luther makes this clear when he says that, although according to secular law there may be reasons for divorce and remarriage, as a way of averting greater evil (WA 32, 377, 37), Christians must know "that through divorce they would no more be Christians but heathen, and in a state of damnation" (WA 12, 119, 10f.). The rejection of divorce for Christians is intended to keep open the possibility of reconciliation through forgiveness, which a new marriage would make impossible (cf. 1 Cor. 7:11). Consequently, there can be at most a separation from bed and board.[117] It was in accordance with this principle when, right down to the nineteenth century, the consistorial courts dealt restrictively with the exceptional cases of possible divorce and remarriage.

In the light of the Tridentine condemnations, we have to ask what the decision of the Reformers means in principle for the theological standpoint, when they permit divorce in exceptional cases. Where present Protestant doctrine is concerned, this question cannot be clearly answered. At the same time, it may be said that today's practice, which is determined by the social order, is guided by reflections starting from the aspect of guilt and forgiveness. Divorce and remarriage are not in accordance with God's will but are an expression of human sinfulness. In this sense, Jesus' saying in Matt. 19:8 belongs to these reflections. But after the Fall, because of sin, God permitted ways for human beings to live together which would seem to be impossible in the light of the original order. Jesus points to this cleavage. This is the way in which the parallelism of Matt. 5:32; 19:8f.; Mark 10:5–9, 11f.; and Luke 16:18 is to be understood. The radical rejection of all divorce stresses the fundamental validity of the way marriage was intended to be in creation. The exception clause points to the fact that with his commandment God is not compelling people to remain in a marriage that has broken down because of their guilt, merely for the sake of the given order, but that in his mercy he shows them a new way to life. Hence the early church modified Jesus' saying appropriately. Protestant doctrine and practice see themselves as scriptural, pointing to Matt. 5:32; 19:8f. For the reasons given, remarriage cannot for Protestant theology be generally described as adultery—contrary to Tridentine can. 7 (*DS* 1807). Nor is separation for an unlimited time, which the Catholic law of marriage envisages (cf. Tridentine can. 8: *DS* 1808), considered on the Protestant side to be in every case appropriate. In relation to the practical questions involved in our problem, the forgiveness of sins, which is the center of the Christian proclamation, means permitting divorce and remarriage as emergency expedients.

c. *Possibilities of Agreement*

Protestant and Catholic doctrines are at one in their conviction that divorce can never be a normal solution, because marriage is concluded for life. Even when a marriage is going through a crisis, the bond should continue to be upheld; that is why a lax practice should not be encouraged, on grounds of Christian compassion. They are further agreed that there are situations where people can no longer be asked to live together in marriage. They draw different conclusions from this fact, however, since Catholic doctrine does not permit divorce but only separation—temporary or permanent—from bed and board. Yet in spite of considerable differences of doctrine and practice, the two churches are not irreconcilably divided on this question. A consideration of the theological closeness of the two positions outlined above makes this clear. At the same time, in the present state of doctrine, their viewpoints do not permit any convergence that could be called agreement.

However, it should at least be asked whether the mutual condemnations or rejections have to be considered as still valid in a church-dividing sense. Protestant and Catholic positions both appeal to biblical pronouncements; in each case they are in accord with a central aspect of marriage (indissolubility in principle—practical realization of the intensive community); in each case they lead to a different impasse. The possibility of divorce (*dissolutio*) or separation (*separatio*), understood as emergency expedients, brings theological reflection and church practice face-to-face with a dilemma for which there is no solution satisfactory to all sides. On the one hand, the impression is given that the indissolubility of marriage is not taken seriously enough. On the other hand, the permanent character which belongs to marriage in principle is in actual fact called into question through the separation, and the impression is given that the formal marriage tie is being maintained, without taking the human emergency into account. In view of the signs of general disintegration, both Catholic and Protestant churches are together challenged to practice such rulings as will bring out both the enduring nature of the institution and God's compassion with his fallen creatures.

3. Celibacy and Marriage

The rejections on the subject of celibacy have a different weight from those just considered, since they do not touch directly on the doctrine of the sacraments but have to be discussed in the ecclesiological context because of their relation to the ministry and to monasticism. Nevertheless, these rejections mark a profound difference between the churches down to the present day. This applies to practice and to legal questions, however, rather than to theological reasoning.

Whereas the Council of Trent pronounces a church-dividing condemnation in this question, the Protestant Confessions and the Reformers themselves—in spite of all their polemic against pre-Reformation positions—consider the matter to be basically open to discussion. The Council of Trent, Sessio XXIV, can. 10, anathematizes those who maintain that the married state is to be preferred to the state of virginity or celibacy, and that it is not better and more blessed *(melius ac beatius)* to remain in virginity or celibacy than to enter into marriage *(DS* 1810). Here it should be noted, first, that it is not simply marriage and celibacy that are being compared; it is the two as "states" or conditions. This is superficially directed against critical remarks made by the Reformers about conditions among the clergy at that time; but over and above that it is leveled at the Reformers' view (developed in a polemical context) that marriage is a way of living more in accordance with human nature than celibacy, and that the latter neither enjoys higher moral dignity before God nor has any merit relevant for salvation. The Confessions reject enforced celibacy as an impermissible intervention in God's order.[118]

They are in favor of the marriage of priests because (1) it "is based on God's Word and command," because (2) "history demonstrates that priests were married" (i.e., until well into the Middle Ages), and (3) because "the vow of celibacy has been the cause of so much frightful and unchristian offense, so much adultery, and such terrible, shocking immorality and abominable vice" (CA 23.18: *BC* 54).

If the argumentation based on practical problems is left out of account (although even today, under different circumstances, it is not theologically irrelevant), the following agreement about the fundamental points may be pointed out. The Reformers and the Confessions also recognize, in common with certain passages of Scripture (esp. Matt. 19:12 and 1 Cor. 7:32–38), that "virginity is a gift that surpasses marriage," although it is not a means by which one can merit justification before God (Apol. 23.38: *BC* 244). Luther stressed that the voluntary renunciation of marriage for the sake of a more intensive commitment on behalf of the gospel is one of the special gifts of God's grace.[119]

Like 1 Cor. 7:38, Luther considered the celibate state to be "better" inasmuch as "the celibate may better be able to preach and care for God's Word" (WA 10 II, 302, 12ff.; *LW* 45, 17ff.). "It is God's Word and the preaching which make celibacy . . . better than the estate of marriage. In itself, however, the celibate life is far inferior" (ibid.). Calvin also recognized the higher value, properly understood, of celibacy, inasmuch as it lends greater independence and readiness for the service of God and the works of piety (*CR* XLIX, 426 on 1 Cor. 7:38). The functional reference does away with the conclusion that the celibate state is superior to marriage in principle. It is in accordance with the Protestant viewpoint that the value of celibacy should have been recognized in recent times in Protestant churches—especially in connection with the rediscovery of forms of community life.

From this standpoint it must be said that the Protestant view falls under the Tridentine condemnation only if the Council's concept *melius ac beatius* ("better and more blessed") implies a higher value in principle, a special holiness, or even greater merit before God. But if, on the one hand—with Vatican II's Decree on the Life and Ministry of Priests—the sacred vocation of married priests is recognized (in connection with the Eastern churches) (*PO* 16), and if, on the other hand, celibacy is viewed as a form of life appropriate to the special tasks of the ministry and as a special gift of divine grace (*LG* 42; *PO* 16), then the condemnation pronounced in Trent can. 10 can no longer count as church-dividing today, even if no agreement is reached about the ecclesiological evaluation of celibacy.

4

MINISTRY

The Differences between the Churches
in the Doctrine of
the Ministry

1. Concept and Starting Point

In the Roman Catholic Church, and also in the Lutheran and Reformed churches, the ministry of the church is distinguished from the general priesthood of all the baptized. Through baptism, all Christians participate in Christ's priesthood, and together they are a single priestly people (*Ministry* 13). But the ministry of public proclamation of the gospel and the administration of the sacraments in the church (a ministry that includes a special responsibility for the unity and hence for the guidance of the congregation: *Ministry* 17) is not entrusted to all. For this, according to the Lutheran and Reformed view, just as from the Roman Catholic standpoint, "a regular call" (CA 14: *BC* 36; cf. Apol. 14: *BC* 214)[1] or an "ordination" (*LG* 20) is required, irrespective of the varying ways in which this may be interpreted.

According to Roman Catholic doctrine, this charge goes back to Jesus Christ and was entrusted by his apostles to their successors (*LG* 20). "Since ancient times" (*ab antiquo*) it has been carried out in various different ministries (*LG* 28), the bishops enjoying a special position, because to them "the fullness of the sacrament of Orders" (*sacri ministerii summa*) has been passed on (*LG* 21). "In God's stead [they preside] over the flock of which they are the shepherds in that they are teachers of doctrine, ministers of sacred worship and holders of office in government" (*LG* 20). This divine mission, it is said, cannot be derived from the priesthood of all the baptized; the office which proceeds from that mission differs from the general priesthood "essentially and not only in degree" (*LG* 10), although the two are ordered in relation to each other.

The Protestant churches should also be able to affirm that the difference between the ordained ministry and the general priesthood of all the baptized is a difference of kind, not a difference of degree of participation in Christ's priesthood (*Ministry* 20, n. 23). For the Reformation's criticism was directed precisely against the assumption of a difference of *degree*, an increase in the priest's personal state of grace through ordination, compared with the rest of the baptized. But according to the Protestant view also, the ordained ministry is different in *kind* from other ministries, and also from the individual testimony of faith to which every Christian is empowered and which is every Christian's duty; for it is a ministry (*ministerium*) which serves the Word of the gospel and the administration of the sacraments, and which has been instituted by God for the whole church. The ordained ministry cannot be traced back to the congregation. It has its origin in a divine commission and institution (CA 5: *BC* 31). So—according to the

Protestant view also—in performing their charge, the holders of the office do not act in their own name but represent the person of Christ,[2] according to the promise: "Whoever hears you, hears me."[3] The one who really acts in Word and Sacrament is Jesus Christ himself, through the power of the Holy Spirit.[4]

Through its close connection with the pure teaching of the gospel and the right administration of the sacraments, "the ministry, also in the Lutheran understanding of it, serves the unity of the church" (*Ministry* 29). And here the ordained office "*is not on the same level* as the preaching of the gospel and the dispensing of the sacraments" but "is rather ordered to them both in a ministerial capacity."[5]

Differences arose in the Reformation period in the view taken of the ordained ministry. Over against the tendency to narrow the ministry down to the concept of *sacerdos* (priest) and his *potestas* (power or authority) in the offering of the eucharistic sacrifice, the Reformation stressed the primacy of the task of proclamation, to which it assigned the function of administering the sacraments. The Reformers turned against the notion that the ministry was a sacrificial priesthood, because they rejected the view that the sacrifice of the mass was a human work, a (bloodless) repetition or complement of the one sacrifice of Christ. The Council of Trent, on the other hand, while making it clear that the eucharistic sacrifice was to be viewed as a sacramental representation (*repraesentatio*) of Christ's sacrifice on the cross, which was once and for all (*DS* 1740), still held fast in its doctrinal decrees to the concept of *sacerdos*, or priest, and the relationship of this to the sacrifice of the mass (*DS* 1752). At the same time, in the reform decrees the task of preaching was stressed, and its practice emphatically encouraged (e.g., Sess. 5, Decree on Biblical Studies and on Preaching [Decr. super lect. et praedic.], n. 9; also Sess. 23 c. 1).

Today the antithesis of that earlier century, with its one-sided stresses on both sides, has been softened by two developments. On the one hand, the Second Vatican Council describes the priestly office in the light of the office of bishop, and as participation in that office (*LG* 21 and 28, as well as *PO* 2 and 7); and here it once again, and particularly strongly, stresses the fundamental and outstanding importance of the task of proclamation.[6] This again has its foundation in the theology of the Word, which was emphasized by the Council (*DV*). Accordingly, the terms *ministerium* (ministry) and *munus* (office or function) are placed in the foreground, where the ministry of the church is concerned. This supplements, but does not reduce, the traditional views about the priestly office in its reference to the eucharistic sacrifice.

On the other hand, in the ecumenical dialogue an understanding begins to emerge with regard to the link between the concept of sacrifice and the Eucharist as an anamnetic participation of the celebrant or minister and the congregation in the one sacrifice of Christ. Anamnesis does not mean merely remembrance in the subjective sense. In this anamnesis Christ, rather, makes himself present by virtue of his promise that "this is my body," "this is my blood." Agreement in this question makes it possible for the churches of the Reformation to dispense with their protest against the sacerdotal interpretation of the spiritual office, now that there is recognition of the fundamental and outstanding importance of the charge of proclamation for the understanding of the ministry of the church. The churches of the Reformation, for their part, according to the evidence of their Confessions and also their contemporary practice, see the ministerial office, not as a mere preaching ministry but always also as a ministry for administering the sacraments (CA 14: *BC* 36; HC 83). In this respect, Tridentine can. 1 (*DS* 1771), which condemns the narrower view, is not applicable. In the canon, the authority (*potestas*) of the office is related to the eucharistic consecration and offering, as well as to the absolution in the sacrament of penance; but even in the Tridentine reform decree (see above) this is already supplemented by the charge to proclaim the divine Word. The Second Vatican Council even names the proclamation of the gospel of God as "the first task of priests as co-workers of the bishops" (*PO* 4). The canon stressed an antithesis between a priestly authority related to the eucharistic consecration and offering (as well as to the power of the keys) and Luther's view, which maintained that those who are ordained to offer the sacrifice of the mass but do not preach are not Christian priests (WA 6, 564, 16f.). But this antithesis no longer exists today, since in most Protestant churches ordination is acknowledged in their own confessions as the precondition for the administration of the sacraments.

2. The Sacramental Character of Ordination

According to Roman Catholic doctrine, ordination is a sacrament (*DS* 1773), the fullness of which is conferred through episcopal consecration (*LG* 21: *episcopali consecratione plenitudinem conferri sacramenti Ordinis*). In his early days (WA 6.564ff.) Luther disputed the sacramental nature of ordination; but here he presupposed that the rite of ordination had a liturgical form and a theological interpretation which is no longer accepted in the Roman Catholic Church today; this earlier view concentrated on the handing over of the eucharistic vessels and the anointing of the hands.[7] Luther, for his part, did not do justice to the biblical point of departure for a ceremony in which the office is passed on through the laying on of hands and through prayer (Acts 6:1–6; cf. 1 Tim. 4:14; 2 Tim. 1:6).

The Lutheran Reformation later thought it possible to recognize as sacrament an ordination carried out through prayer and the laying on of hands, provided that the office was understood as a ministry (*ministerium*) of proclamation and the administration of the sacraments, and was not defined as a sacrificial ministry (in the sense of the sacrificial concept which the Reformation rejected);[8] for according to the Protestant view also, the ministry, understood in this way, undoubtedly rests on a charge given by Christ. Here attention was drawn particularly to Luke 10:16; John 10:21f.; and Mark 16:15; as well as to Eph. 4:10ff.

In the framework of this interpretation, it might well also be noted that the Tridentine view was concerned to stress the (implicit) institution of the ministry through the command for repetition passed down in the context of the eucharistic words (Luke 22:19; 1 Cor. 11:24f.) (cf. *DS* 1740 and 1752).

Although the churches of the Reformation have not taken over the *nomenclature* that terms the act of ordination a sacrament, they have kept the essential components of the act itself (which was termed a "sacrament" in the closer sense of the term for the first time by the medieval church). At the same time, in the countries in which the Reformation originated, the Protestant churches departed from the requirement that ordination be carried out by the bishop. The reasons are discussed in sec. 5 below. Constitutive for the act of ordination is the invocation of the Spirit, which takes place in connection with the laying on of hands.[9] "Through the laying on of hands and through prayer (*epiklesis*) the gift of the Holy Spirit is offered and conveyed for the exercise of ministry" (*Ministry* 32).

Ever since 1947, the Roman Catholic Church has also made it clear that it is not the handing over of the eucharistic vessels that must count as constitutive for the act of ordination (*DS* 1326) but solely the consecratory prayer of the church, in connection with the laying on of hands (*DS* 3859). The anointing of the hands, which the Reformers criticized and which the Council of Trent still stressed (*DS* 1775), is today ascribed merely the function of an "explanatory rite," like the assumption of the liturgical vestments.[10]

This clarification of the significance of the rite of ordination, together with the interpretation not only of the episcopal office but of the priestly office as well (irrespective of its connection with the eucharistic sacrifice, which no longer needs to be a matter of controversy today, in view of the ecumenical understanding achieved), means that the most important reasons for Protestant criticism of ordination and its sacramental character have been eliminated. Consequently, the condemnations of the Council of Trent which were leveled at this criticism (cf. *DS* 1773-75) are no longer applicable today either. On the other hand, for the Roman Catholic Church the question arises whether the wide degree of agreement about essential components of the act of ordination does not justify recognition of the sacramentality of the ordination carried out in the Protestant churches, provided that an understanding can be reached about the observance of the apostolic succession in this act.

3. The Effect of Ordination

Theological tradition teaches that ordination, just like baptism and confirmation, imposes a permanent mark *(character)* on the soul of the recipient. It is therefore never repeated. Pope Eugene IV introduced this doctrine into the Decree for the Armenians *(DS* 1313). Luther disputed this traditional teaching (WA 6, 408.11f., 562f., 567) because, in association with the concept of priest, he saw it as an assertion that the ordained person enjoyed a higher spiritual state than the laity; while—contrary to any such view—he emphasized the general nature of baptismal grace.[11]

The Council of Trent, on the other hand, stressed that through ordination the Holy Spirit was conferred and that because of this the person ordained was permanently marked *(imprimi characterem)*; and it condemned any opposing view *(DS* 1774).

It is in fact true that in 1520 Luther related the anointing of the Holy Spirit solely to baptism, and hence to the priesthood of all believers. From 1522 onward, however, he talked about a special gift of the Holy Spirit in connection with the laying on of hands, among other places in his ordination formulary of 1535.[12] Even though the prayer for the gift of the Spirit at ordination is related to the ministry of the future office-bearer, and not to his personal state of grace as it were, he is nonetheless equipped for his ministry by the Spirit, and this means a permanent claim on his person; for ordination is not repeated. This means that "Lutherans in practice have the equivalent of the Catholic doctrine of the 'priestly character'" (Malta 60). And Calvin's comparatively positive utterances on this subject suggest a similar interpretation *(Inst.* IV, 19, 31; cf. IV, 3, 16). If this concept is seen "more in terms of the promise and mission which permanently mark the ordained and claim them for the service of Christ" (*Ministry* 37), then it does not have to be rejected by the Protestant churches. According to Luther's earlier utterances, there is no more than a distinction of function and work between those who have been ordained and other Christians, not a difference of "estate"; so that a deposed priest is nothing but "a bad layman" (WA 6, 408, 23f.; for the contrary view, cf. *DS* 1774). But these remarks are not directed against the claim made by ordination on the person ordained, which comprehends that person's whole life history (cf. *Ministry* 36, 38, and 32; *AÄDO* I, 4, 1).

The categories of the traditional Roman Catholic view were often interpreted in terms derived from Aristotelian ontology. But because they were really concerned with the ministerial function of the ordained person, they can also be expressed through functional definitions, which for their part, however, imply an ontology that is more strongly historically and personally orientated. This preserves the intention for faith of the doctrine about sacramentality as a permanent effect of ordination, as well as the preeminence of the divine effect on the human being that precedes all human activity; and this was the intention of the ontological description.

4. The Ordering of the Ministry and the Ministerial Succession

The Roman Catholic Church teaches the unity of the divine mission, which proceeds from Jesus Christ and which was transferred from the apostles to their successors (*LG* 20 and 28). But according to Roman Catholic doctrine, the one ecclesiastical office (*ministerium ecclesiasticum*) instituted by God is exercised in different degrees (*ordinibus*) by those who "even from ancient times" have been distinguished as *bishops, priests, and deacons* (*LG* 28). This pointer to the historical character of the varying names gives more precise form to the formulation of the Council of Trent, according to which the hierarchy of the three offices, even though it is not divinely instituted, is nonetheless divinely ordered (*divina ordinatione*: *DS* 1776).

The Lutheran churches stressed the unity of the ministry of the word (*ministerium verbi*, CA 5: *BC* 31), and especially the unity of the office of bishop and priest which originally obtained, according to their view of the tradition of the ancient church, for which they appealed to Jerome (Treatise 60ff.: *BC* 330ff.). The Reformed churches stress more strongly the plurality of offices in the church (*AÄDO* I, 2, 2), a stress that especially follows the listing of apostles, prophets, evangelists, pastors, and teachers in the Epistle to the Ephesians (Eph. 4:10f.; cf.

Calvin, *Inst.* IV, 3, 4). The threefold division of ministries in the ancient church was associated with this (*Inst.* IV, 1). But Lutherans too do not reject the division of the one ecclesiastical office into different ministries which has developed in the history of the church (Apol. 14.1: *BC* 214). For the Lutheran churches, it is at least left open as to whether this is not a development which could have taken place under the guidance of the Holy Spirit, and is more than a matter of arbitrary human choice; for according to the Lutheran view also, the Spirit is at work in the church and its history. Calvin, on the other hand, viewed the development of the triple division of offices in the ancient church quite explicitly as a development of what is said in the New Testament about offices in the church.

The Lutherans also declared especially that they were prepared to accept for themselves, as a matter of ecclesiastical order, the distinction between bishops and pastors given through a right to ordain reserved for bishops (Treatise 64 and 73: *BC* 490 and 493; AS III.10, 1ff.: *BC* 324), the provision here being that the bishops should tolerate Protestant doctrine and accept Protestant pastors (CA 28.69ff.: *BC* 93f.; Apol. 14.1ff.: *BC* 214f.). To this extent, therefore, the condemnation at the beginning of the Council of Trent's can. 7, which was directed against a denial of any subordination of priests to bishops (*DS* 1777), is not applicable.

According to the statement in the same can. 7 of the Tridentine Decree on Order, bishops are *superior* to priests because they have the authority (*potestas*) to confirm and to ordain. The canon explicitly disputes that they share this authority with priests. At the same time, the then disputed question as to whether this superiority was a matter of divine law was left open by the Council, inasmuch as the gradation of the ministry is not traced back to divine institution but is presented only as resulting from divine ordainment (*divina ordinatione*). On the other hand, the Council rejects the validity of ordinations without ecclesiastical and canonical consecration and commission (*aliunde venerunt*).

The doctrinal decree (*DS* 1768; NR* 711) added that part of the superiority of bishops was that they "can exercize very many other functions for which the owners of a lower level of consecration (*inferioris ordinis*) have no authority." Accordingly, the bishop's superiority is also a superiority of *jurisdiction*.

The Reformers tried to preserve this order. The Augsburg Confession stresses that the churches "are bound by divine law to be obedient to the bishops" (CA 28.21: *BC* 84), in respect of their commission to proclaim the gospel and administer the sacraments, forgive sins, condemn doctrine contrary to the Gospel, and exclude notorious sinners from the community (CA 28.21: *BC* 84). Even where the distinction between the office of bishop and the office of pastor was viewed as a matter of church order, not divine law (in the sense of being instituted in the gospel itself),[13] Luther and Melanchthon tried to preserve the episcopal office. But because the bishops "force our priests to forsake and condemn the sort of doctrine we have confessed" (Apol. 14.2: *BC* 214) an emergency situation arose for the Reformers. In order to supply pastors for the Lutheran congregations that had come into existence, they took the step of allowing ordination through ordained pastors, appealing to the original unity of the office of pastor and bishop. They believed that in an emergency situation of this kind they were entitled to do this without surrendering the rule of apostolic succession because— appealing to Jerome—they assumed the original unity of the office of bishop and priest.[14]

It must also be remembered here that for the second generation of Reformers, as the Reformed churches struggled to renew the structures of the ministry on the basis of the statements of Holy Scripture, the question about the historical continuity of the episcopal office no longer presented itself in the same way, because of the breach that had meanwhile occurred. Yet Calvin too remained concerned to link the order of ministries with the ancient church, relating the office of pastors and doctors in Eph. 4:11 (*Inst.* IV, 3, 4f.) to the office of presbyter in the early church, and—like the Lutheran Reformation—appealing to Jerome for the original unity of the offices of bishop and priest (*Inst.* IV, 4, 1ff.). Nor did even Calvin fundamentally deny the institution of superior offices, although he inclined rather to set up synods, because of the danger that superior offices may degenerate and come to involve claims to power (IV.4, 4). A section of the later Reformed tradition, on the other hand (Conf. Helv. Post. 18, Niederländ. Bek. 31), explicitly rejected the episcopacy as superordinated, supervisory office, above the parish ministry and with regional competence. In all cases, however, it is stressed that the bishop belongs to the collegiality of the presbytery.

In today's *ecumenical discussion*, Lutherans can recognize that the distinction between local and regional offices in the church was "more than the result of purely historical and human developments, or a matter of sociological necessity" but was "the action of the Spirit" (*Ministry* 45). This is true particularly of the episcopal office. According to the Lima declaration, today "churches, including those engaged in union negotiations, are expressing willingness to accept episcopal succession as a sign of the apostolicity of the life of the whole Church. Yet, at the same time, they cannot accept any suggestion that the ministry exercised in their own tradition should be invalid until the moment that it enters into an existing line of episcopal succession" (Lima, Ministry 38). In addition, in ecumenical documents the churches are asked to reconsider the possibility of restoring the link with the historical episcopal succession as a sign of the unity of faith.[15]

The Second Vatican Council described the office and position of the bishop in detail (*LG* III; *CD*): the bishops are not deputies of the pope; each of them has his own authority over his own local churches, or a regional group of local churches, in which he serves as teacher of doctrine, and has the office of sanctification and the duty of ruling. Among their chief tasks the proclamation of the gospel has pride of place (*eminet: LG* 25; cf. *CD* 12). This interpretation of the episcopal office is also in line with the Reformers' statements about the ecclesiastical office in general and the episcopal office in particular (CA 28.5: *BC* 81f.). The Second Vatican Council sees the bishops as a "college" which has taken the place of the apostles as shepherds of the church. The position of the bishops is described by Luke 10:16 (LG 20), a saying of the Lord which was also fundamental for the Protestant interpretation of the authority of the episcopal office (CA 28.22: *BC* 84) and of the ordained ministry in general (Apol. 7.28: *BC* 173). According to Roman Catholic doctrine, the bishops represent the visible principle and the foundation of unity in the particular, individual churches in which and out of which the church consists. They have the duty of caring for the church as a whole. As a total body or college, in communion with the pope as its head, the bishops are teachers and witnesses of the divine truth. They "proclaim infallibly the doctrine of Christ [when] they are in agreement that a particular teaching is to be held definitively and absolutely" (*LG* 25).

Where the relationship of bishops to priests is concerned, the Second Vatican Council talks about their differing tasks rather than about the superiority of the bishops. The fullness of the sacrament of consecration is conferred by episcopal consecration (*LG* 21 and frequently), and in this the priests also participate "in a subordinate degree" (*PO* 2 and 7). Together with the bishop, the priests form a single sacerdotal college (*presbyterium*). Priests and bishops are joined through the sacrament of ordination: in the local congregations the priests make the bishop present, as it were; they make the universal church visible in their locality (*LG* 28; *SC* 42). This points to the immense amount which the office of bishop and the office of priest have in common, irrespective of what Catholic opinion sees as the different gradation in their common participation in the priesthood of Christ and in the divine mission of the one eccesiastical ministry which is based on that. (*PO* stresses especially—more strongly than *LG* 28—the cooperative relationship between the two offices.)

The question about the degree of this common ground has not yet been conclusively answered, even in the Roman Catholic view. Trent still maintained explicitly that the bishop is the sole proper dispenser of confirmation (*DS* 1630). But Vatican II calls bishops "the original ministers."[16] In many cases, named by *CIC* in 1983, confirmation is today also dispensed by nonepiscopal ordained persons (priests).[17] This is also the tradition of the Eastern churches. The question about authority to ordain is more difficult. According to Catholic doctrine, ordination is reserved for bishops (*DS* 1768, 1777; *LG* 21). Ordinations that do not conform to this ecclesiastical and canonical order count as illegitimate (*DS* 1777). Vatican II talks about a *defectus ordinis* (a "lack" or "deficiency" in the sacraments of orders) in the Reformation churches and ecclesial communities (UR 22).

According to the law and the practice of the Protestant churches, leading clergy are as a rule responsible for ordination—in this sense, that is to say, the incumbents of episcopal offices. Yet how far this fact is the expression of a substantial agreement with Roman Catholic practice is a matter that still has to be examined, especially since this regulation does not in general count as something that is essential and therefore binding for the ministry of the churches (cf. *Kirchengemeinschaft in Wort und Sakrament*, report of a bilateral R.C./Evang.-Luth. working party [Paderborn and Hannover, 1984], 67). On the other hand, the Protestant churches and ecclesial communities have never denied the existence of the ministerial office in the Roman Catholic Church (Malta 64).

In spite of a whole series of notable new viewpoints, therefore, no full consensus exists as yet about the question of the bishop's sole right to ordain (Malta 63f.; *Ministry* 74ff.). Nonetheless, in view of the history and the present discussion, it is possible, indeed necessary, according to Roman Catholic conviction also, to clarify more precisely the relationship between the offices of bishop and priest.

5. The Church's Ministry and the Papacy

For the churches of the Reformation, as for the Roman Catholic Church, "it is essential to be aware of the interrelationship of the individual local and regional churches" (*Ministry* 72, cf. 68; also Calvin, *Inst.* IV, 4, 4). The churches of the Lutheran Reformation recognized the need for a "ministry of leadership and of pastoral supervision" (*Ministry* 42; *AÄDO* IV, 2) which stands above the local congregations. This recognition was already given when "visitors" *(visitatoren)* were introduced in 1527–29. The Reformed tradition inclines rather to synodal arrangements, also seeing the episcopal office of the ancient church as linked with the presidency of the college of presbyters (Calvin, *Inst.* IV, 4, 2). Even the possibility of an office to serve Christian unity on the level of the universal church was never excluded by the Reformation as a matter of principle (*AÄDO* IV, 4). It is impossible here to go into detail about the development of the Reformation position with regard to the papacy; but it must at least be said that the pope is not Antichrist.

The Reformation's opposition to the pope—which the apocalyptically colored thinking of Luther expressed by the term "Antichrist"[18]—grew up only out of the experience of the way papal authority was exerted against Protestant doctrine. This attitude was bound to appear to the Reformation as directed against the doctrine of the gospel itself. Today the mutual condemnations require revision on both sides. As far as the term "Antichrist" is concerned, the real heart of the reproach it contains is the accusation that the papacy puts itself above Scripture. As a polemical assertion, this reproach was substantially unjustified even under the conditions of the sixteenth century, if the way in which the papacy saw itself is precisely evaluated.

Today, on the Protestant side too, the application of the expression "Antichrist" to the papal office, as well as the history of mutual abuse that resulted, is a matter of regret. But the use of the expression in the Reformation period is of course explicable in the context of the late medieval tradition of ecclesiastical criticism and in the controversial situation of the Reformation period. It is especially understandable in the light of the experience of what the Reformers saw as the condemnation of the gospel itself by the very office called to serve it at the highest level. Opposition to the papacy was linked with criticism of the view of the church as *monarchia externa suprema* ("supreme outward monarchy," Apol. 7.23: *BC* 172), which the Reformers saw expressed in the historical claims of the papacy to authority over worldly governments, in the power deduced from the medieval title *vicarus Christi in terris* (Christ's deputy on earth), as well as in the claim to a universal episcopacy over the whole of Christendom (Treatise 1–5: *BC* 320; Calvin, *Inst.* IV, 6, 14). Modern Protestantism saw itself confirmed in this protest against the papacy by the statements of the First Vatican Council. But even this protest could in no way continue to justify the

Protestant description of the pope as Antichrist. All Christians and churches have cause to fear the appearance of the Antichrist among themselves and must pray to be preserved from it. But no office can as such be identified with the Antichrist.

With regard to the factual controversy about the papal office, the Second Vatican Council has developed viewpoints which open up possibilities of understanding; for it talked about the subordination of the magisterium to the Word of God (*DV* 10), taught the collegiality of bishops, and stressed the particular local churches, in which and out of which "the one and unique Catholic Church exists" (*LG* 23). It also calls to mind the ancient patriarchal churches "as mothers in the faith" (*matrices fidei: LG* 23; cf. *OE* 7ff.). The Constitution on the Church calls the diocesan bishops *vicarii et legati Christi*, deputies and ambassadors of Christ (*LG* 27). At the same time, cans. 331ff. of the *CIC* of 1983 show that considerable differences about this subject still exist.

The community of bishops, according to Roman Catholic doctrine, expresses the fact that every local church "is a realization and representation of the one church of Jesus Christ" (*Ministry* 68). In church history this community has taken its bearings from a few congregations which enjoy particular prominence because of their apostolic origin. Among these the congregation in Rome, with its bishop, enjoyed particular precedence from ancient times. Even the Reformers did not dispute this (cf. Calvin, *Inst.* IV, 6, 16). Agreement with Rome and with the incumbent of the episcopal see in Rome could be viewed as one criterion for unity with the whole church. But it was never the sole criterion. In particular, the presupposition was also that the bishop of Rome himself was in agreement with the gospel.

However, the judgment of the Reformation about the pope can find no application to a papacy whose office is subordinated to the gospel. Today, rather, even Protestant Christians welcome the fact that in the Roman Catholic Church the Petrine office is seen and lived as a ministry for the unity of the church which has its foundation in the gospel. In addition, the Lutheran churches too are asking themselves about such a "service to the unity of the church at the universal level" (*Ministry* 73). Here the "possibility" begins to emerge that, in addition to the institution of the ecumenical council and other forms of supra-regional community between the churches, "the Petrine office of the Bishop of Rome also need not be excluded by Lutherans as a visible sign of the unity of the church as whole 'insofar as [this office] is subordinated to the primacy of the gospel by theological reinterpretation and practical restructuring' " (*Ministry* 73; cf. Malta 66).

APPENDIXES

I. THE RESULTS OF THE VOTING

Between April and September 1985 the Ecumenical Study Group of Protestant and Catholic Theologians submitted all the individual documents separately to the vote of its members and to the members of the working parties, the results of the voting being as follows:

1. Introduction

Votes cast	40
Yes	35
No	2
Abstentions	0
No vote cast	3

2. Justification

Votes cast	41
Yes	35
No	2
Abstentions	0
No vote cast	4

3. Doctrine of the Sacraments in General

Votes cast	42
Yes	38
No	1
Abstentions	0
No vote cast	3

4. Eucharist/Lord's Supper

Votes cast	42
Yes	38
No	1
Abstentions	0
No vote cast	3

5. Confirmation

Votes cast	42
Yes	34
No	2
Abstentions	2
No vote cast	4

6. Anointing of the Sick

Votes cast	42
Yes	33
No	4
Abstentions	2
No vote cast	3

7. Marriage

Votes cast	42
Yes	34
No	2
Abstentions	2
No vote cast	4

8. Ministry

Votes cast	42
Yes	34
No	3
Abstentions	0
No vote cast	5

Note:

A deliberate distinction was made between "Abstentions" and "No vote cast." An abstention represents a verdict on the substance of the individual document. Some members voted "No vote cast" because they had joined the Ecumenical Study Group at a later point, or had been prevented for grave reasons from participating consistently in the project. "No vote cast" therefore does not generally represent a judgment about the substance of the document in question. On the contrary, many of those who chose this course welcomed the trend and direction of the documents.

Since it was found impossible to reach agreement with the Protestant members of the Ecumenical Study Group about the section page 142, second paragraph, in the document on "Marriage," or on the section page 158, lines 2–32, in the document on "Ministry," Professor Reinhard Slenczka, Erlangen, withdrew his signature from all the individual documents (letter of 16 June, 1986). For technical reasons, it was no longer possible to take account of this in the results of the voting printed above. However, Professor Slenczka feels that it is important that the change in his position should be publicly put on record.

II. MEMBERS OF THE
ECUMENICAL STUDY GROUP OF
PROTESTANT AND CATHOLIC THEOLOGIANS
(as of spring 1985)

Protestant Members
1. Bishop Hermann Kunst (Chairman), Bonn
2. Prof. Wolfhart Pannenberg (scholarly director), Munich
3. Prof. Horst Bürkle, Munich
4. Prof. Heinrich Greeven, Bochum
5. Prof. Wolf-Dieter Hauschild, Münster
6. Prof. Martin Hengel, Tübingen
7. Prof. Eberhard Jüngel, Tübingen
8. Bishop Martin Kruse, Berlin
9. President Hartmut Löwe, Hannover
10. Prof. Bernhard Lohse, Hamburg
11. Prof. Harding Meyer, Strasbourg-Kehl
12. Bishop Prof. Gerhard Müller, Wolfenbüttel-Brunswick
13. Dr. Reinhard Mumm (d.), Grafing, Munich
14. Prof. Reinhard Slenczka, Erlangen
15. Prof. Odil Hannes Steck, Zurich
16. Prof. Gunther Wenz, Munich
17. Bishop Ulrich Wilckens, Lübeck

Corresponding Members
1. Prof. Hans Freiherr von Campenhausen, Heidelberg
2. Prof. Gerhard Friedrich (d.), Kiel
3. Prof. Heinz-Dietrich Wendland, Hamburg

Catholic Members
1. Hermann Cardinal Volk (Chairman), Mainz
2. Bishop Prof. Karl Lehmann (scholarly director), Mainz
3. Prof. Peter Bläser, MSC, Paderborn
4. Prof. Franz Böckle, Bonn
5. Prof. Alfons Deissler, Freiburg
6. Prof. Karl Suso Frank, OFM, Freiburg
7. Prof. Heinrich Fries, Munich
8. Prof. Alexandre Ganoczy, Würzburg
9. Prof. Erwin Iserloh, Münster
10. Prof. Walter Kasper, Tübingen
11. Msgr. Gerhard Krems, Schwerte
12. Prof. Emil Lengeling (d.), Münster
13. Prof. Otto Hermann Pesch, Hamburg
14. Prof. Vinzenz Pfnür, Münster
15. Prof. Josef Pieper, Münster
16. Prof. Richard Schaeffler, Bochum
17. Bishop Prof. Paul-Werner Scheele, Würzburg
18. Prof. Karl Hermann Schelkle, Tübingen
19. Prof. Gerhard Schneider, Bochum
20. Prof. Theodor Schneider, Mainz

Corresponding Member
Joseph Cardinal Ratzinger, Prefect of the Congregation for the Doctrine of the Faith, Vatican City

Minutes Secretaries
Dr. Peter Walter, Tübingen
Hermann Kalinna, Bonn
Dr. Achim Dunkel, Tübingen

III. MEMBERS OF WORKING PARTIES I—III

Members of the Working Party on Justification (I)
1. Bishop Prof. Karl Lehmann (Chairman), Mainz

2. Prof. Friedrich Beisser, Mainz
3. Prof. J. F. G. Goeters, Bonn
4. Prof. Erwin Iserloh, Münster
5. Prof. Karl Kertelge, Münster
6. Prof. Bernhard Lohse, Hamburg
7. Prof. O. H. Pesch, Hamburg
8. Prof. Vinzenz Pfnür, Münster
9. Prof. Reinhard Slenczka, Erlangen
10. *Minutes Secretary:* Dr. Peter Walter, Tübingen

Professor O. Hofius, Tübingen, resigned from the working party after a brief membership. Professor F. Hahn, Munich, resigned from the Ecumenical Study Group after about half the meetings, and hence also from this working party.

Members of the Working Party on the Sacraments (II)
1. Prof. Theodor Schneider (Chairman), Mainz
2. Prof. Horst Bürkle, Munich
3. Prof. Balthaser Fischer, Trier
4. Prof. Heinrich Greeven, Bochum
5. Prof. Wolf-Dieter Hauschild, Münster
6. Prof. Alasdair Heron, Erlangen
7. Prof. Wilhelm Neuser, Münster
8. Prof. Vinzenz Pfnür, Münster
9. Prof. Gerhard Schneider, Bochum
10. Prof. Heribert Schützeichel, Trier
11. Prof. Gunther Wenz, Munich

Members of the Working Party on the Ministry (III)
1. Prof. Wolfhart Pannenberg (Chairman), Munich
2. Prof. Gerhard Friedrich (d.), Kiel
3. Prof. Heinrich Fries, Munich
4. Prof. Karl Suso Frank, Freiburg
5. Prof. Alexandre Ganoczy, Würzburg
6. Prof. Klaus Ganzer, Würzburg
7. Prof. Walter Kasper, Tübingen
8. President Hartmut Löwe, Hannover
9. Prof. Helmut Merklein, Bonn
10. Prof. Harding Meyer, Strasbourg-Kehl
11. Bishop Prof. Gerhard Müller, Wolfenbüttel-Brunswick
12. Landessuperintendent G. Nordholt, Leer/Ostfriesland

DOCUMENTATION

I. OFFICIAL DOCUMENTS OF THE
JOINT ECUMENICAL COMMISSION WITH REGARD TO
THE ASSIGNMENT
"THE CONDEMNATIONS IN THE
PROTESTANT CONFESSIONS
AND IN THE DOCTRINAL DECISIONS
OF THE COUNCIL OF TRENT
WHICH NO LONGER APPLY TO OUR PARTNER TODAY"

For a better understanding of the task assigned to the Ecumenical Study Group, excerpts from a number of documents are printed below. These were also made available in this form to the members of the Ecumenical Study Group during their deliberations.

1. From the Minutes of the First Meeting of the Joint Ecumenical Commission held in Munich on 6 and 7 May, 1981 (p. 3):

In the evening (6 May, 1981), Bishop Lohse put forward the conviction of the Protestant side that it was now time for the churches affected to establish, not merely in personal dialogue but in binding form, that *the condemnatory pronouncements formulated in the sixteenth-century Confessions* about the doctrine, form, and practice of the Roman Catholic Church are no longer applicable to today's partner. An analogy may be found in the relationship of the Protestant churches to one another expressed in the Leuenberg Concord (or Agreement). Here it is not a question of a mere change of terminology, still less of a frivolous relationship to our own history. On the contrary, it means that, accepting our own history, we also accept the new insights that have meanwhile emerged, new challenges and new experiences.

Cardinal Ratzinger thought that a corresponding reexamination of the doctrinal decisions of the Council of Trent was also necessary. It was important to formulate here what is always already presupposed in Protestant-Catholic dialogue: that new realities have come into being, and that the old massive dissensus to all intents and purposes no longer exists.

The commission expressed itself in favor of asking the so-called Stählin-Jaeger Group to take over the extensive preliminary theological work required. For this, the group would have to be expanded (Reformed theology would have to be taken into account, and various different trends represented). Work would have to be divided between subcommittees, and meetings would have to be more frequent. The present chairmen of the group, Bishops Volk and Kunst, together with the theological directors, Professors Lehmann and Pannenberg, were asked for their opinions and for suggestions as to how best the task could be mastered (see the letters appended below).

It was agreed that the correction of the past would also open up new possibilities with regard to contemporary problems (mixed marriages, ecumenical services, intercommunion).

2. Letter from the two Chairmen of the
Joint Ecumenical Commission to the Chairmen and
Theological Directors of the Ecumenical Study Group
of Protestant and Catholic Theologians
(undated; received on 11 June, 1981):

Archbishop Joseph Cardinal Ratzinger   Bishop Eduard Lohse
Kardinal-Faulhaber-Str. 5 (= 7)   Herrenhäuser Str. 2 A
8000 Munich 2   3000 Hannover 21

To
Cardinal Hermann Volk, Mainz
Bishop Emeritus Dr. Hermann Kunst, Bonn
Professor Karl Lehmann, Freiburg
Professor Wolfhart Pannenberg, Gräfelfing, Munich

Dear Sirs, dear Brethren,
On the occasion of the visit of Pope John Paul II to the Federal Republic of Germany, it was agreed that a Joint Ecumenical Commission should be set up, which then met for its constituting meeting in Munich on 6/7 May of this year. The purpose of the commission is to overcome immediate problems between the churches and, above all, to strengthen the common witness of the two churches. During the discussions in Munich, it once again became clear that our common witness is counteracted by judgments passed by one church on the other during the sixteenth century, judgments which found their way into the Confessions of the Lutheran and Reformed churches and into the doctrinal decisions of the Council of Trent. According to the general conviction, these so-called condemnations no longer apply to our partner today. But this must not remain merely private persuasion. It must be established by the churches in binding form. The path entered upon in the Leuenberg Agreement between the Lutheran and Reformed

churches ought to find a corresponding continuation between the Protestant churches and the Roman Catholic Church.

To say this is to formulate a task for which the Joint Ecumenical Commission first of all, and later the leaders of the churches themselves, will require expert theological help. Since an excellent instrument for taking up common tasks in theology and the church has existed for years in the form of the Ecumenical Theological Study Group founded by Bishops Jaeger and Stählin, we are permitting ourselves to suggest that this group might work out a proposal for solving the problem briefly set out above. It will probably be necessary to form subcommittees and also to co-opt additional members. But we do not wish here to anticipate your own ideas in this matter.

We should be very grateful if you could give a favorable reception to our inquiry and could assure us of your help. We are readily prepared to meet for a discussion, in order to explain the request of the Joint Ecumenical Commission and to discuss working methods and the period of time that should be envisaged.

With kind regards,

Yours sincerely,

Eduard Lohse   Joseph Cardinal Ratzinger

3. Extract from the Minutes of the Second Meeting of the
Joint Ecumenical Commission held on 14 and 15 September, 1982,
in Loccum (pp. 2–4):

On the point "Condemnations in the Protestant Confessions and in the doctrinal decisions of the Council of Trent which no longer apply to our partner today," Professor Lehmann, speaking also on behalf of Professor Pannenberg, reported as follows:

The members of the Stählin-Jaeger Group had not up to now been informed about the task which is to be entrusted to them. However, the next meeting would consider this subject. The assignment was faced with a fundamental impasse: the Confessions remain valid; yet at the same time they are no longer in all their parts applicable to the state of doctrine in the other church today. Behind this impasse are recognitions which are the result of historical research; but there are also non-theological factors and a change in ways of thinking. In order to lend the assignment greater precision, Professor Lehmann, put a number of *questions*, which then became the subject of discussion:

1. Is it sufficient simply to approach the condemnations by them-

selves? For the sake of the total context, must not the positive content of the doctrine be treated as well?

The commission realized the inner connection between negative and positive statements, all of which have their place in a total survey. It was important that the paper to be laid before the deciding bodies should be of a size suited to consultations in synods, and so forth. This meant limiting it to twenty to twenty-five pages. However, this authoritative paper might be accompanied by a series of less extensive studies, less binding in nature, similar, for example, to the compendium of papers accompanying the Malta report.

2. At present only Lutherans were represented in the Study Group on the Protestant side. This raised the question of Reformed participation in the context of questions affecting the Reformed Confessions. What form should this cooperation take, on an institutional level?

Since the Ecumenical Study Group already comprises about forty members, a general co-optation for the purpose of this particular assignment would not seem advisable. The Study Group had incidentally hitherto been autonomous in its choice of members. But since subcommittees would in any case have to be formed (because of the ramifications of the subject), there could be no objection to a cooperation by Reformed theologians in these subcommittees. It would be best for names to be discussed with Moderator Esser. . . .

Details about the frequency of meetings would be a matter for the Ecumenical Study Group. A result, however, should be presented in three years. Necessary technical help should be provided by the Secretariat of the German Episcopal Conference and the offices of the EKD.

3. How was the scope of the task to be defined? A strict limitation to the Protestant Confessions and the Council of Trent would not be possible, because certain developments only reached maturity at a later point (Vatican I, modern Protestantism), and have a retroactive effect on the interpretation of the sixteenth-century texts.

The commission pleaded that the assignment should be restricted, while seeing that more modern developments would have to be present in the background and would have to be taken into account (e.g., the dogmatic formulation of papal infallibility).

4. What significance would a "regional concord" or agreement have in the Catholic Church?

Here Cardinal Ratzinger pointed to the theological weight and the well-known cautious attitude of the German Episcopal Conference. Any consensus reached between the German Episcopal Conference and the Protestant churches would sooner or later make itself felt in the Roman

Catholic Church on a worldwide level. Here there was no need for anxiety.

In the general discussion about the questions involved, the autonomy of the Ecumenical Study Group was underlined, but a continual feedback to the Joint Ecumenical Commission was requested. There was deliberately no attempt to pin down the terminology to a "concord" or "consensus." A concord might be too ambitious, but even a partial consensus would have to be judged as being a positive result. At all events, positive formulations (consensus) and the superseding of earlier condemnations of our partner are two sides of the same coin and must be carried out simultaneously. The problems must not remain on the academic level but must be radically simplified, although the differentiations of the question must not be forgotten in the desire for a consensus. The fields to be considered must be realistically defined and demarcated, and they must include the following problem complexes: the decree on justification; the doctrine of the Eucharist (including what was said about sacrifice); penance and confession; *ordo*; Scripture/tradition. Here the consensus texts already in existence may and should be drawn upon.

Cardinal Volk asked how the question had actually been arrived at. What had meanwhile occurred in theology and the church? The claim to a body of belief must surely be no less today than in the sixteenth century. Moreover, the men who were locked in controversy at that time were not simply fools, nor did they simply misunderstand one another. But above all, the relationship between the confession of faith as it was formulated and the praxis of the church must be borne in mind (e.g., with regard to the Eucharist).

Bishop Lohse pointed to the common ground shared between the two churches. This had never been felt to this extent in earlier times. A limited, precise assignment ought to serve our common Christian witness.

It was agreed that more must be attained than is to be found in note 80 of the Heidelberg Catechism; that the genre "concord" should not be aimed at; but that positive statements should go even beyond a concord, and should as a whole reap the harvest of the hitherto existing consensus texts. The quality of the dissent must also be considered here, since this will be judged differently today, compared with the sixteenth century (Kruse).

Professor Lehmann, together with a small preparatory group, will prepare a thematic outline for the next meeting of the Ecumenical Study Group, this outline to concentrate on limited, realistic steps. A report will then be submitted to the Joint Ecumenical Commission at its May meetings (1983).

4. The Assignment "An Examination of Already Existing Consensus Texts"

a. Page 5 of *the Minutes of 6/7 May, 1981*, under point 6 of the agenda (where future assignments are discussed), reads as follows:

Examination of existing *consensus texts:* What declarations in the agreed statements that have been worked out by theologians can be received by the churches, and how can this reception find expression? (The Ecumenical Commission of the German Episcopal Conference will make a proposal.)

b. Pages 5f. of *the Minutes of 14/15 September, 1981*, under point 3 of the agenda, read (following a written proposal by Bishop P.-W. Scheele):

In the succeeding discussion the following aspects emerged.

• It should be the special task of the Joint Ecumenical Commission to promote and coordinate efforts to arrive at consensus texts, and also to promote and coordinate their reception.

• It was asked whether the work directed toward the reception should not also be taken up by the Stählin-Jaeger group and whether the assignment already given should not be modified accordingly. Greater thematic precision in the assignment given to the Stählin-Jaeger group was in any case required (with regard to "the condemnations in the Protestant Confessions and in the doctrinal decisions of the Council of Trent which no longer apply to our partner today").

• A distinction must be made between the work of the theologians, the churches' reception of the consensus texts formulated by the theologians, and the development of the awareness of the faith in the congregations. It was pointed out that reception cannot simply be commanded from above; although it is equally true that the actually existing state of congregational awareness is not as such normative either. Reception requires a mutual process between theology, the church's ministry, and congregational belief. Within this structure the commission ought to try to be actively encouraging.

• A list of previous attempts at a reception on the Protestant and the Catholic side was thought to be necessary.

As a result of the discussion, the following points were established, and these also provided subjects to be considered at the next meeting:

1. Some fundamental facts touching on the reception (based on Bishop Scheele's introductory paper);
2. Report on steps toward a reception undertaken up to now
   —by the Catholic Church
   —by the Protestant churches (including a list of synodal statements on consensus texts);
3. Discussion of the text "Wege zur Gemeinschaft. Alle unter einem Christus" ["Ways to Fellowship. All under the one Christ"] (Paderborn and Frankfurt, 1980). Which proposals in this text seem possible and should be jointly recommended? Attempt to coordinate further steps toward a reception.

II. CORRESPONDENCE BETWEEN THE CHAIRMEN OF THE JOINT ECUMENICAL COMMISSION AND THE ECUMENICAL STUDY GROUP AT THE CONCLUSION OF THE STUDY

Ecumenical Study Group of Protestant and Catholic Theologians
—from the Chairmen—

Maria Laach, 25 October, 1985

To the Chairmen of the
Joint Ecumenical Commission
Bishop Prof. Eduard Lohse
—Chairman of the Council of the EKD—
Bishop Prof. Paul-Werner Scheele
Re: *The submission of the result of the study on "The Sixteenth-Century Condemnations"*

Dear Mr. Chairman, dear Bishop Scheele,

On 6/7 May, 1981, at its first meeting in Munich, the Joint Ecumenical Commission resolved to ask the Ecumenical Study Group of Protestant and Catholic Theologians for a major study project. This request had the following starting point: "that our common witness is counteracted by judgments passed by one church on the other during the sixteenth century, judgments that found their way into the Confessions of the Lutheran and Reformed churches and into the doctrinal resolutions of the Council of Trent. According to the general conviction, these so-called condemnations no longer apply to our partner today. But this must not remain merely private persuasion. It must be established by the churches in binding form" (letter of the then chairmen Bishop Lohse and Archbishop Joseph Cardinal Ratzinger, addressed to the leaders of the Ecumenical Study Group in June 1981). Our study group agreed to this request and from early autumn 1981 discussed the specific plan of the work with you in a series of meetings. The two scholarly directors of our group, Professor Karl Lehmann (since 1983 bishop of Mainz) and Professor Wolfhart Pannenberg of the University of Munich, participated as experts in the discussions on the subject at the meetings of your commission, so that agreement and harmonization was always possible. We ourselves were also able to take part in an advisory capacity in the final deliberations of the Joint Ecumenical Commission. We should like to express our sincere thanks for this excellent cooperation.

As you know, the Ecumenical Study Group, with your consent, set up three working parties, to which, in an appropriate balance, Lutheran, Catholic, and also Reformed theologians were appointed (the latter in cooperation with the moderator of the Alliance of Reformed Churches). Together with you, we decided that the main subjects should be justification (baptism, faith, repentance), sacraments, and ministry (including Scripture and tradition). The three working parties, about thirty-five theologians in all, were led by the two scholarly directors Professor W. Pannenberg (ministry) and Bishop K. Lehmann (justification), and by Professor T. Schneider, Mainz (sacraments). About fifty theologians in all participated in the exchange of views and in the voting process, which lasted from April to September of this year.

Many meetings of the working parties and the plenary session were devoted exclusively for a period of four years to the subjects passed on to us by you. The theologians set aside much of their own personal scholarly work in order to cooperate in this project. Now the time has come when the work on the eight individual documents could be completed. With his letter of 18 October, 1985, Bishop K. Lehmann passed on to you, in a separate folder, the detailed results of the voting.

Today we are submitting to you, as the result of our endeavors, a volume of over two hundred pages, with all the individual documents. It accompanies this letter.

With this our study group has fulfilled the request passed on to it within the time envisaged and hopes that it may thereby have made an important contribution to a convergence between our churches. You will see from the voting results that our members were to a large degree able to assent to the whole project and to the individual documents, which have been continually and untiringly revised. For all the bodies who now and in the future concern themselves with this result, this undoubtedly imposes a serious obligation to make the conclusions that have been worked out here fruitful in bringing about a still more profound unity between Christians.

We could have worked on the task entrusted us for a still longer period. Many things could still be improved and deepened. But there was pressure for a result, both from outside and in the nature of the matter itself. We are also prepared to continue accompanying the project in the future, if this can further ecumenical endeavors.

For ourselves, we consider that priority must be given to a formal examination and harmonization of the eight individual documents, with a scholarly commentary on the texts, accompanied by the essential studies required. This should also be made available to a wider public. The date of publication will of course be determined upon in agreement with you. In this connection we should like gratefully to revert to your offer of financial support in the appointment of a scholarly assistant.

We should like once more to express our gratitude for the friendly spirit in which our work together was carried on. We respect the theological efforts and the results achieved. We would remind ourselves and the readers of the documents of the prayer for the gift of the Holy Spirit, who leads us into all truth. It is our hope that our work may be blessed with abundant fruits, and we remain, with kind regards to you and to all the members of your commission,

Yours sincerely,
Hermann Cardinal Volk   Hermann Kunst

The Joint Ecumenical Commission
—from the Chairmen—

Hannover/Würzburg
Beginning of November 1985

To the Chairmen of the
Ecumenical Study Group of
Protestant and Catholic Theologians
Hermann Cardinal Volk, Mainz
Bishop Hermann Kunst, Bonn

Dear Cardinal Volk, dear Bishop Kunst,

At the last meeting of the Joint Ecumenical Commission held in Maria Laach on 25 and 26 October, you presented to us the results of the study on "The Sixteenth-Century Condemnations." In the name of the Joint Ecumenical Commission which was set up by the German Episcopal Conference and the Council of the Evangelical Church in Germany, we should like to express to you our most sincere and warmest thanks for this valuable gift. These thanks go out to all members of the Ecumenical Study Group, but more especially to the two scholarly directors, Bishop Karl Lehmann and Professor Wolfhart Pannenberg. We realize that with the request it made over four years ago to the Ecumenical Study Group, the Joint Ecumenical Commission presented it with a task that was by no means easy. We are deeply impressed by the results, which have been so conscientiously worked out and which have now been entrusted to us. We would therefore beg you to pass on to the scholarly directors and to all members of the Ecumenical Study Group our respect and our grateful recognition. Almost forty theologians, all of them engaged in scholarly work, have selflessly set aside their own personal projects and have devoted themselves with the greatest helpfulness to a joint ecumenical task in the service of our churches. This presents us with an example of growing ecumenical fellowship between our churches which should encourage us all.

The service which the Ecumenical Study Group has shown our churches could certainly not have been completed in so relatively short a time had not so strong a confidence grown up during the almost forty years during which the group has met for regular conferences, together with an increasing awareness of the fellowship that binds us together in Christ. We therefore congratulate the study group on the fact that in the power of the fellowship given us in Christ it has been able to bring to completion, and with so large a measure of agreement, the study that has now been submitted to us. The Joint Ecumenical Commission has composed a final report which we shall lay before the German Episcopal Conference and the Council of the Evangelical Church in Germany, together with the study entrusted to us, asking them to give the document with which we have been charged the greatest possible degree of church recognition. We confidently hope that the merciful God in his grace will bless the work to which we have been permitted to commit ourselves together in the years behind us.

Yours sincerely,
Paul-Werner Scheele   Eduard Lohse

III. FINAL REPORT OF THE
JOINT ECUMENICAL COMMISSION
ON THE EXAMINATION OF THE
SIXTEENTH-CENTURY CONDEMNATIONS

I

Times have changed, and during the last fifty years we have become aware, not only of the differences between the Roman Catholic and the Protestant forms of the Christian faith, but still more of what we have in common. It has become clear that the commission given by the Lord to his church requires the common testimony of faith and the common search for the visible unity of the church. The changed situation of Christianity in modern times, in which a worldwide atheism and secularism threaten the Christian faith, our common bitter experiences in the Third Reich, the witness of the martyrs, the encounters of Christians belonging to different denominations—all these things have brought it about that members of our churches experience one another as brothers and sisters in Jesus Christ. The Christian faith will not fulfill its charge to spread the gospel if it comes to the nations and different cultures divided and disunited.

After the end of the Second World War, because of these insights and experiences, the Roman Catholic and Protestant churches in Germany have worked together in many sectors. Refugee congregations were hospitably received by congregations belonging to the other denomination. Charitable help was developed in many forms of cooperation. In the new form of civil government that grew up after the war, both churches assumed responsibility, which continually also took the form of common declarations and a cooperation that became a matter of course. The duty to help in the development of state and church was jointly recognized and assumed. Participation in the worship of the other church, the celebration of ecumenical services, joint study of Holy Scripture, the new beginning brought about by the Second Vatican Council, impulses from the ecumenical movement—all these things showed Protestant and Catholic churches that they are bound together as members in the body of the Lord, and made them ask how this common ground of faith, love, and hope was to be reconciled with the traditional divisions.

During the visit of Pope John Paul II to the Federal Republic of Germany in 1980, these growing ecumenical ties also led to a meeting in Mainz between the pope and the Council of the Evangelical Church in Germany. During this notable conversation, which gave happy expression to our ecumenical ties, a Joint Ecumenical Commission was agreed upon, its task being to delineate, deepen, and strengthen the degree of Christian fellowship and community between the churches that had been achieved. The commission was composed of representatives of the German Episcopal Conference, the Vatican's Secretariat for Promoting the Unity of Christians, and the Council of the Evangelical Church in Germany. Since 1981 it has met twice a year for working sessions. In 1981 it set forth in a declaration for both churches and for the public what the Christian faith confessed in Nicaea-Constantinople in 381 means today. In a further declaration of the same year, it encouraged people in our country, especially the younger generation, to give an unreserved assent to marriage as a form of living. In a common statement "Celebrating Sunday," it affirmed that not only the church but the world as well is in need of Sunday and Sunday worship. Finally, in 1985 it issued a common statement about the responsibility of the churches for mixed marriages.

However, the mutual condemnations pronounced in the sixteenth century still stand between the churches, hindering a closer fellowship between them. Consequently the Joint Ecumenical Commission set itself as main task the examination of these condemnations. The investigation was to discover where they applied to the partner of that earlier time and whether they are still applicable to our partner today. Condemnations were pronounced in the sixteenth century in confessions and official doctrinal documents about the doctrine and practice of the other church, and became anchored in the awareness of church members as divisive differences. They are binding on clergy and teachers of the faith down to the present day, and—because they were once made officially authoritative—cannot simply be passed over in silence, or given a different interpretation, merely as we think best.

The Ecumenical Study Group of Protestant and Catholic Theologians, which came into being in 1946, was asked to devote its attention to this complex.

II

The Catholic-Protestant Study Group agreed to this request, and, with the cooperation of further expert theologians, worked out a detailed document in which the condemnations pronounced in the sixteenth century were intensively examined. The investigations bring to light a wide spectrum of differentiated judgments. The general trend of the results is this: a series of condemnatory pronouncements rest on misunderstandings about the opposing position; others no longer apply to the doctrine and praxis of today's partner; in the case of still others, new factual insights have led to a large degree of agreement: but where some of the condemnatory pronouncements are concerned, it cannot be said that there is as yet any agreement at the present day.

Yet the history that lies behind us, with its disputes about the truth, is still important. We cannot simply ignore the condemnations pronounced in the past. They retain their importance as salutary warnings, in two ways: in our own tradition, in each given case, they are a warning against falling behind the clarifications arrived at in the sixteenth century; and those belonging to the other church are warned against so interpreting and expressing their own tradition that the antitheses which recent theological development has shown to be surmountable break out once more in their ancient acrimony. If the ancient condemnations remain as permanent warnings today, both to Christians of our own church and to those of the other, then church leaders are faced with the task of asking themselves whether—in view of the changed relationship between the churches and their members—the church-dividing effect of the condemnatory pronouncements still has to be maintained. At the same time, further agreement about the positive content of doctrine, about worship, and about the community of the church is still required, on the way to full unity. Even if the condemnations of the Reformation period lose their divisive effect, this does not mean that all the conditions for a full fellowship of the churches are already given; but it does mean that the path to negotiation about these conditions has become free.

The still existing differences must certainly not be underestimated, let alone denied. Our history has run in opposite directions for centuries; and during that time different denominational cultures have developed which put their stamp on the behavior of men and women right down to everyday life. The relationship to the community of the church, church order, the form and importance of church services, the tension between the individual decision of faith and the common praxis of faith, life lived from the sacraments and from Holy Scripture—all these things still distinguish Protestant from Catholic Christians. The fundamental common ground of faith, of which people have become aware, and which is described in what follows here, needs time before it can find its matter-of-course expression in the everyday life of Christians. But the differences in the doctrine and praxis of faith which obviously exist must not mean that theological antitheses have to be asserted about fundamental things, when these antitheses do not actually exist.

The Study Group has drawn its results preeminently from three subject complexes. It was on these that the sixteenth-century controversies were concentrated, and they are still of central importance for the understanding of faith in the churches, and for church life. These complexes are: justification (faith, baptism, repentance), the sacraments (generally, and especially the Lord's Supper), and ministry (including the ecclesiological presuppositions and the question about Scripture and tradition). Other open questions—for example, mariology, the veneration of saints, celibacy, and monastic vows—were not to be explicitly included here. The doctrine of the church, especially its connection with the understanding of the ministry, and the importance of the dogmas of the nineteenth and the twentieth century for the whole of the Christian faith, are not considered as separate subjects. Here tasks remain for future binding doctrinal discussions.

Important new insights arising from theological studies and official interchurch dialogues make their contribution to the already given community between Catholic and Protestant Christians which is experienced; and these throw new light on the antitheses formulated in the sixteenth century. For example, on the Roman Catholic side the theology of the Word was taken up and the importance of preaching in church services stressed; while on the Protestant side the Eucharist as essential component of the life of worship has been recognized and a corresponding new order begun. On both sides there is agreement that Jesus Christ, as he is testified to in the gospel, is the source, center, and norm of Christian life. A renewed and deeper study of the Holy Scriptures of the Old and New Testaments has brought Catholic and Protestant theologians together and has contributed more than anything else to the surmounting of old questions of controversy. Further impulses have been contributed by historical research in the fields of church, liturgical, and dogmatic history. As well as liturgical renewal, work on patristic theology has played an important part. This has allowed a number of connecting threads to be seen more distinctly today. A clearer distinction can be made between the New Testament origins and the later developments of the patristic and medieval periods. A better historical understanding makes it possible to grasp more precisely the different ways of thinking and different conceptualities on both sides which have made mutual understanding more difficult, especially in the doctrine of justification but also, for example, in the interpretation of the Lord's Supper as eucharistic sacrifice.

One direct result of progress in biblical studies and historical research is the insight that different words can apparently not infrequently mean the same thing, but also that the same words may mean something different. Antithetically formulated statements have to be related, on the one hand, to the specific questions and alternative possible answers of the time of their origin, and on the other, to the common biblical foundation. They are then moved into a new perspective. And only then does it become possible to perceive more clearly the historically conditioned character of the confessional statements as well as the condemnations that correspond to them.

After the investigations of the Ecumenical Study Group, important controversial questions appear in a new light.

1. The Reformers taught that in the *justification* of the sinner all cooperation on the part of the human being himself is excluded. A person is righteous before God solely because God bestows on him his grace in Jesus Christ; and this grace can be received only in faith. The doctrine of the Roman Catholic Church, on the other hand, stressed that a human being who is touched by God's grace also cooperates for his own part, inasmuch as he freely assents to God's justifying action and accepts it.

Today, when we consider the doctrine of justification in the different forms it took in the sixteenth century, the following must be said. No one can condemn those who, in experiencing the misery of their sin, their resistance toward God, and their lack of love for God and their neighbor, put their trust solely in the God who saves, are assured of his mercy, and try to make their lives match up to this faith. But on the other hand, no one can condemn those who, deeply penetrated by the unlimited power of God, stress more than anything else, even in the event of justification, God's glory and the victory of his gracious activity in men and women, and who hold the failure and halfheartedness of human beings toward this gracious activity to be, in the strict sense, of secondary importance.

This tense community in faith, which was certainly sensed in germ in the sixteenth century but could never find common expression, can today be expressed as the common testimony of both churches to the pardoning justification of God. Both churches are concerned to make it clear that toward God human beings can in no way look to their own efforts, but that they are nonetheless penetrated by justification wholly and entirely. The response of faith is brought about by the Holy Spirit through the Word of promise which comes to men and women. Cooperation cannot be a matter of controversy, if it means that in faith the heart is involved, when the Word touches it and faith is created. On the other hand, the faith of which it is said that it justifies the whole life of the human beings brings men and women into a trustful acceptance of the promise of God in Christ. Because today there is agreement between the churches about this, it must be asked whether the condemnatory pronouncements on justification that were formulated on each side in the sixteenth century, against the doctrine of the other, still have to be maintained today in their church-dividing effect.

2. Apart from justification, *the Eucharist* was at the center of the conflicts of the Reformation period. What was especially in dispute were questions about the sacrifice of the mass, the transformation of substance, and the function of the priest. The criticism of the Reformers was not directly solely against the doctrine of transubstantiation; it was also made a subject of reproach that the doctrine of the sacrifice of the mass falsified the eucharistic celebration into a human work, so that the mass could be termed a "damnable idolatry."

By going back to the statements of the New Testament, in the doctrine of the Eucharist both churches have arrived at a common understanding about the celebration of the Lord's Supper through which these ancient differences and conflicts can be overcome. Here what is particularly important is a deepened understanding of the Lord's Supper as anamnesis (remembrance or memorial) of the sacrifice of Jesus Christ on the cross. From this point a new understanding is possible today about the connection between the presence of Christ and participation in his sacrifice. Both churches acknowledge that Jesus Christ himself is really present in the celebration of the Lord's Supper. Historical investigation shows that, in the different development of this biblical testimony both through the doctrine of transubstantiation and through the doctrines of the Protestant churches, a common fundamental concern was pursued: to express the mystery of the real presence of Jesus Christ in the Eucharist. These different ways of conceptualizing the biblical truth could not be reduced to a common utterance in the sixteenth century. Each of these conceptions has evident strengths and weaknesses, but none of them can of itself claim exclusive validity of such a kind that the other form of doctrine in any given case must automatically be condemned as heretical. In view of the common conviction of faith about the true and real presence of the Lord in the Eucharist, it must be asked whether the remaining different emphases in the theology and spirituality of the Eucharist—emphases that have been molded through denominational tradition—must still be termed divisive of the churches.

3. In the doctrine of *the ministry* the Catholic Church firmly retains

the concept of priest, as it was substantially determined through its relationship to the performance of the sacrifice of the mass. Only through the consecration of the bishop can a Christian receive the authority to celebrate the Eucharist. Protestant doctrine was directed against an interpretation of the priestly office understood solely in the light of the sacrifice of the mass, and stressed in contrast the preeminence of the task of proclamation, to which it assigned the charge to administer the sacraments. The regional episcopal office, with its functions of leadership and pastoral superintendence, was not considered by the Reformation to be fundamentally different from the commission given to the minister. This had consequences in the conviction about the legality of an ordination of ministers by ministers, at least in the sense of an emergency regulation, when the Protestant congregations required clergy and not enough priests who had been consecrated by bishops were available. A proper call or ordination, which brought out the fact that the ministry originated with Jesus Christ (over against delegation by the congregation), was required by the Reformation as a matter of course.

Fundamentally speaking, there was more common ground with regard to the doctrine of the ministry in the period of the Reformation than is generally realized today. It was never disputed that the ministry originated with Jesus Christ and that the necessary ordination took place through the church, in the succession of the apostles. There is agreement today in the rejection of the worldly jurisdiction of bishops and about their concentration on their spiritual and ecclesiastical tasks. Earlier antitheses, with their one-sided stresses on both sides, have also been softened by two developments. On the one hand, the Second Vatican Council, in describing the priestly office in the light of the episcopal office and as participation in that office, has emphatically stressed the fundamental and preeminent importance of the task of proclamation. On the other hand, in the ecumenical dialogue agreement begins to emerge about the link between the concept of sacrifice and the Eucharist, in the sense of a participation of celebrant and congregation in the one sacrifice of Christ. It must therefore be asked whether such an agreement does not make it possible for the Protestant churches to dispense with their objection to a priestly interpretation of the ministry (which was oriented toward a notion of sacrifice which was rejected), now that the fundamental and preeminent importance of the task of proclamation for the interpretation of the ministerial office has been unequivocally stressed. The churches of the Reformation for their part, according to the evidence of their Confessions and also their contemporary practice, do not see the ministerial office as merely a preaching office, but always as at the same time an office for the administration of the sacraments.

For the churches of the Reformation just as for the Roman Catholic Church, the sense that the individual local and regional churches belong together is of essential importance. The churches of the Reformation have hence for their part also realized the need for offices of leadership and pastoral oversight which are above the local congregations. The community of bishops, according to Roman Catholic doctrine, expresses the fact that every local church is a realization and representation of the one church of Jesus Christ, while yet being woven together with the other local churches. In the history of the church this community of bishops has been orientated toward certain congregations that have a particularly prominent position because of their apostolic origin. Among these the congregation in Rome and its bishop has had a special prominence since ancient times.

The Reformation did not fundamentally reject the possibility of a supreme office of leadership in the church, although the Reformers were not able to see the primacy of the bishop of Rome as a divine ordinance founded on the Lord's commission to Peter. Their rejection of the papacy, to the point of terming the pope Antichrist, must be viewed as a reaction to the condemnation of the Protestant doctrine of justification by Rome, in which the Reformers saw the rejection of the gospel itself. However, through the softening of antitheses in the doctrine of justification and in the doctrine of the Eucharist, as well as through the changes in the relationship of the churches to one another in general, the reasons for the Reformation judgment about the papacy now no longer apply; and the Protestant churches can accept that to term the pope the Antichrist, who sets his own authority above the Scripture and the gospel, is not appropriate. As a polemical assertion this reproach was not justified even under the conditions of the sixteenth century, if the way in which the papacy interpreted itself is precisely evaluated. Today both churches have cause to look back with shame to the history of mutual vilification, which found expression in this term for the papacy and in corresponding judgments about the Reformation. Protestant Christians too can understand today that in the Roman Catholic Church the papal office is understood and lived as a ministry for the unity of the church, a unity which has its foundation in the gospel. The critical judgment of the Reformation about the pope can find no application to a papacy whose office is subordinated to the gospel.

III

The Joint Ecumenical Commission has received with thanks the study which the Ecumenical Study Group of Protestant and Catholic Theologians has submitted on the subject of the sixteenth-century condemnations. It is laying this important document before the German Episcopal Conference and the Council of the Evangelical Church in Germany, with the request that it be examined and that practical consequences should be drawn from it for the judgment of the churches about one another. The struggles of the Reformation period, in the dispute about the truth, led to different, indeed antithetical, forms of church doctrine. In the acrimony of the dispute, condemnations were uttered which, according to our now commonly acquired recognition, were even at that time the expression of an incomplete understanding of the facts on both sides. At all events, they no longer apply to today's partner. This means that the conditions have been created for clearing away severe hindrances which stand in the way of a closer community between the divided churches and for taking joint steps which can lead to a further strengthening and cementing of ecumenical community.

The Joint Ecumenical Commission therefore asks the leading bodies of the churches involved to express in binding form that the sixteenth-century condemnations no longer apply to today's partner, inasmuch as its doctrine is not determined by the error which the condemnation wished to avert. Even where no full consensus has as yet been achieved in all the questions involved, the ancient antitheses have been softened, so that an abandonment of the once-usual contradiction is enjoined, at least under certain conditions. An initial partial, if not as yet complete, consensus is a spur toward finding still further agreement, in order then to be able to express full unity in our common faith. Polemical and inapplicable terminology used against the others and their doctrine must be retracted and avoided in the future.

The churches, their teachers of theology, and their clergy should interpret the Protestant Confessions and the statements of the magisterium of the Roman Catholic Church in the light of the recognitions formulated here. Ancient denominational prejudices and antitheses which were unjustly maintained may count as having been surmounted; and this means a radical change in the attitude of one church to the other. As Christians belonging to the two churches encounter one another, they learn how to see the heritage of the other church in a new way. They direct their gaze toward the goal before them, which is to arrive at full community. On the road to that goal, new and great tasks must still indeed be mastered. The decisions which were taken in the era of separation have to be absorbed in a positive way. The dogmas of the Roman Catholic Church which were formulated in the nineteenth and the twentieth century must be investigated with a view to what they really say and mean, and the consequences for the whole understanding of faith and the church. Developments in Protestantism, which have led away from the binding character of the original Confessions, require understanding and have to be worked through. Faith as it is lived every day in both churches has to be taken into account.

If both churches take the next steps recommended in these studies, and declare in binding form that the condemnatory judgments pronounced in the sixteenth century can no longer be reiterated today, they will be on the way to a fellowship which will bind them ever closer together; and they will be emphasizing their conviction that what binds us together is stronger than that which still divides us.

Maria Laach, 26 October, 1985

The Protestant and Catholic Chairmen of the
Joint Ecumenical Commission:

Eduard Lohse   Paul-Werner Scheele

The above "Final Report of the Joint Ecumenical Commission on the Examination of the Sixteenth-Century Condemnations" was presented to the public at a press conference in Bonn by the two chairmen, Bishop Eduard Lohse and Bishop Paul-Werner Scheele.

NOTES

EDITORS' PREFACE

1. Cf. *Papst Johannes Paul II. in Deutschland*, Verlautbarungen des Apostolischen Stuhls 25, ed. by the Secretariat of the German Episcopal Conference (Bonn, n.d.), p. 78.

2. The Ecumenical Study Group of Protestant and Catholic Theologians, convened for the first time on 2/3 April, 1946, in Werl, Westphalia, originally consisted of two groups of Protestant and Roman Catholic theologians who had been invited by the then Bishop of Oldenburg, Professor Wilhelm Stählin, and the later Cardinal Lorenz Jaeger, Archbishop of Paderborn (hence briefly known as the Jaeger-Stählin Group). It was not until 1968 that this body was given its present form as the Ecumenical Study Group of Protestant and Catholic Theologians (Ökumenischer Arbeitskreis evangelischer und katholischer Theologen). Up to 1986, forty-eight working conferences had been held, each lasting three to four days. For an interim report, cf. *Pro Veritate. Ein theologischer Dialog. Festgabe für L. Jaeger und W. Stählin*, ed. E. Schlink and H. Volk (Münster and Kassel, 1963). For basic information, cf. also the preface contributed by the two chairmen, Bishop Hermann Kunst and Hermann Cardinal Volk, to *Glaubensbekenntnis und Kirchengemeinschaft* (Freiburg and Göttingen, 1982), pp. 5f., this being vol. 1 of the series Dialog der Kirchen published by the Ecumenical Study Group.

3. On the preparation, consultation, theological discussion, and reception of the Leuenberg Agreement (or Concord), cf. the comprehensive account by E. Schieffer, *Von Schauenburg nach Leuenberg. Entstehung und Bedeutung der Konkordie reformatorischer Kirchen in Europa*, Konfessionskundliche und kontroverstheologische Studien XLVIII (Paderborn, 1983). There cf. also the documentary appendix.

4. The formulation chosen in another connection by the Ecumenical Study Committee of the VELKD, *Die Verwerfungen der Confessio Augustana und ihre gegenwärtige Bedeutung* (1980), sec. V, no. 16.

CHAPTER 1: INTRODUCTION

1. Cf. A. Lang, "Der Bedeutungswandel der Begriffe 'fides' und 'haeresis' und die dogmatische Wertung der Konzilsentscheidungen von Vienne und Trient," *Münchener theologische Zeitschrift* 4 (1953): 133–46; P. Fransen, "Reflexions sur l'anathème au Concil de Trente," *Ephemerides Theologicae Lovanienses* 29 (1953): 657–72, and idem, "Die Formel 'Si quis dixerit,'" *Scholastik* 25 (1950): 492–517; also H. Lennerz, "Notulae Tridentinae," *Gregorianum* 27 (1946): 136–42; and as summary survey of the research, A. Amato, *I pronunciamenti tridentini sulla necessità della confessione* (Rome, 1974), 128–40.

2. SD X.28: *BC* 615; cf. SD X.10: *BC* 612.

3. Pope Paul VI on the Council of Lyons of 1274 (cf. esp. *DS* 850): *AAS* 66 (1974): 620–25, esp. 623.

4. Ökumenischer Studienausschuss (Ecumenical Study Group) der VELKD, *Die Verwerfungen der CA und ihre gegenwärtige Bedeutung*, no. 4. Cf. no. 6/2 on the interpretation and the presuppositions of the opposite procedure adopted by the CA which "did not utter any anathemas against the opponents holding the old faith." Cf. here also no. 12.

5. Ibid., no. 16.

6. Cf. here *Confessio Augustana. Bekenntnis des einen Glaubens. Gemeinsame Untersuchung lutherischer und katholischer Theologen* (Paderborn and Frankfurt, 1980); also *Das katholisch-lutherische Gespräch über das Augsburger Bekenntnis. Dokumente 1977–1981*, ed. H. Meyer (Geneva, 1982) = LWF Report 10.

7. Among these documents the following deserve particular mention: *Report of the Joint Lutheran/Roman Catholic Study Commission on "The Gospel and the Church"* (Malta Report), published in *Worship* 46 (1972): 326–51, in *Lutheran World* 19 (1972): 259–73, and in H. Meyer and L. Vischer, eds., *Growth in Agreement: Reports and Agreed Statements of Ecumenical Conversations on a World Level* (New York: Paulist Press; Geneva: World Council of Churches, 1982); the text and position papers discussed over five years also appear in H. Meyer, ed., *Evangelium—Welt—Kirche. Schlussbericht und Referate der römisch-katholisch/evangelisch-lutherischen Studienkommission "Das Evangelium und die Kirche" 1967–1971* (1975); *The Presence of Christ in Church and World: Final Report of the Dialogue Between the World Alliance of Reformed Churches and the Secretariat for Promoting Christian Unity, 1970–77* (1977); *The Eucharist: Final Report of the Joint Roman Catholic–Lutheran Commission* (1978); *The Ministry in the Church: Final Report of the Joint Roman Catholic–Lutheran Commission* (1981); *Baptism, Eucharist and Ministry*, Faith and Order Paper No. 111, World Council of Churches [Lima text] (1982); G. Gassmann, ed., *Vom Dialog zur Gemeinschaft. Dokumente zum anglikanisch-lutherischen und anglikanisch-katholischen Gespräch* (1975); *Anglican-Roman Catholic International Commission, The Final Report (1982)*; *Bilaterale Arbeitsgruppe der Deutschen Bischofskonferenz und der Kirchenleitung der VELKD: Kirchengemeinschaft in Wort und Sakrament* (Paderborn and Hannover, 1984).

8. Malta Report (cf. n. 7 above) 17. Cf. Montreal sec. II, 45.

9. Cf. the commentary by J. Ratzinger on *DV* 8, *LThK* suppl. vol. II, 518ff.

10. Cf. A. Grillmeier, *LThK* suppl. vol. II, 537ff., on *DV* 12; he points out the relationship to the encyclical *Divino afflante Spiritu* of 1943 (cf. there esp. *DS* 3826ff.).

11. *DV* 12: "Cuncta enim haec, de ratione interpretandi Scripturam, Ecclesiae iudicio ultime subsunt, quae verbi Dei servandi et interpretandi divino fungitur mandato et ministerio" ["For, of course, all that has been said about the manner of interpreting Scripture is ultimately subject to the judgment of the church which exercises the divinely conferred commission and ministry of watching over and interpreting the Word of God"]. Cf. *DS* 1507.

12. Thus Luther says particularly of the "external clarity" of Scripture, which serves to strengthen those whose faith is weak and to confute opponents, that it is a matter for the preaching office ("in verbi ministerio posita": WA 18, 609, 5). Cf. WA 18, 653, 24f., where, talking about judging the spirits and opinions of all men ("spiritus et dogmata omnium")—a judgment that is founded on Scripture—Luther writes: "Hoc iudicium est publici ministerii in verbo et officii externi" ["This judgment belongs to the public ministry of the Word and to the outward office"].

13. According to the introduction to the Formula of Concord ("A Summary Epitome...."), the Holy Scriptures are "the only judge, rule, and norm" according to which all doctrines are to be judged (Epit. 3, 7: *BC* 465). The creeds (symbols) and "other writings" are no more than "witnesses and expositions of the faith, setting forth how at various times *(singulis temporibus)* the Holy Scriptures were understood by contemporaries in the church of God with reference to controverted articles, and how contrary teachings were rejected and condemned" (ibid., 8: *BC* 465).

14. FC SD "Articles concerning which there has been a controversy" *(BC* 506, 14ff.).

15. Cf. here also *Verbindliches Lehren der Kirche heute: Arbeitsbericht aus dem Deutschen Ökumenischen Studienausschuss und Texte der Faith-and-Order Konsultation Odessa 1977* (Frankfurt, 1978), *Ökumenischen Rundschau, Beiheft* 33.

CHAPTER 2: JUSTIFICATION

1. "*Credimus,* docemus atque confitemur peccatum originis non esse levem, sed tam profundam humanae naturae corruptionem, quae nihil sanum, nihil incorruptum in corpore et anima hominis atque adeo in interioribus et exterioribus viribus eius reliquit."

"Credimus, quod hominis non renati intellectus, cor et voluntas in rebus spiritualibus et divinis ex propriis naturalibus viribus prorsus nihil intelligere, credere, amplecti, cogitare, velle, inchoare, perficere, agere, operari aut cooperari possint. . . . Inde adeo naturale liberum arbitrium ratione corruptarum virium et naturae suae depravatae, duntaxat ad ea, quae Deo displicent et adversantur, activum et efficax est" (Epit. I, Affirmative Theses III: *BC* 467; SD II.7: *BC* 521).

2. "Liberum arbitrium post peccatum res est de solo titulo—immo titulus sine re—et dum facit quod in se est, peccat mortaliter" (WA 1, 354, 5–6; cf. 18, 756, 7; the intensification in the inserted phrase is a response to the papal rejection: WA 7, 146, 3–5).

3. "Si quis liberum hominis arbitrium post Adae peccatum amissum et exstinctum esse dixerit, aut rem esse de solo titulo, immo titulum sine re, figmentum denique a satana invectum in Ecclesiam: an. s.

"Si quis dixerit, gehennae metum, per quem ad misericordiam Dei de peccatis dolendo confugimus vel a peccando abstinemus, peccatum esse aut peccatores peiores facere: an. s." (Council of Trent, Decree on Justification, cans. 5, 7, 8: *DS* 1555, 1557–1558; NR* 823, 825f.; Deferrari 258f., 815, 817, 818).

4. "Clare enim appellant [sc. testimonia Augustini et Pauli] concupiscentiam peccatum, quod tamen his, qui sunt in Christo, non imputatur, etsi res sit natura digna morte, ubi non condonatur" (Apol. 2.40: *BC* 105).

5. "Reiicimus ergo et damnamus dogma illud, quo asseritur . . . concupiscentias pravas non esse peccatum, sed concreatas naturae conditiones et proprietates quasdam essentiales, aut defectus illos et malum ingens a nobis paulo ante commemoratum non esse peccatum, propter quod homo Christo non insertus sit filius irae" (FC, Epit. I.11–12: *BC* 467; cf. SD I.17–18: *BC* 511).

6. "Manere autem in baptizatis concupiscentiam vel fomitem, haec sancta Synodus fatetur et sentit; quae cum ad agonem relicta sit, nocere non consentientibus et viriliter per Christi Jesu gratiam repugnantibus non valet. Quin immo 'qui legitime certaverit, coronabitur' [2 Tim. 2:5]. Hanc concupiscentiam, quam aliquando Apostolus 'peccatum' [cf. Rom. 6:12ff.; 7:7, 14–20] appellat, sancta Synodus declarat, Ecclesiam catholicam numquam intellexisse, peccatum appellari, quod vere et proprie in renatis peccatum sit, sed quia ex peccato est et ad peccatum inclinat. Si quis autem contrarium senserit: an. s." (Council of Trent, Decree on Original Sin, can. 5, pt. II: *DS* 1515; NR* 357; Deferrari 246f., 792).

7. "Sic humana voluntas in medio posita est, ceu iumentum, si insederit Deus, vult et vadit quo vult Deus. . . . Si insederit Satan, vult et vadit, quo vult Satan, nec est in eius arbitrio, ad utrum sessorem currere aut eum quaerere." (*De servo arbitrio*, WA 18, 635, 17ff.; *LW* 33, 65f.).

8. "Ad conversionem suam . . . prorsus nihil conferre potest (sc. homo). Et hac in parte multo est deterior lapide aut trunco, quia repugnat verbo et voluntati Dei, donec Deus eum a morte peccati resuscitet, illuminet atque renovet" (SD II.59: *BC* 532).

9. "Si quis dixerit, liberum hominis arbitrium a Deo motum et excitatum nihil cooperari assentiendo Deo excitanti atque vocanti, quo ad obtinendam iustificationis gratiam se disponat ac praeparet, neque posse dissentire, si velit, sed velut inanime quoddam nihil omnino agere mereque passive se habere: an. s." (Council of Trent, Decree on Justification, can. 4: *DS* 1554; NR* 822; Deferrari 258, 814).

10. "Cur non exponunt [sc. adversarii] hic gratiam misericordiam Dei erga nos?" (Apol. 4.381: *BC* 165 [trans. slightly altered]).

11. "Gratiam accipio hic proprie pro favore dei, sicut debet, non pro qualitate animi, ut nostri recentiores docuerunt" (*Antilatomus*, WA 8, 106, 10; *LW* 32, 227).

12. "Si quis dixerit, homines iustificari vel sola imputatione iustitiae Christi, vel sola peccatorum remissione, exclusa gratia et caritate, quae in cordibus eorum per Spiritum Sanctum diffundatur atque illis inhaereat, aut etiam gratiam qua iustificamur, esse tantum favorem Dei: an. s." (Decree on Justification, can. 11: *DS* 1561; NR* 829; Deferrari 259, 821).

13. "Quod homines non possint iustificari coram Deo propriis viribus, meritis aut operibus, sed gratis iustificentur propter Christum per fidem, cum credunt se in gratiam recipi et peccata remitti propter Christum, qui sua morte pro nostris peccatis satisfecit. Hanc fidem imputat Deus pro iustitia coram ipso, Rom. 3 et 4" (CA 4.1–3: *BC* 30).

14. AS II.1: *BC* 292.

15. "Si quis dixerit, sola fide impium iustificari, ita ut intelligat, nihil aliud requiri, quo ad iustificationis gratiam consequendam cooperetur, et nulla ex parte necesse esse, eum suae voluntatis motu praeparari atque disponi: an. s.

"Si quis dixerit, fidem iustificantem nihil aliud esse quam fiduciam divinae misericordiae peccata remittentis propter Christum, vel eam fiduciam solam esse, qua iustificamur: an. s." (Decree on Justification, cans. 9, 12: *DS* 1559, 1562; NR* 827, 830; Deferrari 259, 819, 822).

16. "Cur dixit Christus: Quorum remiseritis peccata, remittuntur eis, nisi quod non sunt remissa ulli, nisi remittente sacerdote credat sibi remitti? . . . Non etiam sufficit remissio peccati et gratiae donatio, sed oportet etiam credere esse remissum" (*Resolutiones zu den Ablassthesen, Conclusio* VII, WA 1, 543, 14–15, 22–24; cf. *DS* 1460).

17. "Dixi, neminem iustificari posse nisi per fidem, sic scilicet, ut necesse sit, eum certa fide credere sese iustificari et nullo modo dubitare, quod gratiam consequatur. Si enim dubitat et incertus est, iam non iustificatur, sed evomit gratiam" (*Acta Augustana*, WA 2, 13, 7–9).

18. "Sola fides, quae intuetur in promissionem et sentit ideo certo statuendum esse, quod Deus ignoscat, quia Christus non sit frustra mortuus etc., vincit terrores peccati et mortis. Si quis dubitat, utrum remittantur sibi peccata, contumelia afficit Christum, cum peccatum suum iudicat maius aut efficacius esse, quam mortem et promissionem Christi" (Apol. 4.148f.: *BC* 127).

19. "Si quis dixerit, omni homini ad remissionem peccatorum assequendam necessarium esse, ut credat certo et absque ulla haesitatione propriae infirmitatis et indispositionis, peccata sibi esse remissa: an. s.

"Si quis dixerit, hominem a peccatis absolvi ac iustificari ex eo, quod se absolvi ac iustificari certo credat, aut neminem vere esse iustificatum, nisi qui credit se esse iustificatum, et hac sola fide absolutionem et iustificationem perfici: an. s." (Decree on Justification, cans. 13, 14: *DS* 1563, 1564; NR* 831, 832; Deferrari 259, 823, 824).

20. "Dicunt enim se de condigno mereri gratiam et vitam aeternam. Haec est simpliciter impia et vana fiducia" (Apol. 4.146: *BC* 127).

21. "[Iustitiarii] gratiam et vitam aeternam non volunt gratis accipere ab eo [sc. Deo], sed illa mereri suis operibus" (*Lectures on Galatians* 1531 [1535], WA 40 I, 224, 30–32; *LW* 26, 127).

22. "Impie philosophantur contra Theologiam . . . qui dicunt, hominem faciendo, quod in se est, posse mereri gratiam Dei et vitam" (*Disputatio de homine*, WA 39 I, 176, 21–23).

23. "Si quis dixerit, iustificatum peccare, dum intuitu aeternae mercedis bene operatur: an. s.

"Si quis dixerit, hominis iustificati bona opera ita esse dona Dei, ut non sint etiam bona ipsius iustificati merita, aut ipsum iustificatum bonis operibus, quae ab eo per Dei gratiam et Jesu Christi meritum (cuius vivum membrum est) fiunt, non vere mereri augmentum gratiae, vitam aeternam et ipsius vitae aeternae (si tamen in gratia decesserit) consecutionem, atque etiam gloriae augmentum: an. s." (Decree on Justification, cans. 31, 32: *DS* 1581, 1582; NR* 849, 850; Deferrari 261, 841, 842).

24. *Justification by Faith*, Lutherans and Catholics in Dialogue VII, ed. H. G. Anderson et al. (Minneapolis, 1985), *Common Statement*, §156.1 (p. 71).

25. Cf. CA, Conclusion of pt. I: *BC* 47f.; AS, Conclusion of pt. I: *BC* 291f.; Council of Trent, Decree on Justification, cans. 1–3, in association with cap. 1–4.

26. *DS* 1555, 1557f.

27. SD I, rejections 1, 3–7: *BC* 511f.; cf. Epit. I.11, 13–17: *BC* 467f.; SD II, rejections 1–3, 6–8: *BC* 535ff.; cf. Epit. II, rejections 2ff.: *BC* 471f.; cf. also HC 2, 5–8, 12–14.

28. AS III.I: *BC* 302f.; cf. Apol. 2.8: *BC* 101f.

29. Cf. Apol. 2.7, 14, 24: *BC* 101ff.

30. "Quod [peccatum originale] tollatur quoad formale, sed maneat quoad materiale" (cf. E. Iserloh, ed., *Confessio Augustana und Confutatio* [Münster, 1980], 364; cf. Apol. 2.27ff.: *BC* 103ff., with the confirmatory quotations from Aquinas and Bonaventure).

31. "De quo quidem morbo in renatis inter nos convenit, quod maneat materiale peccatum originis, formali sublato per baptismum. Materiale autem vocamus peccati, quod fiat ex peccato, quod ad peccatum inclinet, et ipsam humanae naturae depravationem, quae quod ad rem ipsam attinet, est quiddam repugnans legi Dei, quemadmodum Paulus quoque peccatum appellat. Ad eandem rationem in scholis compendio doceri solet, manere in baptizato originalis peccati materiale, formale vero, quod reatus est, auferri" (*CR* IV, 32; 86. Cf. Eck, *Apologia* 154).

32. *BC* 536; cf. Epit. II: *BC* 471f.

33. Cf. Apol. 2.9–11, 17f.; 4.287–97, 316–18: *BC* 102f.; 150–53, 156; and already Apol. 2.8–13: *BC* 101f.

34. *BC* 548; cf. Epit. II: *BC* 46ff.

35. *BC* 550; cf. Epit. III: *BC* 472ff.; cf. HC 56–60, 86, 115, 126.

36. Cf. *DV* 5 as well as the Declaration on Religious Liberty *Dignitatis humanae* 10.

37. "Et rursus, quoties nos de fide loquimur, intelligi volumus obiectum, scilicet misericordiam promissam" (Apol. 4.55: *BC* 114).

38. "Et quia sola haec fides accipit remissionem peccatorum, et reddit nos acceptos Deo, et affert spiritum sanctum: rectius vocari gratia gratum faciens poterat, quam effectus sequens, videlicet dilectio" (Apol. 4.116: *BC* 123).

39. "Remissio peccatorum fit per gratiam gratum facientem et fidem formaliter" (*Acta der Sieben Vorordneten*, Öster. Nationalbibliothek Cod. 11817, Fol. 174ᵛ–175ʳ; cf. Iserloh, *Confessio*, 366f., n. 110).

40. "Si ipsi fidem formata vocarent veram et Theologicam vel, ut Paulus, α ʼνυπόκριτον, quam Deus fidem vocat, nihil me offenderet haec ipsorum glossa. Tunc enim fides non distingueretur contra charitatem, sed contra vanam opinionem fidei, quo modo et nos distinguimus inter fidem fictam et veram" (WA 40 I, 421, 17–21).

41. AS III, 3.42: *BC* 309f.; cf. also CA 12, 7f.: *BC* 35.

42. Cf. WA 56, 298, 24ff.; 8, 114, 21f.

43. Cf. Decree on Justification, cap. 9, 12: *DS* 1533f., 1540.

44. But cf. SD III. 30; IV. 12; Epit. III. 12: *BC* 544, 553, 474; cf. also Apol. 4.148f.: *BC* 127 (cf. I.6 above).

45. Cans. 3, 4 of the Decree on Original Sin: *DS* 1513f.; cans. 7, 9 of the Decree on Justification: *DS* 1557, 1559, in association with cap. 6: *DS* 1526.

46. Cans. 14, 29: *DS* 1564, 1579.

47. CA 12, 13: *BC* 34–36.

48. Apol. 12.41, 98–101; 13.4: *BC* 187, 197, 211.

49. Decree on Justification, cap. 14 and can. 29: *DS* 1542f., 1579; can. 1 on the sacrament of penance: *DS* 1701.

50. LC IV.6, Baptism, 80–82: *BC* 446; and even earlier *De captivitate Babylonica*, WA 6, 529, 22–34.

51. CA 12.7: *BC* 35; Apol. 4.219, 222: *BC* 137, 137f.; AS III, 3.42: *BC* 309f.

52. CA 12.8: *BC* 35.

53. LC IV.6, Baptism, 82: *BC* 446.

54. "Non recusamus, tres partes paenitentiae ponere, scilicet contritionem quae significat terrores incussos conscientiae agnito peccato, Confessionem, sed in hac oportet respicere absolutionem et illi credere. Non enim remittitur peccatum, nisi credatur, quod propter meritum passionis Christi remittatur. Tertia pars est satisfactio videlicet digni fructus paenitentiae. Sed propter satisfactiones concorditer sentimus, non remitti peccata, quoad culpam; uerum de hoc nondum conuenit, utrum necessariae sint satisfactiones ad remissionem peccati, quoad poenam" (*Acta der Sieben Vorordneten*, Öster. Nationalbibliothek Cod. 11817, Fol. 175ʳᵛ; cf. Iserloh, *Confessio*, 368, n. 116).

55. "Solum est verbalis et non realis differentia," "expertise" proffered by Eck, Giessen Univ. Library, Cod. 296, Fol. 117ᵛ; cf. Iserloh, *Confessio*, 368, n. 117.

56. K. E. Förstemann, *Urkundenbuch zu der Geschichte des Reichstags zu Augsburg im Jahre 1530*, vol. II (Halle, 1835), 228; cf. Iserloh, *Confessio*, 369, n. 123; cf. Förstemann, op. cit., II:292; Iserloh, *Confessio*, 371, n. 136.

57. "Nudum ministerium pronuntiandi, et declarandi, remissa esse peccata confitenti, modo tantum credat se esse absolutum."

58. "Ad instar actus iudicialis . . . velut a iudice sententia pronuntiatur": *DS* 1685; NR* 654. Cf. Deferrari 277, 902.

59. Cf. Thomas Aquinas, *STh*, Suppl. 9, 2.

60. Cf. can. 978, 1 *CIC* 1983 = unaltered can. 888, 1 *CIC* 1917, taken from the Rit. Rom. 1614, tit. 4, cap. 1 n. 2.

61. Cf. *Ordo Paenitentiae*, 2 Dec., 1973 = *Die Feier der Busse*, Studienausgabe 1974, Einführung 10.

62. Cf. *DS* 1709 and *Reconciliatio et Paenitentia* no. 31, II, with reference to Luke 5:31f; 9:2; Isa. 54:4f., Augustine and the Ordo Paenitentiae.

63. Apol. 12.117, 118: *BC* 199. "Satisfactio est operatio laboriosa . . . ad placandam divinam offensam."

64. Cf. esp. *LG* 11, 28; Apostolic Constitutions *Paenitemini* of 17 Feb., 1966, and *Indulgentiarum doctrina* of 1 Jan., 1967, n. 4.

65. E.g., CA 11: *BC* 66; CA 25: *BC* 61ff.; Apol. 11.5: *BC* 181; SmC, Confession and Absolution: *BC* 349ff.; probably also LC, Confession, 13: *BC* 458.

66. Cf., e.g., *Inst*. III, 1, 22; 4, 14; IV, 11 passim; HC 83–85.

67. Cf. here the Decree on Justification can. 29 in conjunction with cap. 14; Decree on Penance can. 2 in conjunction with cap. 2; *DS* 1579 in conjunction with 1542f.; 1702 in conjunction with 1671f.

68. "Regnum meretur filios, non filii regnum," WA 18, 694, 27, picking up Matt. 25:34.

69. Cf. the word index to the Second Vatican Council under the catchword "merit," in the light of *LG* 14, middle section.

70. Cf. WA 30 II, 670; HC 86 and pt. III passim.

CHAPTER 3: THE SACRAMENTS

1. CA 13: *BC* 35f.; Apol. 13.5: *BC* 211f.: *testimonium* (witness), *verbum visibile* (visible word).

2. Cf. CA 4.2: *BC* 30; 5.3: *BC* 31; Apol. 4.381: *BC* 165; cf. also Justification, pp. 47f. above.

3. *DS* 1605; see p. 79f. below and esp. 50f. above.

4. *DS* 1655; see Eucharist/Lord's Supper 4.2, pp. 111ff. below.

5. Cf. Eucharist/Lord's Supper 1 (The Sacrifice of Jesus Christ in the Lord's Supper) and 4.3 (Masses for the Dead).

6. See Calvin's comment in *Inst*. IV, 14, 5–13, which is clearly directed against Zwingli and in part also against Bucer.

7. The sacraments of baptism, penance, and consecration (ordination) will not be treated separately in the following text since they are considered elsewhere; cf. pp. 56ff., 150f., and the subject index.

8. Cf., e.g., CA 13 (Ed. pr.): *BSLK* 68; CA 24.28f., 30ff.; *BC* 59f.; Apol. 13.18ff.: *BC* 213f.; Apol. 24.11f., 14, 27ff., 48, 60: *BC* 251, 251, 254f., 258, 260; AS II.2: *BC* 293ff.

9. Cf. Apol. 4.210: *BC* 136, with the reference to Biel.

10. Cf. CA 24.21, 25ff.: *BC* 58; Apol. 24.56ff., 62f.: *BC* 259f.; cf. Confessio Scoticana (The Scots Confession) 22; HC 80.

11. Cf. *DS* 1740 (NR 597): "Sacrificium, quo cruentum illud semel in cruce peragendum repraesentaretur eiusque memoria in finem usque saeculi permaneret, atque illius salutaris virtus in remissionem eorum, quae a nobis quotidie committuntur, peccatorum applicaretur" ["A sacrifice . . . whereby that bloody sacrifice once to be completed on the cross might be represented, and the memory of it remain even to the end of the world and its saving grace be applied to the remission of those sins which we daily commit"].

12. Present-day theology explains this aspect as follows: the eucharistic Real Presence always means at the same time the presence of the exalted One as the master of the feast ("commemorative personal presence") and the presence of his sacrifice on the cross ("actual presence"). Cf. the Ökumenischer Arbeitskreis evangelischer und katholischer Theologen (Ecumenical Study Group of Protestant and Catholic Theologians), "Das Opfer Jesu Christi und die Kirche. Abschliessender Bericht," in *Das Opfer Jesu Christi und seine Gegenwart in der Kirche*, ed. K. Lehmann and E. Schlink (Freiburg and Göttingen, 1983), Dialog der Kirchen 3, 215–38. These 4.3.2, p. 234 (from now on cited as *Opferthesen*).

13. *Eucharist*, thesis 56.

14. Cf. *Opferthesen*, 3.3.2.

15. Ibid., 3.4.2.

16. Cf. Apol. 24.53ff.: *BC* 259f.; FC Epit. VII.8: *BC* 482; SD VII. 74: *BC* 583.

17. Cf. *Opferthesen*, 4.2.3.

18. Ibid., 4.2.2.

19. Ibid., 4.4.3.

20. Cf. Apol. 24.14f.: *BC* 251f.

21. Vatican II's Constitution on the Liturgy entitles chap. II *De sacrosancto Eucharistiae mysterio* ("The Most Sacred Mystery of the Eucharist") and chap. III *De ceteris sacramentis* ("The Other Sacraments"). The new *CIC* treats *De sanctissima Eucharistia* ("The Most Holy Eucharist"), like the code of 1917, in Title III of the section *De sacramentis* ("The Sacraments"), but it no longer distinguishes between *De sacrae Missae sacrificio* ("The Sacrifice of the Holy Mass") (cap. I) and *De sanctissimo eucharistiae sacramento* ("The Most Holy Sacrament of the Eucharist") (cap. II), but unites the two in cap. I under *De eucharistica celebratione* ("The Celebration of the Eucharist").

22. Cf. Lima, Eucharist 26 and 27.

23. Cf. esp. Apol. 24.16ff., 68ff.: *BC* 252ff., 261ff.

24. The anamnesis texts in the new eucharistic prayers, which follow the Lord's words, are all concerned to make it clear that the sacrifice of the church means that the church enters into the sacramentally present, unrepeatable sacrifice of the cross (cf. already the characteristic DE TUIS DONIS AC DATIS in the first eucharistic prayer). No new sacrifice is offered from below

upward, as it were. What is brought is Christ's sacramentally present sacrifice on the cross, laid in the hands of the church through Christ's command that it be repeated in remembrance.

25. Cf. *CT* V, 869, 16f.; VII/1, 111, 12; cf. *CT* XIII, 123–130.

26. Cf. *CT* V, 869, 16.

27. CA 10: *BC* 34; Apol. 10: *BC* 179f.; cf. AS III.6: *BC* 311; FC Epit. VII.2ff., 6f., 15f., 26ff.: *BC* 481f., 482, 483f., 485, par SD; Wittenberg Article of 1536, ed. G. Mentz (1968), 48.

28. "Mysteriis . . . quodammodo annexa" (*Inst.* IV, 17, 5).

29. Cf., e.g., Calvin's balanced judgment on the dispute between Luther and Zwingli in his *Petit Traicté de la Saincte Cene de Nostre Seigneur Iesus Christ* of 1541.

30. Cf. *Inst.* IV, 17, 30.

31. "Cum pane et vino vere exhibeantur corpus et sanguis Christi vescentibus in coena Domini" (*BSLK* 65, 45f.).

32. Cf. *Inst.* IV, 17, 33.

33. Leun. C. §18.

34. *The Presence of Christ in Church and World*, nos. 70, 91, 83 in Meyer/Vischer.

35. Lima, Eucharist 14.

36. "Reiicimus atque damnamus unanimi consensu . . . Papisticam transsubstantiationem, cum videlicet in papatu docetur panem et vinum in sacra coena substantiam atque naturalem suam essentiam amittere et ita annihilari atque elementa illa ita in Christi corpus transmutari, ut praeter externas species nihil de iis reliquum maneat" ["We unanimously reject and condemn . . . the papistic transubstantiation, when it is taught in the papacy that the bread and wine in the Holy Supper lose their substance and natural essence and are thus annihilated, in such a way that they are transmuted into the body of Christ and that only the exterior appearance remains"] (FC Epit. VII.21f.: *BC* 484; FC SD VII.108: *BC* 588; cf. FC SD VII.14: *BC* 571f.; FC SD VII.35: *BC* 575).

37. Cf. A. Gerken, *Theologie der Eucharistie* (Munich, 1973), 80f., 86.

38. "Et comperimus non tantum romanam ecclesiam affirmare corporalem praesentiam Christi, sed idem et nunc sentire et olim sensisse graecam ecclesiam. Id enim testatur canon missae apud illos, in quo aperte orat sacerdos, ut *mutato pane* ipsum corpus Christi fiat. Et Vulgarius, scriptor ut nobis videtur non stultus, diserte inquit, panem non tantum figuram esse, sed vere in carnem *mutari*. Et longa sententia est Cyrilli in Johannem cap. 15, in qua docet, Christum corporaliter nobis exhiberi in coena" ["We know that not only the Roman Church affirms the bodily presence of Christ, but that the Greek Church has taken and still takes this position. Evidence for this is their canon of the Mass, in which the priest clearly prays that the bread may be changed and become the very body of Christ. And Vulgarius, who seems to us to be a sensible writer, says distinctly that 'the bread is not merely a figure but is truly

changed into flesh.' There is a long exposition of John 15 in Cyril which teaches that Christ is offered to us bodily in the Supper"] (Apol. 10.2:*BC* 179). Cf. also Calvin, *Inst.* IV, 17, 14; cf. Luther, WA 2, 794, 12; 8, 435, 1; 8, 438, 3; 30 I, 122, 20f.; 38, 248, 28 (cf. V. Vajta, *Die Theologie des Gottesdienstes bei Luther,* 2nd ed. (Göttingen, 1954), 182–95; Religious colloquy at Regensburg, 1541, Protestantes de Transsubstantiatione: "Hanc. *conversionem* declarari vellemus. Nos enim adfirmamus, corpus vere praesens esse, *converti* autem seu *mutari* panem *mutatione mystica*, id est, qua iam vera fit exhibitio praesentis corporis post consecrationem. Et intellegimus *mutationem* mysticam, non tantum significativam, sed eam, qua corpus Christi fit praesens" ["We wish this to be declared *a conversion*. For we affirm that the true body is present, but that the bread is *converted* or *changed* in a *mystical change.* . . . And we understand a mystical *change* . . . [to be] of such a kind that the body of Christ is present"] (*CR* IV, 263; cf. *CR* IV, 264: "*Non est conversio physica*" ["It is not a physical conversion"]: Martin Chemnitz, *Examen Concilii Tridentini* (pars II, locus IV, sectio IV, 20: "Veteres dicunt in Eucharistia fieri *mutationem seu conversionem* panis et vini . . . nos *mutationem Sacramentalem* intelligimus" ["The ancients say that in the Eucharist there is a change or conversion of the bread and wine . . . we understand a *sacramental change*"].

39. Cf. H. Jorissen, *Die Entfaltung der Transsubstantiationslehre bis zum Beginn der Hochscholastik* (Münster, 1965).

40. "Ore et corde profiteor . . . panem et vinum, quae in altari ponuntur, post consecrationem *non solum sacramentum, sed etiam verum corpus* et sanguinem Domini nostri Jesu Christi esse, et *sensualiter, non solum sacramento, sed in veritate*, manibus sacerdotum tractari et frangi et fidelium dentibus atteri" ["I, Berengarius, in my heart believe and with my lips confess . . . that the bread and wine which are placed on the altar are after consecration not merely a sacrament but also the true body and blood of our Lord Jesus Christ, and are physically, not merely sacramentally but in truth, handled by the priest and broken and eaten by the faithful"] (*DS* 690).

41. Thomas Aquinas, *STh* III q. 75 a. 5 ad 2: "Intellectus, . . . cuius est proprium objectum substantia" ["Our intellect, which is properly concerned with the substance of a thing"]; *STh* III q. 76 a. 5 corp: "Dicendum quod . . . corpus Christi non est in hoc sacramento secundum proprium modum quantitatis dimensivae, sed magis secundum modum substantiae. . . . Unde nullo modo corpus Christi est in hoc sacramento localiter" ["As we have already said, Christ's body is not in this sacrament in the normal way as an extended body exists, but rather as if it were purely and simply substance]; *STh* III q. 80 a. 3 ad 3: "Dicendum quod etiamsi mus vel canis hostiam consecratam manducet, substantia corporis Christi non desinit esse sub speciebus, quamdiu species illae manent. . . . Nec hoc vergit in detrimentum dignitatis corporis Christi . . . praesertim cum mus aut canis non tangat ipsum corpus Christi secundum propriam speciem, sed solum secundum species sacramentales. . . . Nec tamen dicendum est quod animal brutum sacramentaliter corpus

Christi manducet quia non est natum uti eo ut sacramento" ["Even were a mouse or dog to eat the consecrated host, the substance of Christ's body would not cease to be under the species so long as the substance of bread remained. . . . This does not cast indignity on Christ's body . . . more especially since the mouse or dog does not touch Christ under his own species, but only under the sacramental species. . . . All the same, that the animal eats the body of Christ sacramentally should not be held, since it is not of a nature to use it as a sacrament"].

42. Calvin's rejection of the doctrine of transubstantiation was already mentioned above (2.1). Cf. also below, 2.2, Excursus, item 8: Three Forms of Doctrine.

43. AS III.6: *BC* 311.

44. Just because Luther is (sometimes) prepared to allow the doctrine of transubstantiation to stand as the opinion of a certain school (WA 6, 456; 6, 508; WA Br 10, 331; differently WA 10 II, 208, 31), he leaves no doubt about his view that the doctrine of transubstantiation must not be viewed as an article of faith. No one is guilty of a heresy because he believes that what is on the altar is true bread and true wine (WA 6, 456; 6, 508).

45. Cf. FC Epit. VII.22: *BC* 484; SD VII.107f: *BC* 588.

46. Cf. WA 6, 510, 13f.; H. Hilgenfeld, *Mittelalterlich-traditionelle Elemente in Luthers Abendmahlsschriften* (Zurich, 1971), 407, n. 73.

47. Apparently the rejection of the view that "the body and blood of Christ are *localiter*, that is, *spatially* enclosed in the bread" (FC SD VII.14: *BC* 571 [slightly altered]) is based on this misunderstanding of the classic doctrine, which explicitly excluded this *localis inclusio*.

48. FC SD VII.38: *BC* 576.

49. "Ut ipsum non includant, circumscribant aut comprehendant, sed potius, ut ipsas praesentes habeat, circumscribat et comprehendat" ["In such a way that they do not include, circumscribe, or comprehend him, but rather he has them present to himself, circumscribes and comprehends them"] (FC SD VII.101: *BC* 587 [slightly altered]).

50. Christ "alicubi esse potest divino et coelesti modo, secundum quem cum Deo una est persona" (FC VII.101: cf. *BC* 587).

51. Cf. FC SD VIII.9: *BC* 593.

52. Cf. FC SD VIII.12–25: *BC* 593ff.; cf. 27–42: *BC* 596ff.

53. FC SD VII.36.6: *BC* 575.

54. Cf. FC SD VII.36: *BC* 575.

55. It is certainly significant in this context that the decrees of the Second Vatican Council avoid the term "transubstantiation" in general, even where they speak indirectly about the presence of Jesus Christ in the Eucharist (cf. *SC* 5, 6, 7, 47, 48; *LG* 11; *UR* 15, 22). Even the detailed theological argumentation of the instruction *Eucharisticum mysterium* (25 May, 1967), which is frequently cited in Rit. Rom. *De S. Communione et de cultu mysterii eucharistici* (21 June, 1973), dispenses with the term "transubstantiation."

56. Cf. *CT* VII/1, 112, 8f.; 142, 6f.

57. Cf. J. Wohlmuth, *Realpräsenz und Transsubstantiation im Konzil von Trient* (Bern and Frankfurt, 1975), 273, 290.

58. J. Ratzinger, "Das Problem der Transsubstantiation und die Frage nach dem Sinn der Eucharistie," *ThQ* 147 (1967): 129–58, here 153.

59. A similar attempt has become familiar under the name of "trans-finalization." Paul VI's encyclical *Mysterium fidei* of 3 September, 1965, does not condemn trans-signification and trans-finalization in themselves, as interpretations; nor does it reject symbolism—"and no one denies its existence in the most holy Eucharist." It merely states that the Eucharist should not be exclusively interpreted in this way, without mentioning the change of substance (*AAS* 57 [1965]:55; Kaczynski no. 421).

60. Cf. F. Eisenbach, *Die Gegenwart Jesu Christi im Gottesdienst* (Mainz, 1982). On the restoration of the order thus given in the drafts of *SC* 7 and postconciliar documents (an order unfortunately altered for the worse in the final version of *SC* 7), cf. E. J. Lengeling, "Zur Aktualpräsenz Christi in der Liturgie," in *Mens concordet voci*. Festschrift for A.-G. Martimort (Paris, 1983), 518–31. The draft of *SC* 7 contains nothing about the presence in the elements, since it deals with the *action* of the Christ who is present.

61. *Eucharist* 16.

62. Lima, Eucharist 13; cf. *Eucharist* 15 and 16; The Presence of Christ in Church and World, 82–86 (cf. Meyer/Vischer).

63. FC SD VII.85ff.: BC 584ff.; cf. VII.14f.: *BC* 571f.; VII.107f.: *BC* 588).

64. We do not wish to conceal here that the Council of Trent's decree on the Eucharist, cap. 5 (*DS* 1644), interprets the jubilation of the Corpus Christi procession as TRIUMPHUS DE HAERESI (triumph over heresy). It was thus partly responsible for the polemical undertone which belonged to this procession for so long. The fact that this undertone is hardly ever heard on either side today is one remarkable result of the ecumenical climate of opinion.

65. The *celebratio versus populum* (celebration facing the people), which stresses the meal character more strongly, is certainly nowhere enjoined by postconciliar regulation, but it has come to prevail generally. In a letter written on 7 March, 1965, by Cardinal G. Lercaro (as chairman of the Consilium for the Execution of the Constitution on the Liturgy) to the National Commission for the Liturgy, this is termed the "most advantageous solution from the pastoral point of view"; cf. Kaczynski and Rennings 414.

In order to underline the *meal character*, Vatican II (*SC* 55) and the postconciliar documents (cf. "General Introduction to the Roman Missal of 1970," no. 56h: Kaczynski 1451, as well as the ritual fascicle of 1973 on the "Dispensation of Communion and the Adoration of the Eucharist Outside the Mass," no. 13: Kaczynski 3074) advise that in administering communion during the mass, *wafers consecrated in the celebration itself* should be dispensed, not wafers out of the tabernacle. The advice can appeal to similar admonitions given in the

Encyclica *Certiores effecti* of Benedict XIV (1742) and *Mediator Dei* of Pius XII (1947) (*AAS* 39 [1947]:564) (*AAS* 50 [1958]:638).

According to postconciliar regulation, the *tabernacle* is no longer the center in a Catholic church, as earlier. Its place should be if possible not on the High Altar but in a side chapel or, "where this is not possible, on an altar or in some other reverently and solemnly prepared place in the church" ("Gen. Intro. to the Roman Missal of 1970," no. 276: Kaczynski 1671). Cf. *CIC*, can. 838 §2.

66. Pius XII's encyclical *Mediator Dei* (11 Nov., 1947) writes: "Sacrarum specierum conservatio pro infirmis, pro iisque omnibus, qui in mortis discrimen venissent, laudabilem induxit morem adorandi caelestam hanc dapem, quae in templis reponitur" (*AAS* 39 [1947]:509). A decree of the Roman Sacred Congregation for the Sacraments of 1 October, 1949, reads: "Abs re non erit in mentem revocare primarium ac primigenium finem asservandarum in ecclesia sanctarum Specierum extra Missam esse administrationem Viatici" (*AAS* 41 [1949]:509f.). This sentence is repeated word for word in the Instruction *Eucharisticum mysterium* 49 (Kaczynski 947) and in the above-mentioned fascicle of the postconciliar Roman ritual (1973) on the "Dispensation of Communion and the Adoration of the Eucharist Outside the Mass," no. 5 (Kaczynski 3066).

67. Cf. FC SD VII.126: *BC* 591; FC Epit. VII.19: *BC* 484.

68. Lima, Eucharist 32.

69. The Motu Proprio *Pastorale munus* (30 Nov., 1963) makes it possible for the bishop to permit celebrations of the mass outside churches (a possibility previously reserved for the Apostolic See). According to the ritual fascicle "The Celebration of the Sacrament for the Sick" (7 Dec., 1972), no. 26, the viaticum should if possible be received in the framework of a celebration of the mass, so that the sick person can communicate under both kinds (Kaczynski and Rennings 2951). The possibility is already mentioned in 1967 and 1969, being sixth in the list of cases of communion under both kinds (Kaczynski and Rennings 930 and 1637).

According to no. 80, the anointing of the sick can be administered in the framework of a celebration of the mass in the house of the sick person or in a suitable room in a hospital, if the condition of the sick person permits it, and especially if the person desires to receive Holy Communion. It is no longer necessary for the local bishop to give permission (revised version of no. 80 of 12 Sept., 1983, in accordance with can. 932 §1 *CIC* 1983).

70. Cf. Justin, Ap. I, 65, 5; 67, 5; Hippolytus, *Traditio Apostolica* 22, 36; further testimony in A.-G. Martimort, *Handbuch der Liturgiewissenschaft* I (Freiburg, 1963), 460f., 473f.; M. Righetti, *Storia liturgica* III, 3rd ed. (Milan, 1966), 545–52, 554–58; O. Nussbaum, *Die Aufbewahrung der Eucharistie* (Bonn, 1979), 37–61.

71. *Eucharist* 52.

72. Cf. CA 22: *BC* 49ff.; Apol. 22.1, 16: *BC* 236, 238; AS III.6: *BC* 311; FC Epit. VII.24: *BC* 484; SD VII.110: *BC* 588f.

73. "On 16 April, 1564, Pius IV gave way to the urgings of the Emperor and Albert V of Bavaria and granted to the metropolitans of Mainz, Cologne, Trier, Salzburg, and Gran the indult authorizing them to permit the cup to be offered to the laity. But it then emerged that this was no longer a matter of general concern. Whether to offer the cup to the laity had definitely become a distinguishing mark of the churches. It was consequently rejected by the Catholic population, for example, in Bavaria and the Lower Rhine. After 1571 Duke Albert V withdrew the permission once more. In 1584 Gregory XIII suspended the indult" (A. Franzen, "Laienkelchbewegung I" in *LThK* VI, 744).

74. Sacra Congregatio Rituum, *Instructio de cultu mysterii eucharistici* 1967, n. 32 (*AAS* 49 [1967]:558). Cf. the detailed regulations with regard to communion in both kinds in the "General Introduction to the Celebration of the Mass" (nos. 240–52) in the new missal, as well as *CIC*, can 925. The *Caeremoniale Episcoporum* of 14 Sept., 1984, expands considerably the possibilities previously offered (p. 315; see also the index under "Eucharist" and "Elements, of the sacraments").

75. *Eucharist* 64.

76. Cf. Apol. 24.6f.: *BC* 250; CA 24.1–9: *BC* 56; Apol. 24.1–8: *BC* 249f.; FC Epit. VII.9: *BC* 482f.

77. Cf. A. Härdelin, *Aquae et vini Mysterium. Geheimnis der Erlösung und Geheimnis der Kirche im Spiegel der mittelalterlichen Auslegung der gemischten Kelchs* (Münster, 1973), esp. 133–36.

78. Apol. 24.90: *BC* 266; Cf. Apol. 13.22: *BC* 214; CA 24.30–33: *BC* 59f.

79. FC SD VII.109: *BC* 588; cf. FC Epit. VII.23: *BC* 484.

80. Cf. Conciliorum Oecumenicorum Decreta 713, Sessio XXII, Decretum de observandis et vitandis in celebratione missarum. The so-called "Gregorian masses" are unfortunately not affected.

81. Cf. Apol. 24.94: *BC* 267: "Quod vero allegant adversarii patres de oblatione pro mortuis scimus veteres loqui de oratione pro mortuis, quam nos non prohibemus" ["Our opponents quote the Fathers on offerings for the dead. We know that the ancients spoke of prayer for the dead. We do not forbid this"].

82. *Evangelischer Erwachsenenkatechismus* (Gütersloh, 1975), 539.

83. Cf. Ezek. 22:17–22; Isa. 1:25; 48:10; Mal. 3:3; 1 Cor. 3:12–15; 2 Thess. 1:7; Jude 23.

84. Cf. the detailed account on pp. 102–106 above.

85. Apol. 13.6: *BC* 212: "Confirmatio et extrema unctio sunt ritus accepti a patribus, quos ne ecclesia quidem tamquam necessarios ad salutem requirit, quia non habent mandatum Dei. Propterea non est inutile hos ritus discernere a superioribus qui habent expressum mandatum Dei et claram promissionem gratiae" ["Confirmation and extreme unction are rites received from the fathers which even the church does not require as necessary for salvation since they do not have the command of God. Hence it is useful to distinguish these from the earlier ones which have an express command from God and a clear promise of grace"].

86. The rejected position is already so formulated in the list of errors of 1 Jan., 1547. The following passage is cited as evidence: "Melanchthon in locis communibus cap. de confirmatione: 'Sed nunc ritus confirmationis, quem retinent episcopi, est prorsus otiosa caeremonia' " ["But now the rite of confirmation, which the bishops retain, is a completely empty ceremony"] (*CT* V, 838, 31–33). This sentence is first found in the 1543/44 edition of Melanchthon's *Loci communes* (MSA II, 2, 507, 18–20).

Only an isolated quotation seems to have been presented to the conciliar fathers; for it emerges from the context of the sentence quoted that here Melanchthon is not criticizing confirmation itself as an *otiosa caeremonia*, but only contemporary practice. In the preceding passage he talks about the communication of the Spirit through the laying on of hands by the apostles ("donabantur manifestis donis Spiritus sancti": MSA II, 2, 507, 17f.), and in what follows he speaks of the prayer at confirmation, which would not be without effect ("nec ea precatio esset inanis," ibid., 22).

87. Cf. G. Kretschmar, "Firmung," in *TRE* 11, 192–204.

88. The immediately succeeding administration of all three initiation sacraments remained, as it did in the Eastern church, in those Western rites which—like the Eastern church—did not reserve the administration of confirmation for the bishop (Gaul down to the ninth century, Spain down to the eleventh, Milan down to the thirteenth). In the Roman rite the unity was also still prescribed in the case of infants (including the reception of the Eucharist, later unconsecrated wine) at least until the fourteenth century, if the bishop was present. It remained binding if the bishop administered baptism; this practice was restricted to adults only in the Pont. Rom. 1596 (final Editio typica 1962, final rubric); in the case of adult baptism administered by a priest, if a bishop was present (Rit. Rom. 1614; final Editio typica 1952, Tit. II, cap. IV, n. 52).

89. *SC* 64ff.; *AG* 14; cf. also *PO* 5.6; *CIC* 1983, can. 842 §2.

90. *LG* 33; *AA* 3; cf. *CIC* 1983, cans. 225, 759, etc.

91. The "Ceremony for the Incorporation of Adults Into the Church" of 1982 (cf. *CIC* 1983, can. 851), which also includes an order for "Children of School Age" (chap. V; cf. *CIC*, can. 852), envisages that, in the absence of the bishop, the priest performing the baptism will immediately administer confirmation (*ipso iure: CIC* 1983, can. 883), which may only be postponed for grave reasons (preliminary comment 34). "Adults who were baptized as children but who have received no instruction in the faith" are supposed "as a rule" (no. 304), after a catechumenate, which is also liturgically ordered, to receive confirmation at the hands of a bishop or authorized priest on Easter Eve, and to receive the Eucharist (chap. IV, no. 295).

92. If only confirmation is administered, the Constitution on the Liturgy recommends that the reception of the sacrament should be preceded by the renewal of the baptismal promises, "so that the intimate connection of this sacrament with the whole of the Christian initiation may more clearly appear." For this reason it is conferred within the mass, not merely "if convenient" (*SC*

71), but "as a rule" (*Ordo Confirmationis*, Praenot. 13). The unity of the *"initiationis christianae Sacramenta,"* or sacraments of Christian initiation (*PO* 2 [3]), is explained in detail in the remarks prefacing the reformed liturgy and is also stressed in the new *CIC:* "The sacraments of baptism, confirmation and the most holy Eucharist are so closely bound up with one another *(coalescunt)* that they are necessary for the full Christian initiation" (can. 842 §2).

93. Paul VI's Apostolic Constitution *Divinae consortium naturae* introducing the new order of confirmation of 15 Aug., 1971, and the *CIC* 1983, can. 879, take over in slightly differentiated form the description of confirmation in *Lumen Gentium*. They add that those baptized receive the gift of the Holy Spirit (in accordance with the new "formula" for the anointing) and are "signed with the mark of the sacrament" (Paul VI: "sacrament . . . that imprints a mark": can. 879). Canon 879 also adds from the *Ordo Confirmationis*, Praenot. 1, that those who have been baptized "progress on the way of Christian initiation" through confirmation. In substance, and to a great extent in wording, *De initiatione Christiana*, Praen. gen 2 (1969), and *Ordo Confirmationis*, Praenot. 1f. (1971), agree in both expansions.

All the descriptions close by stressing the obligation to bear witness through a special power of the Holy Spirit (cf. the Roman prayer at the laying on of hands). The prayers at the consecration of the chrism, which (similar to the prayers at the consecration of the water at baptism) imply the theology of confirmation, make clear both the gift and the charge. The new alternative chrism prayer (1971) corresponds substantially to the old Roman prayer and to the consecratory prayers of other liturgies: "God . . . thou hast prefigured the sanctifying mystery of the oil in the old covenant [the German version elucidates: "with it hast thou consecrated prophets, priests and kings"; in the old prayer the sequence is better: priests, kings, and prophets], and, in the fulness of time, hast let it shine forth in unique manner in thy beloved Son. For when thy Son, our Lord [the German version supplements from the first Roman and other consecratory prayers: "Him, after his baptism in Jordan, didst thou anoint with the Holy Spirit"], had through the paschal sacrament saved mankind, he filled thy church with the Holy Spirit and furnished her marvellously with heavenly gifts, in order through her to perfect thy saving work in the world. Since that day dost thou distribute the riches of thy grace to men through the holy mystery of the chrism, so that thy sons, born again through baptism, may be strengthened through the sanctification of the Spirit, and, made like in form to thine Anointed One (Christ), may share in his task as prophet, priest and king." In the intercessory section, the prayer includes the following petition: "Pour out in rich measure upon our brethren whom we anoint with this chrism the gifts of the Holy Spirit." Cf. P.-W. Scheele, "Sakrament der Sendung, Bemerkungen zum Spezifikum der Firmung," in his *Alle eins—theologische Beiträge II* (Paderborn, 1979).

94. Thus, e.g., SmC IV, Baptism, 9–14: *BC* 349; LC, Baptism, 41: *BC* 441f.; 65–79: BC 444–46; 83–86: *BC* 446.

95. Cf. for The American Lutheran Church, the Lutheran Church of America, and the Evangelical Lutheran Church of Canada: *Lutheran Book of Worship* (1978), 311; for the Protestant Episcopal Church (U.S.A.): *The Book of Common Prayer* (1979), 30; for the Church of England: *The Alternative Service Book* (1980), 226, 234.

96. The priest is "by law" (*ipso iure: CIC*, can. 883; duty of the administrator of the sacrament: can 885 §2; duty of the recipient: can. 890) the administrator of confirmation, also in the "ceremony for the reception of the properly baptized into the full fellowship of the Catholic Church" (1972), and when a person's life is in danger, also in the case of children (*Ordo Confirmationis* [1971], cap. IV; celebration of the sacraments for the sick [1972], cap. V; *CIC*, can. 891). In mission areas, confirmation by the priest is, largely speaking, the rule. Priests of the uniate Eastern churches can administer to Roman Catholic Christians "the sacrament of chrism" in association with baptism, or independent of it (*OE* 14). Insofar as the Eastern churches have taken over Western practice of administration by the bishop, "the established practice . . . which has existed . . . from ancient times" (the link with baptism) "is to be fully restored" (ibid., 13).

97. "Confirmatio et extrema unctio sunt ritus accepti a patribus, quos ne ecclesia quidem tamquam necessarios ad salutem requirit, quia non habent mandatum Dei. Propterea non est inutile hos ritus discernere a superioribus qui habent expressum mandatum Dei et claram promissionem gratiae" (Apol. 13.6: *BC* 212).

98. "Non licere Apostolum sua autoritate sacramentum instituere, id est, divinam promissionem cum adiuncto signo dare. Hoc enim ad Christum solum pertinebat" ["No apostle has the right on his own authority to institute a sacrament, that is, to give a divine promise with a sign attached. For this belongs to Christ alone"] (WA 6, 568, 12ff.; *LW* 36, 118).

99. "Igitur hoc unctionis extremae nostrum saramentum *non damno*, sed hoc esse, quod ab Apostolo Iacobo praescribitur, constanter nego, *cum nec forma* nec usus nec virtus nec finis eius cum nostro consentiat" (WA 6, 570, 32ff.; cf. *LW* 36, 122).

100. "Ut igitur maxime demus, unctionem Sacramentum fuisse earum virtutum quae tum per manus Apostolorum administrabantur: nihil nunc ad nos pertinet, quibus virtutum administratio commissa non est" (*Inst.* IV, 19, 18).

101. "Quae nec ceremonia est a Deo instituta, nec ullam promissionem habet. Siquidem, quum duo ista in Sacramento exigimus, ut ceremonia sit a Deo instituta, ut Dei promissionem habeat: simul postulamus ut ceremonia illa nobis tradita sit, et promissio ad nos spectet" (*Inst.* IV, 19, 20).

102. "Illis vero praesertim, qui tam periculose decumbunt, ut in exitu vitae constituti videantur, unde et sacramentum exeuntium nuncupatur. Quod si infirmi post suspectam hanc unctionem convaluerint, iterum huius sacramenti subsidio iuvari poterunt, cum in aliud simile vitae discrimen inciderint" (cap. 3).

103. " 'Extrema Unctio,' quae etiam et melius 'Unctio infirmorum' vocari potest, non est Sacramentum eorum tantum qui in extremo vitae discrimine versantur. Proinde tempus opportunum eam recipiendi iam certe habetur cum fidelis incipit esse in periculo mortis propter infirmitatem vel senium" (*SC* 73; cf. *CIC* 1983, can. 1004 §1).

104. "Unctionem numerus pro opportunitate accommodetur, et orationes ad ritum Unctionis infirmorum pertinentes ita recognoscantur, ut respondeant variis condicionibus infirmorum, qui Sacramentum suscipiunt" (*SC* 75).

105. *Die Feier der Krankensakramente*, ed. for the Episcopal Conferences of Germany, Austria, and Switzerland, and for the Bishops of Bozen-Brixen (Bolzano-Bressanone) and Luxemburg (Einsiedeln, Freiburg, Regensburg, Vienna, Salzburg, and Linz, 1974), 14.

106. Cf. *Agende für Seelsorge an Kranken und Sterbenden*, ed. W. Lotz (Kassel, 1949), 165–69; Proposal for an order for the anointing of the sick. More recently (1979) the choice of joining this assurance with an anointing has been officially recognized, for example in the Lutheran churches of the United States and Canada.

107. For a recognition of Christ as, in this sense, the great Physician, cf. Ludwig Heimbold's hymn (1575) "Nun lasst uns Gott dem Herren/Dank sagen und ihn ehren," the fourth verse of which runs: "Ein Arzt ist uns gegeben, der selber ist das Leben;/Christus, für uns gestorben, der hat das Heil erworben."

108. E.g., in the "Horrible, Most Damnable Fruits of the Lutheran Gospel, which bring much perdition" (*Abscheulichen, zuviel Verderben bringenden, verdammtesten Früchten des lutherischen Evangeliums*) we read the following: "Moreover among them slight is the reason for a separation and divorce, it may be no more than that a quarrel has chanced to arise between wife and husband. Thus many apostate monks may be found who have already taken a third wife, having cast off two still living. Moreover Luther taught in the *Babylonian Captivity*: 'If a woman hath a husband too feeble for the pleasures of love, so that he doth not fulfil his marital duty, she may draw upon the help of his brother or another, to slake her desires.' This doctrine was the cause of unheard of shameful deeds and offences. With shame do we repeat what he wrote against virginity: namely that no one can be chaste and remain so. Thus it came about that in several places virgins dedicated to God were torn from and thrust out of the monasteries" (J. Ficker, *Die Konfutation des Augsburgischen Bekenntnisses* [Leipzig, 1891], 186f.).

It must be said, however, that the passage quoted does not correctly render what Luther actually said (De capt., WA 6, 558). Luther thinks that if a woman's husband is incapable of marital intercourse (and is therefore incapable of begetting children), she may, with her husband's permission, conceive children by another man, who are then to count legally as the children of her husband.

Of the twelve articles submitted in Bologna on 26 April, 1547, on extreme unction, ordination, and matrimony, six deal with the sacrament of matrimony

(*CT* VI/1, 98–99). The sources to which they refer are Luther's *De captivitate Babylonica*, *De sacerdotio, legibus et sacrificiis Papae* (= *De abroganda missa privata, pars III*), and *Epithalamion* (= "Das 7. Kapitel S. Pauli zu den Korinthern,*" 1523), as well as the *Büchlein der Kölner Reformation*. The form in which the quotations are cited shows that they are taken from J. Fabri, *Antilogiarum Martini Lutheri Babylonica* (1530) and J. Cochlaeus, *Confutatio excusationis et iactantiae Protestantium* (= *Miscellaneorum libri tertii tractatus quartus*). They are found in the same form in Girolamo Seripando's list of errors of April 1547 (*CT* VI/1, 92–95; cf. the *canones* of Ambrosius Pelargus: *CT* (VI/1, 129). Article 2 of the draft of 26 April, 1547, runs: "Christians are permitted to have several wives at the same time, and no law forbids polygamy" (cf. can. 2: *DS* 1802). The evidence adduced is that "this article is to be found in the Büchlein der Kölner Reformation" (the Booklet of the Cologne Reformation). But this is not in fact a quotation; it is a conclusion which J. Gropper draws in his "Antididagma" (1544), because in the Booklet of the Cologne Reformation marriage is not counted among the sacraments: "And there is no doubt that the authors of the book are not of the opinion that marriage be a true sacrament. But those who think thus permit Christians to have more than one wife at the same time." It is not clear from this passage whether Gropper had in mind Luther's opinion on Philip of Hesse's bigamous marriage (see his "Raten zum Beichtweis" of 10 Dec., 1539: WA Br 8, 638–44; cf. 15, 212).

Article 3—that remarriage is permitted after adultery (cf. can. 7: *DS* 1807)— offers the following as evidence: "In 'De captivitate Babylonica' Luther formulated these words." But the words cited are not Luther's. The first part ("A woman who gives herself to another man has already ceased to be a married woman") was a statement of Erasmus's and was condemned by the Paris theological faculty in 1527 (cf. P. Fransen in *Scholastik* 27 [1952]: 531, n. 30). It is true, however, that in *De captivitate Babylonica* Luther calls in question the prohibition of remarriage after a divorce (cf. WA 6, 559).

It may therefore be said in retrospect that what the conciliar fathers knew about the Reformers' position with regard to marriage was knowledge derived second or third hand.

109. The viewpoint which brings together the two love relationships under the heading of "covenant" may be found in the Roman *benedictio sponsae* of the Gregorian *Hadrianum* (which is testified to at the end of the eighth century but is in fact older). It is also incorporated in the text remolded in 1969 as blessing for bride and bridegroom, where the covenant of marriage (*foedus nuptiarum*) of the order of creation is seen as a prefiguration of the sacrament of Christ and the church. The additional new texts of the ritual (1969) and the missal (1970) express the same idea in several places, in especially comprehensive form in the *Oratio II super sponsam et sponsum*. On the level of the magisterium's texts, this central statement is to be found, e.g., in the Pastoral Constitution of the Second Vatican Council (cf. *GS* 48).

110. In the Roman nuptial blessing, since 1969 "Prayer Over Bride and

Bridegroom," natural marriage is termed *excellens mysterium*, the excellent mystery which God has sanctified *(consecrasti)* and on which he bestowed a blessing (cf. Gen. 1:28) which was not revoked because of Fall and Flood. According to the first alternative prayer of 1969, natural marriage intimates the covenant between God and his people, the sacramental symbolism of which is completed in Christian marriage, in which the "nuptial mystery" of Christ and the church is manifested. According to the encyclicals of Leo XIII and Pius XI on marriage, every marriage has a religious and a sacred character. From "the beginning of mankind onwards it has been instituted *(institutum)* . . . by God as sacred bond of love" (Second Vatican Council, draft on the sacrament of marriage, submitted to the pope after a brief discussion on 20 Nov., 1964. No. 1: *LThK*, "Das Zweite Vat. Konzil" III, 596).

111. Cf. the following text from *STh*, Suppl. 42, 2 in corp. (= In IV Sent. d. 26: 2, 2): "Nature inclines towards marriage, thereby striving towards a good which, however, varies according to the different (historical) states of men. Hence that good thing must be instituted in a different way in the different states of men. In so far, then, as (marriage) is ordered towards the begetting of offspring, which was necessary even then there was as yet no sin, it was instituted before sin. But in so far as it offers a remedy for the wounds of sin, it was instituted after sin, at the time of natural law. Where it has respect to the destiny of persons, its institution was given in the law of Moses. But in so far as it makes present the mystery of the bond between Christ and the Church, it finds its institution in the New Law; and in this sense it is a sacrament of the New Law. But as for the other benefits which spring from marriage, for example friendship, and the mutual help which the spouses render one another, it has its institution in civil law." [This passage is not included in the English translation of Aquinas (Blackfriars) otherwise cited.]

Cf. further documents issued by the magisterium in which the nature and characteristics of marriage are essentially derived from the natural marriage instituted by God, e.g., Leo XIII, *Arcanum divinae sapientiae*, 10 Feb., 1880 (extracts *DS* 3142–46); Pius XI, *Casti connubii*, 31 Dec., 1930 (extracts *DS* 3700–3724); Vatican II, *GS* 48; John Paul II, *Familiaris consortio*, 22 Nov., 1981, no. 11ff.

112. The expression refers to the consent doctrine which is essential for the Catholic understanding of the sacrament of marriage. This appears in the decree *Tametsi* (*DS* 1813) and, in the context of an anthropological view of love, is also stressed by Vatican II through the expression *donatio mutua* ("mutual giving") (*GS* 48 [1]; 50 [2]).

113. Cf. Meyer/Vischer, 366f.

114. *DS* 1805: "propter haeresim, aut molestam cohabitationem, aut affectatam absentiam a coniuge"; *DS* 1807: adulterium.

115. Cf. B. Bruns, *Ehescheidung und Wiederheirat im Fall von Ehebruch. Eine rechts- und dogmengeschichtliche Untersuchung zu Kanon 7 der 24. Sitzung des Konzils von Trient* (Munich, Paderborn, and Vienna, 1976); L. Bressan, "Votum

Tridentino inedito di G. Lainez sul matrimonio," *Gregorianum* 64 (1983): 307–30, 487–513, 683–714, esp. 321f.

116. Cf. here, among others, also H. Dietrich, *Das protestantische Eherecht in Deutschland bis zur Mitte des 17. Jahrhunderts*, = Ius Ecclesiasticum, vol. 10 (Munich, 1971), esp. 69ff. and 105ff.; cf. A. Biéler, *L'homme et la femme dans la morale calviniste* (Geneva, 1961), esp. 69–76.

117. Cf., among other passages, WA 10 II, 291, 15–24; 15, 562, 7–10; 30 III, 243, 31–35; 32, 378, 4ff.

118. CA 23/Apol. 23: *BC* 51ff./239ff.; AS III. 11: *BC* 314f.

119. E.g., WA 10 II, 279, 15; 12, 105, 5.

CHAPTER 4: THE MINISTRY

1. See also "Thesen der reformiert-lutherischen Konsultation in Driebergen 1981 zur Fortsetzung der Leuenberger Konkordie," in *Konkordie und Kirchengemeinschaft reform. Kirchen im Europa der Gegenwart*, ed. A. Birmelé (Frankfurt, 1982), II, 3.2 (58ff.).

2. *Repraesentant Christi personam:* Apol. 7.28: *BC* 173; cf. *DS* 1321; also *LG* 21 and 10, and frequently.

3. Luke 10:16; cf. Apol. 7.28: *BC* 173; also CA 28.22: *BC* 84; also *LG* 20.

4. Cf. also *SC* 6 and 7, *LG* 8, *PO* 5, and frequently.

5. K. Lehmann and E. Schlink, eds., *Evangelium—Sakramente—Amt und die Einheit der Kirche. Die ökumenische Tragweite der Confessio Augustana* (Freiburg and Göttingen, 1982), Dialog der Kirchen 2, 188 (italics added by the Ecumenical Study Group).

6. Even the *CIC* of 1917 already explicitly stressed that proclamation was an episcopal duty (cans. 1327ff.). Cf. also the new codex of 1983 (can. 753).

7. After the introduction of additional rites from Gallic sources into the medieval Roman ordination liturgy, the question of what was constitutive for the rite of ordination became a matter of controversy in Catholic theology. In addition, the ordination of the bishop was frequently not viewed as a special sacrament, whereas the subdiaconate and the minor orders were viewed as belonging to the sacrament of ordination. The controversy found its way into official documents to some degree: the handing over of the vessels as *materia*, the corresponding formulas as *forma* in Eugene IV's union bulls for Armenians and "Jacobites" (1439/1441: DS 1326, 1351 n.). The Council of Trent mentioned the anointing and the formula for the (later introduced) second laying on of hands at episcopal ordination and defends them against the reproach of being unnecessary or without effect (*DS* 1774f.). After Pius XII's decision that at the ordination of bishops, priests, and deacons only the laying on of hands and the central words of the ordination prayers are constitutive (*DS* 3680)—which some modern canonists and liturgists had always maintained—Vatican II, the new rites of ordination, and *CIC*, cans. 266 §1, 375 §2 and 1009 could draw the appropriate conclusion: episcopal ordination now counts as the first stage of the sacrament of orders (LG 26; Constitutio Apostolica *Pontificalis Romani recog-*

nitio, 1968), the minor orders are abolished (Paul VI, Litt. *Ministeria quaedam*, 1972), and the secondary rites are interpreted as explanatory of the essential components of the rites of ordination (Pont. Rom., *De ordinatione diaconi, presbyteri et episcopi*, 1968).

8. Apol. 13.7ff.: *BC* 212f.; cf. Calvin, *Inst.* IV, 19, 28, 31.

9. R. Mumm, ed., *Ordination und Kirchliches Amt* (Paderborn, 1976), 173, 3c; cf. Calvin, *Inst.* IV, 19, 28–31.

10. Ibid., 52.

11. W. Stein, *Das Kirchliche Amt bei Luther* (Wiesbaden, 1974), 90ff., 199f.

12. Ibid., 100f., 194f.

13. Treatise 63–65: *BC* 331; AS III.10: *BC* 314f.; cf. Calvin, *Inst.* IV, 4, 2–4.

14. Apol. 14.1: *BC* 214; Treatise 60ff., esp. 63ff., 72: *BC* 330ff.; cf. AS III.12: *BC* 315.

15. Lima, Ministry 53b; Malta 57; *Ministry* 66.

16. *Ministri originarii: LG* 26; the *CIC* of 1983 calls the bishop *Confirmationis minister ordinarius* (can. 882).

17. As in the East, in non-Roman rites in the West in ancient times confirmation was dispensed by priests (Spain: *DS* 187; for Umbria, cf. *DS* 215; cf. further J. Neumann, *Der Spender der Firmung in der Kirche des Abendlandes bis zum Ende des kirchlichen Altertums* [Meitingen, 1963]). But this is now also the case in the Roman rite "by virtue of general law or by particular permission *(vi . . . concessionis)* of the responsible authority" (*CIC* 1983, can. 882), and goes far beyond the earlier cases which already existed in the Middle Ages (1351: *DS* 1070f.; 1439: *DS* 1318; 1774: *DS* 2588; *CIC* 1917, can. 281f.).

18. AS II.4, 10 and 14: *BC* 300 and 301; cf. Treatise 39 as well as 41, 42, and 57: *BC* 327f. and 330; Apol. 7.24 and 15.18: *BC* 172f. and 217; also FC SD X.20 and 22: *BC* 614f.

INDEX OF SUBJECTS

This index should be used in conjunction with the table of contents.